THE MEDIEVAL VISION

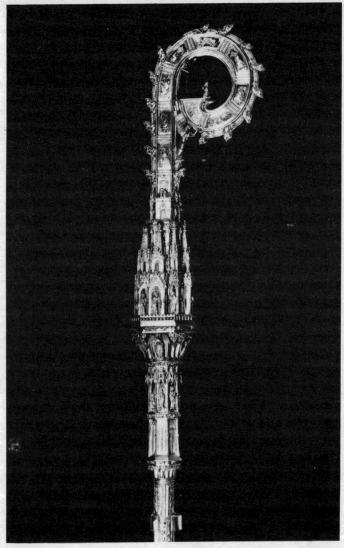

Enamelled staff of William of Wykeham, from C. J. Jackson, *History of English Plate*, (1911), Vol. 1, p. 114, reprinted by permission of the Warden and Fellows, New College, Oxford.

THE MEDIEVAL VISION
Essays in
History and Perception

CAROLLY ERICKSON

New York
OXFORD UNIVERSITY PRESS

PREFACE

When in September of 1970 I began work on an interpretive history of the twelfth, thirteenth and fourteenth centuries I had a very different book in mind than the one I finished four years later. But as I read on in lesser-known chronicles, letters and treatises along with more familiar sources I was confronted again and again by passages that seemed to heighten the remoteness of the medieval past. Many of these passages related visions, or used metaphors of sight to convey abstract thought.

The ubiquitous visionary imagination seemed to me an evocative symbol of the perceptual distance between our own times and the middle ages, and a touchstone for a tentative exploration of that distance. Of course, to construct from source texts a definitive account of medieval perception would be a long and probably presumptuous task, requiring much technical knowledge in fields other than history. Nothing like that is attempted here. Rather I hoped to weave into an overview of some major themes of medieval life hints at how that life was differently perceived by those who lived it.

I have not tried to use these ideas about medieval perception to radically change our understanding of belief, order, personalities or social attitudes in the middle ages. But the visionary imagination has here and there informed each of these themes, and given them fresh nuances.

In the course of working out these ideas I have had much-needed encouragement from Kathleen Casey and Warren Hollister, and from Herbert Mann at Oxford University Press. Several generations of research assistants—Paul Gordon, Cynthia Truant, Valerie Sopher, and Peter Satris—have made an indispensable contribution, and the libraries of the University of California and the Graduate Theological Union have, as always, provided wonderful riches in bibliography.

October 1974   C.E.
Berkeley, California

CONTENTS

Not to prove, but to discover

THE MEDIEVAL VISION

Chapter one

THE ENCHANTED WORLD

A late thirteenth-century manuscript tells the story of three "Mesopotamian monks" who agreed to journey together to find "the place where heaven and earth join." Their destination, the terrestrial paradise, was marked on medieval world maps, though its exact location varied. Some made it an island off the East Indian coast, others the island of Thule, still others placed it in the region of Ethiopia. More often, though, it was located at the easternmost end of the world, at a point no traveler had ever reached.

The monks began their long journey by crossing the Tigris, which led them through Persia into the plains of Asia, where Julian the Apostate was killed. Four months' further travel brought them through the Persian city of Ketissephodo and into India, where they were taken for spies and imprisoned. (Only a short time before this account was written, four Franciscan missionaries had been martyred in India, and their fate had been widely publicized.) For reasons that are not explained in the account, the three monks were spared by the inhabitants (here called Ethiopians), and on leaving the country, they found themselves in unknown lands.

3

Beyond a fruitful region where they refreshed themselves was the country of the "Chananeans," rock-dwellers; a hundred days' further travel brought them to the homes of the "Pichichi," a people less than two feet high who ran from the travelers in panic. A bleak and mountainous country lay beyond, filled with dragons, basilisks and unicorns; amid still higher mountains the monks found elephants, and a region of continual darkness. Escaping with difficulty from this dark land they came upon a memorial column whose markings bore the name of Alexander the Great.

Forty days' journey then brought them to a place of terrible torments. Mournful shrieking came from sinners who had denied Christ, condemned to drown in a noxious lake full of snakes. A giant chained between rock pillars was ceaselessly tortured with fire, while a sinful woman was pinned to the rocks by a coiled snake which bit her tongue when she tried to speak. Passing through these fearful sights, the monks at last came upon signs that they were reaching the celestial country. On the far side of a vale where speaking birdlike animals called continually upon God stood four venerable old men wearing jeweled crowns and carrying golden palms. They were placed there to guard the way, they told the travelers, but allowed them to go on into a beautiful country whose sweet air was filled with singing voices. Light seven times brighter than familiar sunlight streamed around the monks as they approached a wonderful church whose great altar poured forth a milky substance.

Another hundred days brought the monks through a second land of tiny folk, across an immense river, and to a huge cave. Here an aged man with long white hair, who identified himself as St. Macarius, told the three monks that he, too, had sought "the end of the earth and of the pole," but that after an angel led him to the cave, he was warned in a vision not to complete his journey. Though he told them they were only twenty miles from their destination, the monks heeded the warning the saint had been given long before, and, setting out the way they had come, made the long trip back through the marvelous lands to India and Persia, and finally to their monastery.

The account of the monks' journey, which is found in an *imago mundi* manuscript devoted to serious geography, combines several dimensions of reality into a single and continuous landscape. It was a journey through time, in which the death site of the Emperor Julian, the monument of Alexander and the encounters with the creatures of ancient myth marked the passage backward through historical chronology to the beginning of time in the garden of paradise. It was a spiritual pilgrimage, whose landmarks included hell, the earthly paradise, and the unattained "place where heaven and earth join," peopled with the company of sinners, the blessed, and St. Macarius. This theological topography closely parallels those found in medieval vision literature, in which a visionary is shown through hell and paradise while in a trance or a deathlike sleep, or in a dream. In this account, however, the spiritual geography is localized—as it rarely is in the vision literature—and is treated as a part of terrestrial geography.

Finally, the monks' expedition was, as described, a physical journey through the actual and speculative geography of the known world. It combined established locations with those drawn from travelers' lore and legends from antiquity and the earlier middle ages, and it brought them into alignment with the historical and spiritual geography. Though their destination was the gate of heaven, the seam between the earthly and heavenly realms, the monks never left the earth in the course of their travels. All that they saw took place in the realm of day-to-day reality, not in an altered state of awareness or through a miraculous revelation.

The multiform reality which forms a backdrop to the monks' journey may be likened to an enchanted world in which the boundaries of imagination and factuality are constantly shifting. At one time the observed physical limits of time and space may be acknowledged; at another they may be ignored, or, from another point of view, transcended. Yet so constant and so automatic is this expansion and contraction of the field of perceived reality that it goes on unnoted and unreconciled by medieval writers. It belongs to those tacit norms in all cultures which, because they are more basic than perception itself, are rarely explicitly acknowledged.

Of course, the fact that medieval men and women shared this flexibility of perception does not mean that they were unable to distinguish between the imagined and the tangible. Nor does it imply that they were puzzled or deluded about the difference between material and immaterial existence. Here it is our habits of mind which hamper us, accustomed as we are to equate realness with materiality; for us, what is unseen and immaterial is assumed to be unreal until its existence is proved by the verifiable data of the senses. Though they were far from being credulous, the medievals did not ordinarily share this suspicion of the unseen, and used other means than sense perception to authenticate reality.

A different view of reality, then, underlay medieval perception— a view we may compare to the altered reality of an enchantment. It was characteristic of that view that throughout the middle ages the earth was conceived as embracing the geographical locus of unseen truths. Shrines localized the virtues of a saint in the near vicinity of his or her remains. Pious journeys and later military expeditions to the Holy Land allowed medieval people to see and touch the sites where the bodiless reality of God became the embodied Jesus. And since ancient times dread and curiosity had brought many to the mouths of hell—the places, such as Lough Derg in Ireland, from which descent into the lower world was believed possible.

Closely associated with this was a concept of geography which, as with the journey of the Mesopotamian monks, drew no distinction between lands known through exploration and settlement and those heard of but unseen. The mythical Atlantic islands were among the most renowned of these speculative places. The island of Antillia, for example, entered Spanish history when seven bishops fled there with their flocks when the Goths overran Spain. Brasil, which some folk traditions associated with the "Isle of the Undying," was reputed to be a large island in mid-ocean, visible from the Galway coast.

The existence of these and other elusive islands—St. Brandan's Isle, Mayda, the Isle of the Seven Cities, the Isle of Demons— seemed plausible in view of Ptolemy's assertion that the Atlantic held some twenty-seven thousand islands, and long after the discovery of the New World distinguished mapmakers continued to note many of them as real places. This readiness to believe that real lands underlay geographical legends spurred an exploratory mentality that led the thirteenth-century Genoese to discover the Canary Islands and later to conceive a westward voyage to Asia; in 1291 Ugolino Vivaldo headed a Genoese expedition "to the regions of India by way of the Ocean sea."

Later, after ocean expeditions had begun to be incorporated into the economic policies of Western governments, the older view persisted. The reconquest of the Canaries by the French knight Jean de Bethencourt in the early years of the fifteenth century was recorded by his chaplains in the language of a medieval romance— as the quest of a knight "starting on his adventures." In the decade of Columbus' first voyage, the mariners of Bristol were sending out several ships every year to search for Brasil and the Isle of the Seven Cities, and Columbus himself allegedly took in his crew a Galway man familiar with the lore of Brasil. Like those of his contemporaries, Columbus' expectations were shaped by his acceptance of the reality behind the legendary lands, and also by the theological geography of the terrestrial paradise. In his copy of Pierre d'Ailly's *Imago mundi* he noted with care the passages relating to its location, and writing later of his voyages he cited the passages in Isidore of Seville, Bede and Strabo which fixed the site of paradise in the Orient. "I was convinced," he wrote, "that I would find the

7

earthly paradise there, to which no one may come but by God's will."

A second quality of medieval perception is more elusive. It is that medieval people tended to perceive an all-encompassing, multifold reality, knit together by a commonly held perceptual design. All-encompassing, because no part of experience or knowledge was conceived to be alien to the pattern of Christian revelation. Multifold, because it was a cultural habit to endow individual things with multiple identities. And in terms of a common perceptual design, because it was the mutually held network of beliefs, expectations and assumptions about reality that made medieval culture comprehensible to those who lived their mental lives within its bounds.

This perceptual formula is apparent in the narrative of the monks' journey with which this chapter began. The narrator included in his geographical assemblage fragments of history, myth, biblical lore, geographical certainty, legend and hagiography—to us, a jumble of inconsistent data—and strung them together in an all-inclusive landscape. It was, within its own limits, all-encompassing. In addition, the journey itself was given a triple identity: it was simultaneously a spiritual pilgrimage, a physical journey, and a progression backward along the linear shape of time. It conformed, then, to the pattern of multiple identities. And finally, at no point did the narrator lose sight of the overarching design of Christian truth which defined the goal of the journey and gave meaning to each of its landmarks.

A simpler formulation of these ideas is the truism that the medieval world view was holistic. But this abstruse term eclipses the most striking characteristic of medieval perception—the extraordinary perceptual significance attributed to the visionary imagination. But this characteristic forms the subject of another chapter. Here we must turn from the analysis of medieval perception to examine one of the leading influences that shaped it.

What then were the roots of the enchanted world? Here another, very difficult problem must be raised. To whose consciousness does this term refer? Though for convenience "medieval perception" is treated as if it were a blanket awareness shared by all but infants, the senile and the insane, this blanket awareness is a fiction which leaves out of account individual differences. It assumes that the perception of an illiterate eleventh-century crusader was also that of a fourteenth-century Bolognese lawyer, or that a Parisian embroiderer held the same view of reality as a Flemish beguine. In fact, the written records of the middle ages give clear evidence of the mentality of only a very limited segment of the medieval population. Of those records which describe behavior and popular thought—chiefly chronicles, biographies, letters and similar informal sources—most have the unavoidable bias of clerical authorship. And while the medieval churchmen who wrote these accounts were themselves of varying backgrounds and temperaments, their perceptions were marked by the shared distortions of a classical education, a monastic or clerical vocation, and a distinctive institutional and political alignment. And with a few well-known exceptions, nearly all medieval records were written by men.

At best, then, any description of medieval perception is little more than a hypothesis based on a limited quantity of heavily biased evidence. It means interpreting the world view of the overwhelmingly illiterate, secular, and heterogeneous population of the middle ages through the filter of a homogeneous, narrowly literate and predominantly clerical group of observers. It is to an extent as if a researcher of the twenty-first century were to extrapolate the mentality of nineteenth-century European factory workers and peasants from the proceedings of a provincial antiquarian society.

But only to an extent, for once these source limitations have been acknowledged, a legitimate evidentiary base remains. Once it is admitted that any conclusions about medieval perception are really conclusions about the clues to perception a group of contemporaries found worth preserving, the focus of analysis shifts. The aim is no longer to penetrate the consciousness of an aggregate of individuals, but to isolate the characteristics of that consciousness that medieval writers themselves chose to emphasize.

The idea of the enchanted world is, then, a construct built up through exposure to another construct—that of a large group of medieval writers. Put another way, the view of medieval perception offered here is a view of a particular distillation of that perception in a wide variety of source materials. Though this distillation should not be confused with the actual thoughts and sentiments of medieval people—which are irrevocably lost—it may fairly be valued as a guide to some of those thoughts and sentiments.

One further issue remains: the difficulty of citing learned treatises to illustrate the consciousness of the unlearned. While it is absurd to claim that a twelfth-century burgher believed what he did about the shape of the earth or the function of the celestial spheres because he read Macrobius or Chalcidius, it is more plausible to turn the argument around—to see higher culture as in part an outgrowth of commonly held beliefs. Stated this way, we would say that Macrobius was widely read during the middle ages partly because his cosmology was broadly in accord with the established world view. More to the point, it is not absurd to claim that what the learned writers of a given medieval generation believed was wholly divorced from what their unlearned contemporaries held true. Learning imposes artificial attitudes and constraints upon thought, but it does not remove the scholar entirely from his time. Points of congruence between the consciousness of highly educated and uneducated people—and the many shades of cultural awareness in between—are in matters of basic perception very numerous. Or at least that is what is assumed here.

Among the forces shaping the perceptual qualities described above, one complex of beliefs stands out. The ideas ascribed to Plato—many of which were drawn from the writings of the Neoplatonic interpreters of Plato and had little or nothing in common with what Plato actually wrote—were central to the medieval world view. These ideas were found in a few texts—primarily Chalcidius' unfinished commentary on the *Timaeus* and Macrobius' commentary on the *Somnium Scipionis* (an excerpt from Cicero's *De re publica*). These works dealt with a variety of themes—as we shall see, Macrobius' commentary was a major reference work on dreams and visions—but their most basic influence was in setting out a graphic model of the continuous act of divine creation.

This description of how all created things come to be combined philosophical terms from late antiquity with a vaguely Christian view of creation. It was fully in accord with the characteristics of medieval perception to be found in the itinerary of the Mesopotamian monks. It emphasized the primacy of noncorporeal forces; it was an all-embracing explanation which stressed the close links between all created things; and it strongly associated the creative principle with visual imagery, using metaphors of sight to describe both the agents and the process of creation. Here is Macrobius' formulation:

> God . . . created from himself Mind. This Mind, called *nous*, as long as it fixes its gaze upon the Father, retains a complete likeness of its Creator, but when it looks away at things below [it] creates from itself Soul. Soul, in turn, as long as it contemplates the Father, assumes his part, but by diverting its attention more and more, though itself incorporeal, degenerates into the fabric of bodies. . . .[1]

Man, Macrobius wrote, participated in the creative Mind because unlike the other animals his erect posture allowed him to "reach towards heaven and shun earth" and to "gaze with ease at the

11

heavens." Animals, which "have difficulty looking upwards," have only sense-perception and growth, not Mind.

> Accordingly, since Mind emanates from the Supreme God and Soul from Mind, and Mind, indeed, forms and suffuses all below with life, and since this is the one splendor lighting up everything and visible in all, like a countenance reflected in many mirrors arranged in a row, and since all follow on in continuous succession, degenerating step by step in their downward course, the close observer will find that from the Supreme God even to the bottommost dregs of the Universe there is one tie, binding at every link and never broken. This is the golden chain of Homer which, he tells us, God ordered to hang down from the sky to the earth.[2]

Among the conclusions about the nature of reality this passage encourages are these. First, it makes plain that the greater and more powerful among created beings are incorporeal. Not only God himself but Mind, Soul, and many of the multitude of beings between Soul and man have no visible bodies. Corporeality, which is directly related to distance from God and imperfect contemplation of him, is not a norm of existence but an indication of inferiority on the scale of creation. Second, it teaches that between God and man there are infinite levels of existence peopled by beings more incorporeal than man but less so than God. Occupying higher planes on the scale than man, they are closer than he is to enlightenment yet alien to him in nature; as such, they form a mysterious and largely unknown spiritual population powerful enough to influence man's destiny.

Third, the Neoplatonic cosmology states that *all* created things —including those we would term inanimate—participate in the chain of creation and follow its laws. As defined here, life is something other than sentience or reproductive capacity; it is an inescapable quality of existence which is shared by stones, water and fire as surely as it is by trees and angels. All creation is alive, and this life puts an indefinable bond between animate and "inanimate" nature. And fourth, the Neoplatonic vision of creation suggested in its terminology that the forces of divine creation are unleashed by the power of sight. Sight was conceived not as a passive recording of experience but as a form of creative energy. It was through a visual act that Mind, by "looking away at things below," created Soul, and that Soul, by "diverting its attention" from God, created the lower forms. Vision was more than creative energy, however; it determined each being's likeness to God. It was man's visual capabilities, Macrobius wrote, that determined the degree of his participation in the divine mind.

This Neoplatonic formulation of existence was incorporated into the works of a chain of influential medieval thinkers, from Augustine through the mystical theologians of the fourteenth and fifteenth centuries. It was not a fringe doctrine but a part of the mainstream of medieval culture. It encouraged medieval people to accept the existence of a wide range of beings, most of which were invisible most of the time. It strengthened their faith in the actuality of the unseen. It underscored their predisposition to cope with the natural world through magical or occult means, triggering by secret methods the life principle that united all things. And it legitimized the visionary imagination as a primary channel of understanding and revelation. In short, it opened the door to the enchanted world.

During the reign of the English king Richard II a monk of Byland Abbey in Yorkshire set down a number of encounters between the people of his neighborhood and supersensible beings. One of them concerned a tailor named Snowball whose meeting with a disembodied spirit involved him, his neighbors, and the local clergy in a drawn-out transaction with the incorporeal.

Riding home one evening, Snowball saw a raven fly around his head and then fall to earth as if it were dying. When sparks shot from its sides, though, he knew himself to be in the presence of a spirit and crossed himself, in God's name forbidding the creature to harm him. It flew away screaming, but attacked him a second time as he rode on, striking him in the side and throwing him off his horse. "In a swoon and lifeless," the account reads, he lay frightened until, "rising and strong in the faith," he fought with the apparition with his sword. As he did so it changed its form, assuming the shape of a peat stack, and Snowball again conjured it in the name of God not to hurt him.

The tailor then went on, but carried the cross-shaped hilt of his sword ahead of him out of fear. When the being appeared a third time, now in the shape of a dog with a chain collar, he determined to force it "in the name of the Trinity and by the virtue of the blood of Christ from his five wounds" to confess its name, the cause of its punishment and the means to ease it.

> And the spirit, panting terribly and groaning, said, "Thus and thus did I, and for thus doing I have been excommunicated. Go therefore to a certain priest and ask him to absolve me. And it behooves me to have the full number of nine times twenty masses celebrated for me. And now of two things you must choose one. Either you shall come back to me on a certain night alone bringing to me the answer of those whose names I have given you; and I will tell you how you may be made whole, and in the mean time you need not fear the sight of a wood fire.* Or otherwise your flesh shall rot and your skin shall dry up and shall fall off from you utterly in a short time. Know moreover that I have met you now because to-day you have not heard mass nor the gospel of John, and have not seen the consecration of our Lord's body and blood, for otherwise I should not have had full power of appearing to you."
>
> And as he spoke with the tailor he was as it were on fire and his inner parts could be seen through his mouth and he formed his words in his entrails and did not speak with his tongue.[3]

* Encountering light after meeting with a spirit was thought to be harmful.

Telling the tailor to bring with him "the four gospels and the name of victory, namely Jesus of Nazareth" on his return, the spirit warned him of two other spirits in the vicinity, one of which habitually took the form of fire or a bush and another which had the likeness of a hunter. Then, making him swear an oath not to "defame his bones"—reveal his identity—to any but the priests who would celebrate the masses, the spirit left him.

It was several days before Snowball contacted the priests. The encounter had left him ill, but on his recovery he approached the cleric who had excommunicated the spirit, who in turn consulted three other churchmen before finally agreeing to give Snowball the written absolution, which he was to bury at the head of the spirit's earthly grave. On being assured by a friar that the absolution was lawful, he contacted "all the orders of the friars of York" and set them to saying masses for the soul of the excommunicate. In three days they were finished, and the tailor again set out to speak with the ghost. At the appointed meeting place, he "made a great circle with a cross," wearing on his person the four gospels and other holy words. Standing in the center of the circle, he placed reliquaries within it, forming a cross, which had written on them formulaic protective words.

The spirit appeared, first as a she-goat and then "in the likeness of a man of great stature, horrible and thin." It told the tailor that his efforts had been successful, and added that he was now freed of the three devils who had been tormenting him and that "on Monday next" he would "pass into everlasting joy with thirty other spirits." Asked about the two other ghosts he had warned of, he would say only that one was a foreign soldier who because he had killed a pregnant woman was condemned to wander in the form of a bullock without mouth or eyes or ears, the other a religious who appeared as a ghostly hunter. The latter, he predicted, would in time be conjured.

Finally the tailor asked the spirit to tell him of his own

condition, and his future, as it had agreed on their first meeting. It warned him of the scandal he caused by remaining in the area, and advised him to move away, adding that riches would follow. Then, announcing "I can stay no longer talking with you," the spirit cautioned Snowball to keep the protective writings by his head until he went to sleep, and "not to look on a wood fire for this night at least," and disappeared.

This interview too made Snowball ill, but he was well again in a few days; what became of him is not recorded in the monk of Byland's account.

There is nothing distinctively medieval in the broad outline of this ghost story, but its background is clearly that of an age maximally open to belief. The meeting with the spirit was not sought or welcomed; indeed, the tailor would gladly have avoided it. But neither was it "beyond belief," as such an encounter might well be for a twentieth-century Englishman. Seeing the apparition was an unlikely but not totally unexpected situation. It was well within the range of the possible; otherwise how did Snowball know exactly what terms to use in his defense and how to conjure the spirit? Obviously, the tailor had either had a similar experience before or had learned what to do from accounts of people who had. Protection against malevolent spirits was a common theme of medieval as of most folklore; in this case the means of protection mingled ideas of Christian powers with devotional prescriptions and occult practices. Three simultaneous remedies—those of magic, theology and deity—were brought to bear against a force whose existence all three realms of knowledge anticipated.

Snowball's familiarity with the ritual of spiritual confrontation seems more appropriate to a practiced sorcerer than to a Yorkshire tailor. Yet there is no reason to believe he had more knowledge than his neighbors of the mechanics of conjuration or other occult lore. In his awareness of precise "names of power" and other holy words, and above all in his exchange of services with the spirit—

helping it gain absolution in return for revealing something of the tailor's future—the Yorkshireman was probably displaying, not expertise but common knowledge, not a Faustian daring but the mundane intelligence of a man habituated to believe in supersensible beings.

To be sure, this habituation did not prevent him from being fearful. The medieval belief in noncorporeal creatures did not presuppose their beneficence. But the availability of occult and religious counterforces prevented a sense of hopelessness, and made possible a certain accommodation between the visible and invisible worlds. And the church, while condemning certain (by no means all) occult knowledge, in practice cooperated actively in this accommodation.

For if Neoplatonism was one wellspring of medieval perceptual attitudes, biblical angelology and demonology was another. "Compared to the multitude of supernal and angelic beings," wrote St. Jerome, "the mass of humanity is as nothing." [4] Jerome's statement was incorporated into the *Etymologiae* of Isidore of Seville, who in another work, the *Differentiae*, characterized demons as forces which

> unsettle the senses, stir low passions, disorder life, cause alarms in sleep, bring diseases, fill the mind with terror, distort the limbs, control the way lots are cast, make a pretence at oracles by their tricks, arouse the passion of love, create the heat of cupidity, lurk in consecrated images; when invoked they appear; . . . they take on different forms, and sometimes appear in the likeness of angels.[5]

Aquinas found in angels a level of creation which made the whole of creation comprehensible. They were the "separated substances" which linked together the causal network of creation, from the uncaused God to the uncausing, irreducible elements of matter.

Bodiless beings had a secure place in theology, which influenced

17

popular thought far less through its careful categorization of these beings than through the simple fact that they were included in the corpus of Christian truth.

Ghosts, demons and angels are the most familiar denizens of the enchanted world. Their history both precedes and antedates the middle ages, and little imagination is needed to grasp their force in medieval thought. Another trait of this mentality strains the imagination more acutely. Stated broadly, it is the tendency to animize.

Giving names to inanimate objects is a very rudimentary form of this habit of mind. Like people before and since, the medievals named their lands, their houses, their ships and their weapons. A chronicler has preserved the names of the ships the Black Prince took to France on a campaign during the Hundred Years' War. Some were called by human names (*Giliane, James, Margaret of the Tower*), others had religious names (*Gracedieu, Trinity, Saint Mary Boat*, and the Prince's own ship, the *Saint Esprit*), still others had names drawn from chivalric or other sources (*Faucon, Cronipher, Glythe*). Swords were usually named, and the crusaders christened even their siege weapons; on the third crusade, King Philip's mightiest petrary was called "Evil Neighbor." Bells, whose installation in a church tower was preceded by a baptism-like ritual of consecration with chrism, were nearly always named. The great bell of St. Albans, broken in the early fourteenth century and recast in the sacristy amid continual psalms and prayers, was called "Amphibalus" by the monks.

More foreign to our patterns of thought was linguistic imagery which ascribed to concepts or places the character of human or animal form. Describing the shape of the world Isidore of Seville wrote that "as it rises toward the region of the north, so it slopes away toward the south; its head and face, as it were, is the east, and its back part the north." Ancient and medieval cities were sometimes said to have animal shapes: Rome resembled a lion, Gervase of Tilbury wrote, and Carthage an ox, while Troy had the outlines of a horse. The equine shape of Troy is both an animization and a symbolic evocation of the city's best-known legend. In his *Rationale divinorum officiorum*, the ecclesiologist Durandus of Mende used a similar blend of anthropomorphic and symbolic imagery when he likened the interior design of a church to the human body:

> The arrangement of a material church resembles that of the human body: the chancel, or place where the altar is, represents the head: the transepts, the hands and arms, and the remainder—towards the west—the rest of the body. The sacrifice of the altar denotes the vows of the heart.[6]

It was only a little step from applying animate metaphors to inanimate things to actually conceiving them as living. The twelfth-century cosmologist Adelard of Bath wrote that the stars were divine creatures which consumed earth and water drawn up through the atmosphere to the purer realms of the heavens. So purified are these substances by their passage upward, he noted, that they do not hamper the intellect of the stellar creatures which eat them.

Medieval cosmological ideas, undergirded by the Neoplatonic view that all things participate, however imperfectly, in the life of the creator led the medievals to attribute to natural and man-made objects a wide range of capabilities. Bells were thought to have the power to frighten off demons, and to calm storms. The monks of St. Albans fastened a papal seal to the top of the Abbey tower to fend off lightning. The church building at Glastonbury was so mighty, William of Malmesbury wrote, that "if any person erected a building in its vicinity, which by its shade obstructed the light of the church, it forthwith became a ruin."

And where they did not actually cause changes in the affairs of mankind, both living and nonliving things were thought to reflect those changes. The night before one English king died, a chronicler noted, the fish in a certain lake prophesied his fate by dying by the thousands. And Gerald of Wales told how a careful observer might chart the course of Marcher politics by watching the River Dee, whose changes of current reflected the outcome of the constant fighting between the Welsh and English. (The Flemings settled in Wales by Henry I brought with them another form of divination in which future events were read in the right shoulder of rams, boiled and stripped of flesh.)

This confidence in the correspondences between the natural world and human events was the traditional ground logic of sorcery, and a broad catalogue of magical arts were cultivated in the middle ages. A fourteenth-century Bolognese professor left a list of the forms of "prohibited science" practiced in his day. It named several dozen varieties of magic, including geomancy, aerimancy, hydromancy and pyromancy (divination by earth, air, water, and fire), theurgy (sorcery done with the aid of gods, spirits or demons), necromancy (sorcery by means of the dead), augury, poisoning, sortilege (divination by lots), legerdemain, incantation, magic by means of symbols, gyromancy (interpretation of astro-nomical events), palm-reading, fortune-telling, enchantment, the preparation of potions, and illemancy (prediction of the future by means of color interpretation). Still other practices are described in contemporary documents: alchemy, the "notary art" (divination by word forms), and the preparation of protective talismans or charms.

The evidence suggests that most of these arts were widely practiced from the twelfth century on, and that most people relied on the magical properties of charmed objects in their daily lives. Travelers carried formulaic writings inscribed with divine names or biblical phrases intended to ward off attackers. The name of Jesus, the first words of St. John's gospel, or verses that symbolized safe passage were all common; "Jesus passed through the midst of them" was a frequent talisman of English travelers. (The "In principio," the phrase that begins the gospel of John, was thought to embody great spiritual potency. Hearing it on a given day was thought to ensure protection throughout that day from a variety of harms. Tailor Snowball's spirit, it will be recalled, told him he was vulnerable to demonic encounters partly because he had not heard the "In principio" that day.) Along with herbal concoctions and charmed stones, medieval soldiers carried magical writings on their persons, and in Italy, the mercenary captains of the fourteenth and fifteenth centuries were accused of relying on sorcery for their victories.

Champions in judicial duels wore magical tokens and sometimes had occult symbols tattooed or painted on their heads. In one judicial contest between champions representing the bishop and the earl of Salisbury, both fighters were searched for unlawful arms, and "prayers and magical spells" were found sewn into the clothes of the bishop's man. The battle was cancelled, and the bishop lost his case—not because the court censured the talismans, but because it was felt their power would surely make the contest unequal. When the English Chief Justice Tresilian was sentenced to be executed for treason in 1388, he boasted that, as long as he remained clothed, he could not be killed. The executioner found hidden in his outer garments "certain images painted like to the signs of the heavens, and the head of a devil painted and the names of many of the devils wrote in parchment." Stripped of them, he was hanged.

Rings were a frequent agent both of enchantment and protection. Through the curative properties attributed to gems set within them, certain rings were believed able to heal wounds or sicknesses. Passavant, bishop of Mans, took such a ring with him on crusade, and cured many by its power. Other rings were miniature reliquaries, such as the diamond ring with a hair of the Apostle Peter

21

which Gregory VII sent to Normandy to encourage a Norman invasion of England. But they could also be used to call up occult forces; Joan of Arc was accused of using charmed rings to crush her enemies, and one of the charges against the slain duke of Orleans in 1407 was that he had conspired against the king using a ring conjured "in the name of devils." Robert Mauvoison, archbishop of Aix, who was a devotee of a variety of magical practices, including palm-reading and divination, consulted a Jewish astrologer who made symbolic carvings on his pastoral rings to protect him from disease and bring him luck.

Charges and countercharges of sorcery were common in the fourteenth and fifteenth centuries, and became a standard feature of church-state and other political struggles. Philip IV accused both Boniface VIII and the bishop of Pamiers of "demonolatry," and invocation of devils was among the charges against the Templars when their order was suppressed in France. John XXII believed he had found in Hugues Geraud, bishop of Cahors, a magician sent to assassinate him through poison and the use of sympathetic magic, and as a continuing precaution the pope kept on his dining table a knife carved from poison-detecting "serpent's horn" he inherited from his predecessor Clement V. At the French court, a rumor associated the deaths of the dauphin, Louis, in 1276 and every Capetian and Valois king for the next hundred years with poison and supernatural assault. While these were among the best-publicized accusations of political magic, similar fears were recorded at earlier medieval courts. Under Henry III, Hubert de Burgh was accused as a poisoner and sorcerer, and the link between theurgy and treason was well forged long before the execution of Tresilian.

Magic, Roger Bacon wrote, is most creditable when performed under the correct astrological influences. Images and verbal charms, made when the proper constellations are in the ascendant, derive their powers from the force of the stars themselves, and from the power they impart to men. For more than any other single occult science, astrology exerted a widespread continuing influence over the medieval imagination.

Chroniclers writing in many parts of western Europe recorded that in the mid-1180's an astrological panic swept Christendom. A conjunction of planets in the constellation Libra foreshadowed, according to some astrologers, natural disasters, destruction and crime. "Impeded and embarrassed between two evils, Saturn and the Tail of the Dragon," an astrologer in the employ of the constable of Chester claimed, Mars predicted "sorrows, contentions, alarms, catastrophes, murders and spoliation of property." A Saracen interpretation of the coming configuration was more moderate, but the warnings of an astrologer called "Corumphira" were extremely alarming. Some countries would be struck by earthquakes, he said, while cities built in desert lands—particularly in Egypt and Ethiopia—would be made unfit to live in. Corumphira saw two advantages in the stars, however; the Franks were to prevail in the Holy Land while the race of Saracens would disappear, and, after the configuration passed, mankind's life span would increase. In German lands, it seems, these advantages were unknown. The Marbach chronicler wrote that people dug underground caves to live in and the clergy performed additional masses, hoping God would alleviate the suffering they felt to be inevitable.

Neither Saladin's destruction of the Christian kingdom of Jerusalem in 1187 nor the notable absence of longer life spans discredited these prophecies, and along with the appearance of comets, astrological predictions continued to spread alarm in every medieval generation. Many dimensions of the enchanted world—its faith in superhuman forces, its belief in correspondences between the level of creation, its fatalistic accommodation with the unseen—found congenial teachings in the popular and formal

23

science of astrology. As a tool of popular thought, the so-called "judicial" astrology that predicted the futures of individuals and the disasters of multitudes was often condemned by the learned, but they eagerly accepted it as a valuable science on other grounds. Astrologers—many of whom were Moors, Jews or even Saracens— were important functionaries at many royal courts, casting horoscopes and determining favorable and unfavorable times for battles and other important events.

Apologists for astrology liked to cite the ways in which the heavenly science helped the cause of Christianity. Citing the great Arab authority Albumasar, from whose works most western astrological knowledge came, Bacon showed how all major religions took shape under a major conjunction of Jupiter with another planet. The Hebrew faith arose when Jupiter conjoined Saturn; the Moslem when Jupiter and Venus joined. Christianity was born under the joining of Jupiter and Mercury—the event that told the Magi of the forthcoming birth of Christ—and in time a conjunction of Jupiter with the moon would herald the arrival of Antichrist.

A legend circulated among the scholastics which by bringing Plato within the circle of Christian revelation removed the stigma of paganism from his teachings. According to the legend, when Plato's tomb was opened, his corpse bore an inscription written in golden letters and proclaiming "I believe in Christ who will be born of a virgin, will suffer for the human race and will rise again on the third day." Plato was legitimized by the fiction that he had known Christ; in the same way, the validity of astrology was enhanced by the claim that biblical personages and saints had used it to gain knowledge of climatic influences and even to perform miracles. The Italian astrologer Guido Bonatti wrote a treatise in which he showed that the church Fathers and even Jesus himself employed astrological knowledge. The Hebrews, Roger Bacon wrote, were the first to record the zodiacal influences on various earthly regions. Moses used a ring charmed under a potent planetary configuration to escape war in Egypt; Solomon left occult astrological knowledge "written in an enigmatical form" which the Magi have since abused. More significant, Bacon added, was the fact that many Christian miracles were worked by virtue of the combined powers of sanctity and the rational soul making use of astrological influences.

> For when the purpose, desire, and force of the rational soul, which is nobler than the stars, are in harmony with the force of the heavens, of necessity either a word or something else is produced of wonderful force in altering the things of this world. . . . We see this in full measure in the case of saints who have performed miracles, to whom the elements of the world were obedient.[7]

This weaving together of two distinct sources of superhuman ability—the miraculous potency of sanctity and the occult forces triggered by intellectual knowledge of astrology—was only one sign of the general absorption of astrology into the mainstream of scholastic thought. Astronomy, defined narrowly as the study of the movements of celestial bodies, had of course long been part of the medieval curriculum. Expanded through the influx of Arab learning to include astrology—the study of the prophetic meaning and occult influences of celestial phenomena—the entire study was redefined as that science which explained the mechanism connecting earthly events and the movements of the stars. It was seen as a scientific key to the mysterious link that bound together the Neoplatonic chain of created beings, causing them to influence one another. Astronomical knowledge per se was eagerly sought, but was subordinated to the divinatory art of astrology.

The fundamental premise of astrology—that the course of human events may be read in the stars—could easily be seen as a permutation of Neoplatonist views. Animated like all created beings, the stars and planets reflected in their movements the activities of other realms; to believe otherwise was to cast doubt on the very structuring of the cosmos. Astrological concepts were easily harmonized with the leading cosmological texts. Twelfth-century commentators glossed the *Timaeus* in terms of zodiacal influences. The Aristotelian doctrine that earthly happenings are caused by a combination of the daily east-west movements of the fixed stars and the yearly west-east paths of the planets also seemed to underscore astrological theory.

In Italy, astrology quickly became a serious academic profession. The universities of Bologna, Milan and Padua all had chairs of astrology, and their occupants produced a body of learned texts. The furor attending the burning in 1327 of the best-known Italian astrologer, Cecco d'Ascoli, by the inquisition has led to a distorted view of the reception of astrological learning. When set against the unmarred careers of countless other professional astrologers, the harsh fate of d'Ascoli seems atypical. One of his crimes, ascribing Jesus' birth, poverty and death to astrological influences, was a frequent theme of other writers who were not condemned. Two generations later a Bolognese lawyer wrote a life of Christ astrologically interpreted, and the great early fifteenth-century theologian Pierre d'Ailly commented on the astrological speculation that accompanied Jesus' birth.

D'Ailly, who wrote a variety of works attempting to harmonize astrological prediction with both history and theology, concluded that this learning "ought neither superstitiously to be believed nor haughtily condemned," and his judicious openness to astrological learning was shared by many of his contemporaries. While the Italian enthusiasm for academic astrology was not paralleled in northern Europe, scholars there were far from ignorant of its teachings, and the number of their references to planetary influences grew considerably in the fourteenth and fifteenth centuries.

In the lands under Arabic influence, astrology was a fixed

dimension of the world view. When the Portuguese chronicler Azurara listed the causes impelling prince Henry the Navigator to undertake the exploration of the African coast, a zodiacal impulse was prominent among them.

> For his [Henry's] ascendant was Aries, that is in the House of Mars and the Exaltation of the Sun, and the said Mars is in Aquarius, which is the House of Saturn, it was clear that my lord should be a great conqueror, and a searcher out of things hidden from other men, according to the craft of Saturn, in whose House he was.

At the gateway to the New World lay the enchanted perception of the Old.

Medieval perception was characterized by an all-inclusive aware-ness of simultaneous realities. The bounds of reality were bent to embrace—and often to localize—the unseen, and determining all perception was a mutually held world view which found in religious truths the ultimate logic of existence. This perception, which where it is alien to modern consciousness may be likened to an enchantment, was encouraged by Neoplatonist ideas of the power and number of noncorporeal beings, the presence of life in inanimate creation, and the significance of vision as a creative force and as a mode of human understanding. Medieval people lived in a perceptual climate in which noncorporeal beings were a familiar and to some extent a manageable force, recognized alike in theology and popular culture. Believing that both these beings and inanimate objects reflected and could be used to influence human affairs, the medievals cultivated a variety of magical practices and relied on occult protective devices and on astrology in the conduct of their everyday lives.

But the enchanted world held still another realm—one which

27

confirmed and nourished this view of reality. It was the realm of the visionary imagination. Visions erased the shear line between the known and the unknowable, the discoverable and the revealed. They interlocked the simultaneous realities; they made visible the unseen; they clarified the hidden shape of truth.

Chapter two

THE VISIONARY IMAGINATION

fter years of wearisome travel, the Mesopotamian monks in the *imago mundi* account finally came to within twenty miles of their destination—the point where heaven and earth meet. Yet though they were so close, they abandoned all attempts to reach it, at the urging of a vision.

It was not even a firsthand vision. Their host St. Macarius had been warned in a dream not to travel further; the monks took that warning to heart, and returned home. Of course, by inserting the vision the narrator avoided having to describe the joining point itself. But to say that the vision was a narrative device does not explain why medieval readers would have found it plausible.

What lent it credence was the central role of the visionary imagination in medieval consciousness. The perceived reality of the enchanted world predisposed the medievals to special habits of sight. Put another way, belief in a densely incorporeal population that could be glimpsed under special conditions affected the quality of their visual perception. Their sight was different from ours in kind; accepting a more inclusive concept of reality, they saw more than we do.

Furthermore, they reacted differently to what they saw. Confronted with a shape-changing apparition of the kind tailor Snowball encountered, an unexceptional modern man would gasp in helpless terror, confounded more by the shattering of his expectations about reality than by the sight of the numinous. To a medieval man or woman, though the appearance of a noncorporeal being was terrifying it did not challenge the very ground of their perception; if anything it reinforced their world view. Our lexicon associates visions with mysticism, irrationality, occultism, impracticality and madness. From our point of view, the visionary is a person who sees what isn't there; his visions separate him from reality. In the middle ages, visions defined reality.

This puts a basic perceptual barrier between us and the past—a barrier which, though it can never really be crossed, must at least be acknowledged. Understanding the medieval past means coming to terms with a quality of awareness that much of modern education is intended to discredit. The visionary imagination, long a disquieting embarrassment to rationalistic historians, was in the medieval period not aberrant but mundane, not unearthly but natural, even commonplace. It was the most distinctive feature of that lens of cultural illusion I have called the enchanted world.

The medieval past is full of visions. Extraordinary appearances—unusual natural configurations, visual portents, dream messages from the dead, divine and infernal warnings, intellectual illuminations, visions of the future—everywhere complemented ordinary sight. Chroniclers wove the visionary miraculous into the pattern of their histories, and the world they described was thick with noncorporeal beings and superphysical events. Visionary metaphors were the common vehicle for many kinds of formal writings, and the multifold reality of allegory and apocalyptic literature was familiar ground to the men and women of the twelfth, thirteenth and fourteenth centuries.

To impose a pattern on the visionary imagination these texts disclose is deceptive, for except to verify them the medievals did not divide into categories the visions they received. We can without distortion, however, distinguish oracular appearances from more general predispositions of sight, and can separate both of these from a quality of mental illumination or clarification that recurs in many forms in medieval thought.

A thirteenth-century chronicle tells how

> . . . about midnight of the day of our Lord's circumcision, the moon being eight days old, and the firmament studded with stars, and the air completely calm, there appeared in the sky, wonderful to relate, the form of a large ship, well-shaped, and of remarkable design and color. This apparition was seen by some monks of St. Alban's, staying at St. Amphibalus to celebrate the festival, who were looking out to see by the stars if it was the hour for chanting matins, and they at once called together all their friends and followers who were in the house to see the wonderful apparition. The vessel appeared for a long time, as if it were painted, and really built with planks; but at length it began by degrees to dissolve and disappear, wherefore it was believed to have been a cloud, but a wonderful and extraordinary one.[1]

The monks who saw the ship in the sky were looking at the stars to judge the time—a matter of precise and literal calculation. They were not watching for the extraordinary, yet they saw more than the stars and clouds; they saw what appeared to be a ship, not a phantom ship but a solid, timbered vessel, painted and "built with planks." It was not a symbolic apparition—it had no particular meaning or message—and after a time it dissolved as cloud-shapes do. Still, although they decided it was a cloud they had seen, and not a ship, the monks agreed it had been a "wonderful and extraordinary" cloud.

In their enthusiasm for the extraordinary the monks never lost sight of the most natural explanation of what they saw—that it was an unusual cloud shape. But if their familiar acceptance of the supernatural did not blind them to the more ordinary possibility, neither did their skepticism rule out the supernatural. This is what I mean by "seeing more." Their perceptual range was broader than ours. They were aware of more possibilities, because they were less inclined to dismiss any of them as unimaginable.

Seeing mundane phenomena as potentially miraculous was, like the tendency to animize, an important characteristic of the medievals' way of thinking. It was as if they continued a watchful interrogation of the natural world, confident that it would at intervals yield the truths of the supernatural. Both interpretations, in fact, might be appropriate.

In his *Itinerarium Cambriae* Gerald of Wales described a magical lake called Brecheinoi, or Llyn Savaddan, that was famous for its visionary appearances. At times, he wrote, the lake is greenish, at other times "tinged with red, not universally, but as if blood flowed partially through certain veins and small channels." People who lived near the lake occasionally saw buildings, pastures, and gardens rising from its surface, and when covered with ice it sent forth mysterious noises.

> In the winter, when it is frozen over, and the surface of the water is converted into a shell of ice, it emits a horrible sound resembling the moans of many animals collected together; but this, perhaps, may be occasioned by the sudden bursting of the shell and the gradual ebullition of the air through imperceptible channels.[2]

As in the case of the cloud-ship, both a natural and a more imaginative explanation for the sounds is advanced; Gerald, however, did not choose between them.

Eagerness for visions, then, did not close out careful observation; it enhanced it. John of Worcester described in great detail something which was seen in the sky by a variety of observers at Hereford in February of 1130. An "unaccustomed glow" appeared in the sky "at about the point where the sun inclines toward sunset at the summer solstice," and at its center was a roof-shaped cloud exuding a darting brightness, triangular in shape and "colored as if with the colors of the full moon and of a bright flame." Next a flat plank seemed to hover over the cloud, lighting first the cloud itself and then all the lower part of the northern sky. Watchers cried out to all who were in the vicinity, but the light faded quickly until only its glowing imprint was visible. "This was seen," the chronicler concluded, "by clerks of St. Guthlac and shepherds in the village of Hereford and by the guard at Brecon Castle. What they said, I have written; may Christ's grace save us." [3]

This account is significant both for its detail (the description of the vision is fuller than my paraphrase) and because it was carefully recorded despite the fact that it had no specific import. The glowing shape, cloud, and spreading light were not interpreted as a portent, a supernatural appearance or a divine sign. But because those who saw it believed it might have become any one of these, they watched it closely, noted its transformations, and later reported all that they saw.

Prompting the Hereford vision was a quality of image-receptiveness, an openness to visual sensation that complemented the broader range of medieval sight. The Hereford watchers, the chronicler wrote, felt "stupor or fear" at the strange configuration they witnessed, but they must also have felt anticipation, for most visions were charged with significant meanings. Correctly interpreted or heeded, they could forewarn against harm and prevent disaster; unheeded, they might prove fatal.

During the expedition sent against Moorish Lisbon as part of the second crusade, the Christian knights were eager for some graphic assurance of victory. Finally, as their ships entered the Tagus, the sign came.

> A wonderful portent appeared to us in the air. For behold, great white clouds coming along with us from the direction of the Gauls were seen to encounter other great clouds bespattered with blackness coming from the mainland. Like ordered lines of battle with left wings locked together they collided with a marvelous impact, some in the manner of skirmishers attacking on right and left and then springing back into line, some encircling others in order to find a way through, some going right through the others and reducing them to a void like vapor, some being pressed downwards and now almost touching the water, others being lifted upwards and now borne from view in the firmament.
>
> When at last the great cloud coming from our direction and carrying with it all the impurity of the air, so that all on this side appeared as purest azure, pressed back all the others which were coming from the direction of the mainland, and, as a victress driving the booty before her, held all along the mastery of the air, and all the others had either been reduced to nothing, or, if some fragments remained, they appeared to be in flight towards the city, we all shouted, "Behold, our cloud has conquered! They are confounded, for the Lord has put them to flight!" And so at last the squall ceased. And a short time afterwards, about the tenth hour of the day, we arrived at the city which is not far from the mouth of the Tagus.[4]

Anxious to know their fate, the crusaders turned the storm into a visual allegory of battle, seeing in the whirling of the storm-clouds the movements of knights and armies. This kind of vision is very close to divination; it does not see the extraordinary but uses the visionary imagination to read in the world of nature the pattern of the human future. It was by this same deductive logic that during the second crusade the soldiers of Louis VII, traveling without the king at their head, concluded that he was in peril. Seeing "the sun shaped like half a loaf of bread for most of the day," wrote Odo of Deuil, they feared that the king "had been deprived of some part of his light by the treachery of the Greeks."

Where the outcome of battle is at stake, the hunger for visionary occurrences is understandably great. But every sort of crisis had its own visionary remedy, and visions came in times of calm as well as of crisis. That class of visions meant to warn, persuade, or exhort the visionary is best understood as a special communicatory network linking the multiple dimensions of medieval reality.

The Cluniac abbot Peter the Venerable, while in Rome attending to the business of his monastery at the papal court, received a vision in his sleep. William, the recently deceased prior of Cluny, appeared to him, and this was their conversation.

> PETER: How are you, lord prior?
>
> WILLIAM: All is very well with me.
>
> PETER: Have you seen God yet?
>
> WILLIAM: I see him continually.
>
> PETER: Is it certainly true, what we believe about God, and is the faith we hold the true faith, without any doubt?
>
> WILLIAM: Nothing else is so true, or so certain.
>
> PETER: Are the rumors and gossip true that certain men whose identities you know killed you?
>
> WILLIAM: It is true.[5]

For added assurance, the entire exchange was repeated twice more; then William vanished.

Like the vision reported by St. Macarius in the account of the monks' journey to the end of the earth, Peter's vision was preserved for a specific purpose—to publicize the wrongdoing of the prior's murderers. Beyond this, though, it reflects either a revelation Peter was certain he had received or, at least, his conception of what such an interview would be like if it were held. Three of the four questions asked of the dead man's image had nothing to do with his murder; they were intended to verify Christian belief. William's comfort and state of mind after death, his ability to see God, and his witness to theological truth were meant to answer Peter's doubt with a certainty beyond the capacity of living men.

We who assign such things to the fringes of reality cannot easily recognize the awesome import of visions for people who set them at its center. Visions were the inescapable final arbiter of truth—but only if they were authentic. How was the visionary to tell true revelations from nightmares, divine illuminations from demonic delusions? The learned, familiar with antique vision theory, could turn to the discriminatory categories of Macrobius and Augustine's often-cited hierarchy of the modes of sight.

In his commentary on the *Somnium Scipionis* Macrobius defined five categories of dreams.

somnium	enigmatic dream
(Greek *oneiros*)	
visio	prophetic vision
(Greek *horama*)	
oraculum	oracular dream
(Greek *chrematismos*)	
insomnium	nightmare
(Greek *enypnion*)	
visum	apparition
(Greek *phantasma*)	

Two of these, the nightmare and the apparition, originate in the mind of the dreamer. Nightmares reflect only his day-to-day anxieties or longings; apparitions are tricks of the mind caught between slumber and wakefulness in the "first cloud of sleep." Oracular dreams, prophetic visions and enigmatic dreams do, however, help to foretell the future and are a crucial guide to conduct. In an oracular dream, a venerable or religious man (or a god) reveals what is to come and advises the dreamer about how to prepare himself for it. Prophetic visions are glimpses of the future itself, while in enigmatic dreams a particular message is conveyed, though "concealed with strange shapes and veiled with ambiguity."

Macrobius' list was of dreams, not visions; waking revelations were not conceived in his explanation. Furthermore, though the gods were not excluded from his categories he referred only obliquely to religious revelation; spiritual truth was not, in his scheme, the primary object of dreaming. And it is significant that Macrobius underscored the unreliability of visionary information. "All portents and dreams," he wrote,

> conform to the rule that their announcements, threats or warnings of imminent adversity are always ambiguous. Consequently we surmount some difficulties by caution and others we escape by entreaty and propitiation; still others are inevitable, being turned away by no skill or powers.[6]

This fatalistic attitude toward visionary communication left little room for divine compassion, yet though they were in some ways at odds with Christian views Macrobius' dream categories were exhaustively repeated by medieval thinkers.

When applied to the visionary lore of the Bible, however, they were found wanting. In explicating a passage in II Corinthians*, Augustine formulated a theory of vision that supplemented Macrobius. Interpreting Paul's reference to a man "caught up into paradise," "to the third heaven," Augustine explained that the three heavens referred to three kinds of human sight.

corporeal vision (*visio corporealis*)	seeing the incorporeal through natural optical perception
spiritual or imaginative vision (*visio spiritualis* or *imaginativa*)	seeing incorporeal shapes, as in dreaming
intellectual vision (*visio intellectualis*)	direct sight of incorporeal beings and imageless concepts

* II Corin. 12:2–4. Augustine, *De Genesi ad litteram*, Ch. 12.

Where Macrobius had simply defined the viridical merits of dreams, without making qualitative judgments between them, Augustine conceived three distinct orders of sight, each more perceptive than the last. His was a theoretical hierarchy in which increasing clarity of vision was linked to increasing cognition of truth. Seen in this new context, Macrobius' dream types became a subordinate category of Augustine's second level of sight, the one he called spiritual vision. The most important feature of this new framework was that it made human sight congruent with the kind of sight described in the Neoplatonic model of creation. There the Soul or Mind's power of sight, nourished by the vision of God, brought lower beings into existence. In the same way, Augustine wrote that through his power of sight man might ascend through comprehension of the corporeal world to perceive insubstantial beings, and finally to understand formless ideas and God himself. Visual perception thus became an important index of spiritual progress, and it became possible to integrate visions themselves into the pattern of salvation.

Augustine's theory of vision gave the visionary imagination a Christian interpretation, but it did not solve the problem of false visions or delusion. In the realm of theology, in fact, this issue was never fully resolved. The thirteenth-century theologian Albertus Magnus accepted the popular view that, aided by astrological forces, demons could create phantasms to deceive the sight. And in his *De occultis* Aquinas wrote at length about evil "separated substances"—malevolent noncorporeal beings—capable of causing necromantic illusions.

Where man-made illusions were concerned, however, the medievals found ways to weigh the true against the false. The authority given to supersensible phenomena made abuse of these visionary expectations inevitable. The English king William Rufus, whose extreme skepticism about visions was as renowned as it was unusual, once dismissed news of a revelatory dream by pointing out that the dreamer was a monk and, like all monks, dreamed for money. A story contained in a letter of Edward III, sent to the papal court in explanation of events immediately preceding his reign, supports Rufus' slander.

After Queen Isabella's lover Mortimer had taken Edward II's place as ruler of England, Edward's brother the earl of Kent demanded of him whether the king was alive or dead. Though Edward was in fact dead Mortimer assured the earl that he was still living. Doubting his word, the earl went to a friar who was known for his occult powers. The friar, who may well have been in Mortimer's pay, told the earl that in a vision a saint informed him the king was indeed alive, and heartened by this news the earl plotted rebellion and was executed as a traitor. Before he died the earl revealed the deception preserved in Edward III's letter.

Whether or not the friar's deception was subsidized by the court of Isabella and Mortimer, it suggests that clerics and religious exploited popular belief in visionary revelation. But clerics were themselves exploited under the same guise. On his way to Rome a twelfth-century archdeacon was accosted by his creditors and jailed for debt. One night as he languished there his major creditor came to him and announced

> Do not despair, righteous man. God blessed you this night in a vision which I had, in which I saw you exalted to great state and high degree. Therefore I am certain, by reason of what it has been given to me to see, that you will conquer your difficulties.[7]

The archdeacon was released and resumed his journey—after promising to pay exorbitant charges in addition to his existing debts.

Visionary hoaxes by merciless creditors were unfortunate, but deception where sanctity and the miraculous were concerned was dangerous to faith. In the preface to his *De miraculis*, Peter the Venerable was aware of this dilemma. "When I recount these miracles," he wrote, "I rarely if ever include dreams, since they are often false or doubtful, but I do include those dreams which are worthy of credence."

Great care was taken in verifying the signs and miracles that occurred at the tombs of holy men and women. When Innocent III was asked by the monks of Sempringham to canonize their founder, he reminded them that "the evidence of miracles is sometimes misleading and deceptive, as with magicians," and ordered a bishop and two abbots to conduct a thorough inquest into the signs and miracles attributed to the holy Gilbert. He ordered them to proceed together to Sempringham, and

> then, by evidence, by witnesses, by common report and authentic documents, seek diligently for complete certainty about the holiness of his works and his mighty signs.[8]

Informants, who were interviewed under oath, included both monks and lay men and women. Their depositions were sealed and sent to Rome, where papal officials scrutinized them for doubts and contradictions. Six lay witnesses traveled to the papal palace at Anagni to testify about Gilbert's life, and not long after they arrived Gilbert himself appeared to the pope in a vision. Within a few days his canonization was declared.

It should not surprise us that the same age that produced the inquest jury should carefully examine the evidences for sanctity. The very importance of the visionary imagination made it imperative that it be authenticated. Like the Lisbon crusaders, the knights who went to the first crusade were very eager for miraculous signs. Yet when those who followed Raymond of Toulouse discovered the Holy Lance through a dream vision, the Norman knights suspected a hoax and demanded proof through the ordeal. Signs alone were not enough; what they wanted were *true* signs, and to recognize them they had to be both skeptical and critical about extraordinary events.

As we have seen, the critical mentality was not foreign to medieval thought. In the late twelfth century Adam of Eynsham wrote down the vision received by another Eynsham monk who had been found by his brethren lying before the altar "apparently lifeless, without movement in any member of his body." His eyes were sunk deep in their sockets, and both his eyes and nose were bloody. They put him to bed, forcing infusions of spices and herbs down his throat and applying plasters to his breast and arms. But though the monks rubbed the soles of his feet, stuck needles into him and even "caused a great horn to be blown in the room," the visionary did not awaken. After two days and nights he roused himself and told Adam all that he had seen on a journey through purgatory, hell and paradise.

Compared with many similar vision narratives, Adam of Eynsham's account was unusually eloquent and persuasive. Despite this—and the dramatic evidence of the monk's extraordinary physical state during the vision—many Eynsham monks refused to believe their brother's story. Ten years later, Ralph of Coggeshall had to defend its veracity in his *Vision of Thurkill*.

> I do not believe that such a man, so religious and so learned, would have written these statements unless they had been sufficiently tested; he being at that time, moreover, chaplain to Hugh, Bishop of Lincoln, a most holy man; and Thomas, Prior of Binhan, who was then Prior of Eynsham, and who examined the evidence closely, has since assured me that he feels no more doubt of the truth of the vision than of the Crucifixion of Our Lord Jesus Christ.[9]

But after all, he concluded, "every revelation is doubted of by someone."

41

The different visual orientation of medieval people and the visionary climate they inhabited perhaps made inevitable a third characteristic of the visionary imagination. It was that the highest accomplishments of abstract thought were associated with a particular kind of vision. Intellectual discovery was often linked to a falling away of barriers to sight. In his *Vita Anselmi*, the twelfth-century writer Eadmer told how the saint "attained such a height of speculation" that he could

> see into and unravel many most obscure and previously insoluble questions about the divinity of God and about our faith. . . . Hence he applied his whole mind to this end, that according to his faith he might be found worthy to see with the eye of reason those things in the Holy Scripture which, as he felt, lay hidden in a deep obscurity. Thus one night it happened that he was lying awake on his bed before matins exercised in mind about these matters; and as he meditated he tried to puzzle out how the prophets of old could see both past and future as if they were present and set them forth beyond doubt in speech or writing.
>
> And behold, while he was thus absorbed and striving with all his might to understand this problem, he fixed his eyes on the wall and—right through the masonry of the church and dormitory—he saw the monks whose office it was to prepare for matins going about the altar and other parts of the church lighting the candles. . . .[10]

Eadmer was not referring here to the mystical illumination of a contemplative, but to a quality of visual illumination experienced in the course of intense speculative thought. Anselm was aware of a sudden burst of visionary understanding, accompanied by an unaccustomed broadening of physical sight.

When at another time Anselm was struggling to formulate the

proofs of God's existence and attributes he would later set forth in his *Proslogion*, "suddenly one night during matins," Eadmer wrote, "the grace of God illumined his heart, the whole matter became clear to his mind, and a great joy and exultation filled his inmost being." Here too metaphors of illumination are used to convey intellectual clarification.

Bacon underscored the close links between what Eadmer called the eye of reason and physical sight when he listed the seven modes of internal knowledge. Illumination received through rational thought was the first of these modes, "raptures"—the seeing of inexpressible truths—the highest of them. The illumination of the thinker and the rapture of the mystic, to Bacon, differed primarily in degree; to the extent that they were rooted in a special kind of internal sight, they were similar in kind.

Bacon, who along with Pecham synthesized the optical knowledge of the middle ages, saw in the study of vision "the flower of all philosophy" and the "peculiar delight" of man. Among all the senses, he wrote, vision alone leads to differentiation, to learning, and ultimately to wisdom. In his *Opus maius*, he elaborated at length a spiritual allegory of optical perception.

Bacon's analogies between physical and spiritual sight are drawn-out and complex. They take as their starting point the phrase "Guard us, O Lord, as the pupil of thine eye." Like the many biblical references to sight, Bacon notes, this one cannot be correctly understood without knowledge of how the mechanism of corporeal vision corresponds to spiritual enlightenment. The eye's pupil has seven "guardians"—two humors, a web, three coatings, and certain "spirits and forces" from the region of the optic nerve. Corresponding to these are the seven guardians of the soul, the pupil of spiritual sight. Each of these seven guardians—virtues, gifts, beatitudes, spiritual senses, fruits, revelations, and gifts of grace—may in turn be subdivided into seven components, all of which are enumerated. There are seven virtues: faith, hope, charity, justice, fortitude, temperance, and wisdom. There are also seven gifts of the Holy Spirit. There are eight beatitudes rather than seven, but to preserve the symmetry here Bacon adds an eighth guardian of the pupil—the eyelashes.

Exhausting this particular analogy, Bacon moved on to point out how the requisite conditions for physical and spiritual sight are parallel. Physical vision needs a source of light; spiritual vision relies on the light of divine grace. Physical vision requires a moderate distance between the viewer and the object of his sight; spiritual vision demands that the believer maintain a "moderate distance" from God—neither too remote through weak belief or excessive sin nor too close through "excessive presumption of intimacy." Finally, Bacon finds in optics a threefold model of visual perception. Just as a visual image may be seen directly, or through refraction (seen after it passes through an intervening medium), or through reflection (seen indirectly, through an image of the original), so spiritual images may be perceived in each of these ways. Direct spiritual vision belongs solely to God, refracted spiritual vision to angelic beings. Man has by nature reflected spiritual vision—the ability to perceive spiritual truths as they are mirrored in earthly creation. Yet human vision, while reflected as compared to the direct vision of God, may itself be subdivided to form two further sets of parallels to the three optical categories. Men and women who approach sanctity have a kind of direct vision; those less perfect see through refraction; the greatest sinners through reflection. And beyond this, man's theological destiny may be expressed in terms of increasing visual acuity.

> Man has a threefold vision; one perfect, which will come in a state of glory after the resurrection; the second in the soul separated from the body in heaven until the resurrection, which is weaker; the third in his life, which is the weakest, and this is correctly said to be by reflection. As the apostle says, "We now see by means of a glass darkly, but in

glory face to face," and after the resurrection in perfect directness, and before it in a deviation from that directness of vision in our soul.[11]

Bacon's allusion to the beatific vision brings this discussion back to its starting point, to that thirst for the sight of God that lay behind the journey to the terrestrial paradise. At the apex of all human visions was the vision of God. It was this hoped-for climax that justified the cultivation of the visionary imagination.

"During the mass," Angela of Foligno wrote, "while I was trying to penetrate the depths into which God's humility and goodness flung me, in his approaching us through the holy Sacrament of the altar, I was rapt in the spirit, and received for the first time an intellectual vision of the holy Sacrament." A voice told her that Christ's body could exist on all the world's altars at the same moment of time, through the power of the All-Powerful, which was beyond the comprehension of living men. The Scripture, it said, speaks at length of this power, but those who read it do not understand. Those who have a certain feeling for God understand better, but even they know but little. "But a moment will come," the voice concluded, "when you will see the light. Then," she concluded, "I saw in a flash how God enters the holy Sacrament. Neither before nor since have I experienced anything like it."

Angela's "intellectual vision" paralleled Anselm's visionary speculation; the theologian sought rational understanding, the mystic understanding through an intensity of feeling. What came to both was a special inner perception, expressed in the language of sight.

That language was adopted by Nicholas of Cusa to describe the indescribable: the very essence of God. In his *Visio Dei*, Cusa identified God with "Absolute Sight, whence all sight takes its origin." God is that sight which surpasses in acuity, swiftness and strength all other known vision, the "true Unlimited Sight, . . . beyond all comparison more perfect." Since as creator God

45

permeates his creation, he takes part in and is the object of all sight, "seen by every person that seeth, in all that may be seen, and in every act of seeing."

In this rich evocation of the Neoplatonic imagery of sight, all existence becomes an extension of God's own vision. Understood in this context, the beatific vision is more than man seeing God, it is God seeing himself through man's eyes.

Human sight is thus enhanced by the presence of the absolute sight that lies hidden within it. Cusa applied this logic of vision to explain the unique nature of Jesus. Jesus had the full measure of human vision, he wrote; though keener and more perfect than those of all other mortal men, his eyes were nonetheless like other human eyes, "finite and limited to an organ." But insofar as Jesus was both man and God, to his human sight was added an absolute and unlimited sight,

> the sight whereby Thou, as God, didst see alike all things and each, absent as well as present, past as well as future. Thus, Jesu, with thy human eye thou sawest such accidentals as are visible, but, with thy divine, absolute sight, the substance of things. None save thee, Jesu, ever in the flesh beheld the substance or essence of things.[12]

Absolute sight, the vision of the substance or essence of things, was withheld from most men, but not participation in the visionary climate of medieval culture. Imaginative visual habits broadened the range of their perception; informative visions gave them guidance and nourished their faith; illuminative visions clarified and deepened their understanding. The profound truths of the middle ages were to be grasped through the education of the eyes. "My children," Angela of Foligno taught,

> man loves as he sees. The more we see the Man-God crucified, the more our love grows toward perfection, the more we are transformed

into him whom we see. And in the same measure that we are transformed through his love, we are transformed through his sorrow, for our soul beholds this sorrow.

The more man sees, the more he loves; the more he sees the passion, the more he is transformed, through compassion, into the very substance of the beloved one's sorrow. . . . As he is transformed through love, he is transformed through sorrow by the vision of God and of himself.[13]

A broader and different conception of reality is discernible in the middle ages; among its most conspicuous signs was a predisposition of sight I have called the visionary imagination. If differences may be traced in these perceptual patterns, why not in other areas of medieval life as well? While they are in no sense a systematic elaboration of this perceptual hypothesis, the chapters which follow do contain occasional illustrations of it, while highlighting familiar and unfamiliar landmarks of the medieval past.

Chapter three

CANONS, MONKS AND PRIESTS

n the second quarter of the twelfth century an obscure Alsatian canon named Hugo Metellus took it upon himself to chastise the greatest churchman of his day for the sin of pride. "Your life," he wrote to Bernard of Clairvaux,

is a shining light, which lights up not only near places but distant ones as well. Yea, you are as a burning coal; your words give off the fire of love, and are redolent with the sweet nectar of gentleness. . . .

But the cock is crowing, and it is the hour to rise from sleep. . . . I commend to you above all humility, without which he who heaps up virtues will find that he carries only dust. For rarely does such learning, such holiness exist without a certain windy elation. . . . and if a man does not know that he is proud, this itself is certainly pride, and the sorrow of pride.[1]

Without presuming to teach, Metellus said, he was moved to warn Bernard about this, lest without humility his chastity should become a widow, or worse, an adulteress at the hands of pride.

The letter in which this admonition occurs has not been

preserved by chance. Before he died, Metellus prepared the most important of his letters for posterity, ordering them according to the fame of their recipients and the weightiness of their contents. The letter to Bernard was put at the head of the collection, and in it Metellus justified the entire correspondence.

> I have written this, Father, first to praise you, secondly so that through praising you I might commend myself to you, and thirdly, so that through this he who has lain obscure among the infinite and nameless crowd may come to light, because he dared to write to such as you.

Though little known outside his own region, Metellus had reason to put himself within the circle of the great man's light. By his own testimony, he had excelled in all the seven liberal arts in his youth, with the rhetorician Ticelin and later at the chief center of divine studies in his time under Anselm of Laon. There he was in distinguished company. His fellow students William of Corbeil, Robert of Hereford, Thietmar of Bremen, Alberic of Rheims, Hugh of Reading and Matthew of Albano would become bishops and cardinals, while another brilliant contemporary, Peter Abelard, would stay at the school briefly on his way to a different avenue of fame.

Many of Metellus' letters echoed his theological learning. Writing to the monk Gerlandus, he condemned the revival of the Berengarian eucharistic doctrine in which the bread and wine were said to represent Jesus' body and blood only symbolically. Other letters discussed divine foreknowledge, papal infallibility, penance and the efficacy of prayer in easing the sufferings of the damned. Letters to Innocent II, Bernard and Abelard himself denounced Abelard's teachings, though in language suggesting that Metellus had not read Abelard's works. Elsewhere he wrote of the controversy over lay investiture, and criticized the ideas and methods of the schools.

49

But although he christened himself "a new disciple of Augustine," and "Aristotle's *secretarius*," Metellus was in fact a literary dilettante. A lamentably fluent writer, he delighted in acrostics and other puzzle poems and in the prose rhythms of the cursus. "*Venator verborum*," Metellus called himself: "a huntsman of words." Although he left assurances that they were wonderful, most of Metellus' works are lost, and our knowledge of his life and talents must come from his letters. Decorated with puns, rhetorical devices and quotations, they are fundamentally hollow—elaborate husks without kernels. They reflect a life largely without controversy, passion or reflection, undisturbed equally by piety or doubt. The everyday affairs of his church and chapter were left out of his correspondence. As a canon his religious duties were light; in a peaceful community he was left to pass the time in reading and composing letters to celebrated churchmen.

Classicism rather than asceticism ruled Metellus' outlook; he once advised a theologian to "live, be well, rejoice and not look backward." But his religious devotion was sincere, and in a letter to a humble cleric named Rainald he described himself, with a certain self-centered tenderness, as "a new calf in the manger of the Lord."

There were many Metelluses in the twelfth-century church. Canons, bishops and abbots had their finest letters copied and preserved in voluminous collections, and observed in them the obligatory word-play and formal stylistic devices demanded by their rank and education.

But in many of these collections the writer's elegance or inventiveness cannot disguise his continuing preoccupation with the management of secular and ecclesiastical affairs. Metellus was born in about 1080; his younger contemporary Arnulf of Lisieux belonged to the next generation of churchmen, and left a much more extensive epistolary legacy. Although most of the letters Arnulf preserved were personal, their constant themes are church administration and politics and the relations of churchmen with secular authorities. Over the span of a long life, Arnulf remained close to the center of ecclesiastical affairs. An active opponent of Anacletus in the double papal election of 1130, thirty years later he supported Alexander III during the schism and was his valued adviser. A papal legate during the second crusade, Arnulf traveled extensively and was on familiar terms with the leading churchmen of England, France and Italy. Peter the Venerable and Bernard were among his acquaintainces; his enemies were equally celebrated, and included John of Salisbury and Thomas Becket.

Arnulf belonged to a family of Norman clerics whose careers and loyalties belonged to the English kings. He was the heir of his uncle John, whose own apprenticeship had been at the courts of successive bishops of Séez in the late eleventh century, and who in about the year of Arnulf's birth became bishop of Lisieux. John owed his advancement to Henry I, and it was Henry who made him head of the Norman Exchequer. Arnulf was to follow his path to advancement, becoming archdeacon of Séez and bishop at Lisieux, and in time he would pass on the chain of succession to his nephews in their turn. But unlike John of Lisieux, Arnulf was trained at the most celebrated schools of Europe, and emerged at thirty skilled in law and jurisprudence.

The associations he made at Chartres, Bologna, Rome and Paris made him a valuable courtier, and Stephen of Blois sent Arnulf as his emissary to the Lateran Council in 1139. Election to the see of Lisieux soon followed, but after 1141 Arnulf found himself having to serve alternately at the French and English courts, frequently as intermediary between them.

Perhaps because of his legalistic temperament, Arnulf served his lords and fellow churchmen best as mediator—between Louis and the Angevins, between Henry II and Becket. But in any dispute a man who appreciates both sides is loved by neither, and despite his wide acquaintance and constant occupation Arnulf was a lonely figure. Although he sought his advice, Henry withheld his friendship from the bishop of Lisieux, and after a final breach between them Henry took over the see of Lisieux, and Arnulf retired to France. He was by this time nearing seventy, and went to live at lodgings he had built at the monastery of Saint Victor in Paris, dying there in 1182.

To those who admire piety and brilliance in twelfth-century churchmen Arnulf of Lisieux seems self-seeking and dull. He was above all an aristocrat, with a taste for good living and a talent for law and administration. He made no attempt to disguise either his tastes or his loyalties, and if he was successful at reconciling conflict he was equally disposed to begin it. As legate in the Holy Land he quarreled openly with his colleague the bishop of Langres; at home in Normandy he fought Geoffrey of Anjou for his episcopal lands; toward the end of the long estrangement between Henry and Becket he advised Henry to bring together an ecclesiastical coalition against the archbishop.

Arnulf's cultural predilections were those of an aristocratic patron. He rebuilt the cathedral church of Lisieux and the episcopal palace, and also built a chapel for the hospital of the town. Poets looked to him for patronage, and his own poetry was not to be despised.

As a lawyer, Arnulf saw the problems of the church largely in terms of disorder and lack of discipline. He was one of many twelfth-century advocates of the new order of canons regular, and tried to introduce it among the clergy of his own diocese. He dealt firmly, if not always effectively, with monastic discord, and wrote much about the church's need for liberty in the face of secular encroachment. But broader issues than firm enforcement of church law troubled him. Writing to Adrian IV in the late 1150's, Arnulf warned that papal permissiveness was encouraging rebellion. Decisive intervention was needed, he wrote,

> lest audacity grow haughty against the apostolic see, especially because the seeds of contempt are already pullulating against it. . . .

For already the apostolic name, which before was held in reverence and terror in this land, has been turned into a cause for scandal and contempt.[2]

In the ideal monastery, he said in another letter, "the apostolic severity would be respected as though the pope were present." Local authorities deserved the same unquestioned loyalty as the pope. Arnulf chastised an abbot for refusing his request to restore a repentant monk, "lest it be turned to contempt for the episcopal reverence. For you know," he added, "that in matters of religion, disobedience is a crime."

Hugo Metellus and Arnulf of Lisieux seem to flit like ephemeral moths around the steady flames of Bernard, Abelard and Becket. But they and not these glittering exceptions formed the characteristic outlook of the twelfth-century church. Though learned, they turned their learning inward to advance their reputations or defend the rights of their colleagues. They distrusted new ideas out of hand, and were very much concerned about the preservation of old ways and authorities; Metellus championed Augustine over Abelard, Arnulf defended keeping the old law in traditional hands rather than allowing new rights and customs. By birth, training and temperament they were conservative, and it was men like them who brought to trial speculative thinkers like Gilbert de la Porrée, were alarmed about the spread of heresy, and declaimed against the apostolic sects of Italy and southeastern France.

The motto, *diversa, non adversa*—"different, yet not opposing" —appears more than once in Metellus' letters. Because it was also Abelard's phrase, it has been made to stand for the whole of the twelfth century, and for a broadly tolerant attitude toward the discovery of truth. But the Rhenish canon and the celebrated Breton were alike only in their egotism; clearly the motto meant

53

different things to them. In the same way the beliefs and practices of the church were colored and influenced by the experiences and natures of thousands of medieval churchmen over a span of many centuries. It was not as an institution but as an aggregate of individual churchmen that the European church absorbed, debated and reshaped ecclesiastical tradition. As individuals, these men lose the clear outlines of their hierarchical rank and settle into the heterogeneous backdrop of medieval society.

For with the exception of a small corps of great or privileged churchmen, medieval clerics were often similar to laymen in their dress and behavior. A clerical career was not always a matter of vocation; many priests were priests' sons, who inherited their fathers' livings. Ordination was one route to freedom for serfs, and although both canon and secular law forbade the ordination of unfree men, both recognized that once ordained they became free. It is probable that many among the lower clergy began life as serfs, as several bishops certainly did. In the same way, clerical status was not insurmountably difficult to erase. To remove the priestly sanctity, the hair was cut, obliterating the tonsure, and the skin at the fingertips was shaved off at the point where they had been put into holy oil at the priest's consecration.

But if it was possible to admit or exclude men from the priesthood by means of ceremonies, it was not always easy to tell a clerk by his dress. In the twelfth century and later, complaints were heard against men in holy orders who wore "particolored clothes" like laymen, and at the Fourth Lateran Council in 1215 clerics were admonished against wearing garments that were too long or too short, or made of gaudy cloth, or adding to their vestments embroidered shoes and jewelry. Such extravagant dress was called simoniac by the Council—a serious charge—but there is good evidence that it continued throughout the thirteenth century and beyond. In 1237 the chronicler Matthew Paris noted that the dress of churchmen "appeared to be not clerical, but rather military," and warned that unless they reformed, stripping the ornaments from their horses as well as from their own garments, they would lose their benefices. But as with other secular garb, the taste for military apparel and fashionable adornment was traceable throughout the late middle ages; in the fourteenth century an English canon was still chastising priests for wearing armor and shoes with pointed toes.

The lives of medieval churchmen reveal an astonishing diversity of experience and personality. We know most about the greatest of them; lesser men have left few records, except in cases of crime or misfortune. The name of one obscure cleric is preserved in a letter of Innocent III solely because he had the ill luck to cause an unintentional homicide. Another man, a monk named Reimpert, was commemorated in the annals of the monastery of St. Stephen in Bavaria because, wanting to get the ants out of his bed, he tried to burn them, and "the flames caught the straw and then leapt quickly to the flooring, and in this way the entire church and cloister were burned to the ground."

Powerful clerics left more tangible evidence of their existence. Robert Hales, archdeacon of Lincoln, left on his death several thousand marks and silver cups of great value; an archdeacon of Northampton, John de Hotofp, left five thousand marks, thirty gold and silver cups, and "jewels of a large amount." Others of great substance achieved notoriety because they were more skilled at serving kings than at serving mass. Robert Stretton, nominated by Edward III to the see of Coventry and Lichfield, was rejected because of his illiteracy by the bishop of Rochester, by papal examiners at Avignon, and finally by the archbishop of Canterbury himself. Going over their heads, however, the king put pressure on the pope, who in the end consecrated Stretton as bishop "without examination." Forced on a point of form to make a profession of obedience to Edward at Lambeth Palace, another man read the statement for Stretton, "because he himself could not read."

Of course, a man like Stretton was only by courtesy a cleric, for he lacked that combination of political sagacity, feudal loyalty and knowledge of church law and administration that characterized most medieval clerics. For if the church was the most all-inclusive institution of the middle ages, the episcopacy was its most all-inclusive office. The medieval bishop was the cornerstone of the supranational edifice of the church, but he was at the same time an essential part of the network of interlocking secular rulerships that stretched across every medieval state. Particularly in northern Europe, a bishop was expected to fulfill the duties of a secular lord along with those of a spiritual ruler. As a feudatory of his secular overlord, he owed feudal taxes, attendance at court and knight service. His estates were given in fee to men who agreed in turn to fight on his behalf in his lord's army; to his court came knights and peasants as well as the clergy of his diocese.

But his secular obligations did not make the bishop's spiritual career any less important. He needed sufficient knowledge of law and theology to preside over a court of canon law, to conduct synods and guide the formulation of synodal legislation, and to advise his overlord in matters of church law and in his relations with other clergy. He was responsible for the behavior and learning of the clergy of his diocese, and for overseeing monastic discipline and the elections of abbots and priors. For most of the middle ages canonization remained an episcopal prerogative, and even after papal authority became pre-eminent in the recognition of saints the bishop continued to play an important role in authenticating miracles and gathering testimony from witnesses. Bishops were expected to find and to root out heresy and doctrinal error, and were called at intervals to Rome to participate in the formulation of church law and doctrine.

It served no one's interest to appoint to the episcopate men who were unfit either as feudatories or prelates, and bishops like Stretton were exceptional rather than common. But so strong were their secular loyalties that many medieval churchmen retained the outlook and behavior of feudal aristocrats throughout their lives. Clerics frequently kept their seigneurial rights even after entering the church, or accepted civil authority after their religious professions were made. Guido Tarlati, named bishop of Arezzo in 1306, was elected lord of the town of Arezzo in 1321, then "lord for life" by the ruling council of the citizens. Growing more and more powerful, he became allied with the Ghibellines against the papal party, launched an attack against the papal fortress of Città di Castello, and ended by being attacked in turn, his bishopric partitioned and his name anathematized.

Medieval clergymen were conspicuous on the battlefield. Sometimes they fought for religious causes—against heretics or the armies of an antipope. But more often the battles were between kings or feudatories to whom clerics had feudal or other personal loyalties. In the Hundred Years' War, the bishops of Metz and Verdun fought against Philip VI, and at the battle of Neville's Cross in 1346 the bishop of Durham and the two English archbishops made a good account of themselves, while two Scots bishops were taken prisoner on the field. A fourteenth-century bishop of Milan died after he fell from his horse while leading an army in Tuscany against the Ghibellines; a twelfth-century archbishop of Mainz who became embroiled in the factional violence of the city was assassinated by a gang whose watchword was "Meingote."

Some warlike clerics remained redoubtable even into old age. Bertrand, a Gascon patriarch of Aquileia, defended his rights for generations against secular rivals, and remained on guard even during the great church feasts. At eighty, we are told, one Christmas eve he celebrated midnight mass with a cuirass under his vestments, his war helmet on the altar, his army of cuirassed priests in the congregation.

Nor did churchmen abandon these habits when raised to the

57

holy see. Matthew Paris tells how at one point in the long and acrimonious struggle between Frederick II and the holders of the see of Peter, Innocent IV rode out to Castellana to meet with the emperor and negotiate peace. A quarrel arose, and Innocent resolved to get away before violence broke out. He made for Genoa, but, being warned that three hundred Tuscan knights were coming to kidnap him, he was frightened, and "at the time of the first sleep, leaving his papal ornaments, and but lightly armed, he mounted a swift horse, and with a well-filled purse, and almost without the knowledge of his attendants, suddenly and secretly took his departure."

The pope rode alone thirty-four miles the first day of his flight, and coming to the coast, met there twenty-three galleys and sixteen barges, filled with armed men under the command of the podestà of Genoa. They put to sea, but met a heavy storm which delayed and endangered them. Finally, however, they came to Genoa, the pope's native city, where his family and relations turned out in great numbers—indeed the men combed their genealogies for evidence of papal kinship. "The chief men," the chronicler wrote, "of the city all boasted that they were related by kindred or blood to the pope, in order that they might get a reward." Along with the rest of the Genoese, they welcomed him "with ringing of bells, with songs, and musical instruments, all crying out, 'Blessed is he who cometh in the name of the Lord.' "

Innocent did no fighting during his flight, but he showed a soldier's familiarity with physical danger, and planned his strategy and defenses skillfully, to the delight of the Genoese. In popular opinion, a soldierly churchman was something to be admired. It was often at the urging of the people that clerics led other soldiers into battle, and not only in Italy, where city politics were polarized around the imperial Ghibelline and papal Guelf parties, but elsewhere in Europe.

Perhaps the most sought-after fighting cleric of the thirteenth century was William, bishop of Valentia, whose exploits with the armies of Frederick II at the siege of Milan confirmed his reputation as a "man of blood, strenuous in slaughter, prone to bloodshed and wanton in incendiarism." Impressed with what he heard of William, the pope, Gregory IX, determined to win him to the side of the church, offering him the bishopric of Liège to guarantee his loyalty. But William was not satisfied, and used another of his suitors, his brother-in-law Henry III, to convince Gregory to appoint him to the see of Winchester as well. In addition to his spiritual powers, William had the advantage of exceedingly well-placed relatives; besides being uncle to the English queen, he was a blood relative of the highest Dutch and Savoyard aristocracy, and claimed ties by marriage to a host of important feudatories. These combined with his churchly rank to make him, as the chronicler wrote, "a spiritual monster and a beast with many heads." Before he could assume leadership of the papal army as Gregory hoped, William was poisoned at Viterbo, perhaps by an English enemy. The pope was much grieved at the news; Henry III tore his clothes and threw them into the fire.

William of Valentia was a cruel and ambitious man who was also a bishop. This combination was not rare; Sagramoso Gonzaga, natural son of Francesco Gonzaga, ruler of Mantua, became bishop of Mantua at age thirty and showed the utmost contempt for the church, murdering one of his cousin's counsellors and becoming a master of debauchery. Of course, by the late fourteenth century such careers were a commonplace of the Italian church. But the foundations for this sort of exploitation of the religious life were well laid in earlier eras. In the 1230's Honorius III wrote to the bishop of Arezzo that

It is known that there are some who, although they have for many years worn the habit of monks, have yet never made the profession of monks; wherefore, when they are accused by you or others of having

59

private property, and living otherwise irregularly, they are not ashamed to say that they are not bound to be without private property, to continence, and other regular observances, when it is not the habit that makes the monk, but the regular profession.[3]

Although Honorius warned these unprofessed monks against trying "to enter the land by two roads," their hypocrisy was mild compared to the criminous twelfth-century monks at the Norman abbey of Grestain, who while their abbot was in England looking after the monastery's property, fought among themselves, "slashing each other, in some cases to death." Thoroughly drunk, they tried to work a miracle, ducking a woman in cold water seven times to the accompaniment of barbarous songs and then trying unsuccessfully to bring her back to life. One of the monks killed a kitchen servant for slandering the monk's wife, breaking his head open and spreading his blood freely over the convent.

Hearing what was going on in his absence, the abbot feared to return; his proctor, whom he had left behind to preserve discipline, had also been killed when he tried to interfere. The bishop, who, as it happened, was Arnulf of Lisieux, stepped in and succeeded in scattering the monks for a time, but before long they grouped together again and defied him. In the end Arnulf went to Grestain in person, but rather than taking him on, the evil monks "claimed to know nothing of what he was talking about," and he had to appeal to the pope for aid.

The outcome of this particular incident is unclear, but it was not unique. Abelard encountered a nest of murderous monks in Brittany at about the same time, and convent regulations and papal letters confirm the frequency of convent violence. Canons and secular priests were no less savage. In 1154, archbishop William of York was, "by the treachery of his clergy, after receiving the Eucharist, during his ablutions, destroyed by means of some liquid of a deadly nature." It was the issue of clerical crimes that alienated

Henry II and Becket, with Henry insisting that because of their frequency and gravity, accused priests and monks ought to be tried in the royal courts.

The monks of Grestain belonged to the generation that saw the first flowering of the Cistercians, and the earliest legends of the Cistercians are as full of religious innocence as the Grestain account is of depravity. The *Exordium magnum*, a collection of stories about the order's beginnings, tells how a simple brother was always careful to pick up all the crumbs he left behind after eating. One day, though, he began his spiritual reading and became so absorbed in the text that he forgot to eat the crumbs still in his hand. His reading over, he realized that to eat them now would be contrary to his Rule, even though to throw them away was equally forbidden. In his great distress he went to the prior for advice, but when he opened his hand he found it was full of pearls.

Such miracles of the simple and the pure in heart accompanied the founding of most new monastic and religious orders in the middle ages. The stories of Francis of Assisi and his followers, and the continual renewal of Francis' radical ascetic by the Spiritual Franciscans and the Observants, provide the best-known body of these legends. But great churchmen could show a high degree of self-imposed asceticism and discipline as well as the mendicants. Petrochino, a fourteenth-century archbishop of Ravenna, was in externals much like any other cleric of his rank, with an extensive household, lavish vestments and a valuable library immense for its time. But his private life was austere, with frugal meals, rigidly simple surroundings, and an unending succession of charitable concerns. And Mauger, the court physician whom Richard of England appointed to the bishopric of Worcester in 1199, showed a tenderness of conscience admirable in any age.

Mauger had earlier been made archdeacon of Evreux, but felt

61

compelled to bar himself from the higher office of the episcopacy, confessing privately to the archbishop of Canterbury that "for some time he had been conscience-stricken in respect of his birth." At the Lateran Council of 1179, Alexander III expressly forbade men of illegitimate birth from entering the ranks of the higher clergy, and Mauger was the son of a knight and a free woman who had not married until he was four years old. Under these circumstances, he told the archbishop, he felt utterly unwilling to "advance a single step towards an office so exalted and important" without special papal intervention.

Seeking to ease his troubled mind—for Richard's nomination and patronage made it impossible for him simply to withdraw his name—Mauger journeyed to Rome, setting out before Innocent III the nature of his condition and the state of his conscience. Reviewing the canons, the pope found them inconsistent, and in the end granted Mauger a dispensation from the Lateran decree, "finding that he had less in him of imperfection than of perfection." In informing the archbishop of Canterbury of his decision, Innocent wrote that he had been especially struck by Mauger's

> humble devotion in making his confession, for voluntarily and humbly he chose to confess his defect rather than mount the episcopal throne with guilt on his conscience.[4]

Others, alas, had fewer scruples. At the time of Mauger's election, both the archbishop of York and the bishop of Salisbury were certainly bastards, and the illegitimacy of many of their colleagues was a matter of public gossip.

By the end of the middle ages no cleric, no matter how saintly, was immune from popular scrutiny. For if the church was made up partly of sanctified priests, lay believers were coming to play a greater and greater role in ecclesiastical affairs. In the eleventh century, nearly all new saints were monks or other clerics; by the thirteenth, more and more lay men and women were being canonized, and it became increasingly obvious that while churchmen ruled the great ecclesiastical institutions and formulated doctrine, they did not control the direction of revelation. Before the great visionary truths prelates and pious laymen were on equal ground.

In 1353 a young Hungarian nobleman ended a long journey of penance which had taken him from southern Italy into France, to the papal palace at Avignon, to Compostella, north again along the western coast of France and across into England, continuing westward and crossing into Ireland and at length to Lough Derg in Donegal. Although he was only twenty-four the young man, George Grissaphan, was a very great sinner; he had fought in Apulia for King Louis of Hungary, where by his own admission he killed and robbed hundreds of victims. Grissaphan came to Lough Derg because of its fame as the site of a cave giving entrance to Saint Patrick's Purgatory, the entrance to hell.

First associated with the penitential visions of a knight named Owen in the twelfth century, the Purgatory was guarded by a convent of Augustinian canons, and descent into the cave was said to be hazardous in the extreme. But both the archbishop of Armagh and the bishop of Clogher gave Grissaphan their approval to make the descent, and he began a series of solemn preparations for the journey into hell. For fifteen days he fasted on bread and water; for five days more he came to the canons' church morning and evening, covered with a black cloth, and heard the office of the dead and a requiem mass sung over him as if he were a corpse. Finally he was led by the prior and canons to Saint's Island in the lake, a cross was put in his hand and final rituals performed, and at last he began the descent into the cave, sealed off from the world by a door at the cave mouth.

According to the record of his journey, Grissaphan was guided by St. Michael through twenty-six visions on Saint's Island, and divine messages were sent through him to the archbishop of Armagh, King Edward of England, King John of France, Innocent VI, and the sultan of Babylon. When he emerged, he immediately sought confirmation of his descent and the revelations he received from the prior of Lough Derg and the local bishop. Next he set about delivering his messages, sending word to the archbishop that he had news for him about matters concerning his own welfare and that of his diocese.

The archbishop's reaction is worth recording. As he wrote to Grissaphan,

> Know that last Monday at Vespers we received letters from our Archdeacon of Armagh with the news that you could not wait for our arrival in those parts longer than Tuesday last elapsed. Having received and read these letters, we rose from our bed at midnight, and that same Tuesday we came to Dundalk, having accomplished a more severe day's journey than any we have done for a great time, and this Wednesday we are much fatigued from our journey at our manor of Dromiskin.[5]

"We implore you from our inmost heart," he continued, "that we be not deprived of the fruits of the revelation made to you," and he offered Grissaphan horses to make the journey to Dromiskin to meet him. Archbishop Fitzralph, a powerful churchman, sometime curial lawyer and theologian who was not given to bursts of enthusiasm or extravagant piety, left his bed to travel nearer to the pilgrim, and was clearly eager to hear the message he carried. His age, his sophistication, his archiepiscopal dignity were as nothing compared with the treasure brought from the Purgatory by a foreign layman who had been a notorious murderer.

Grissaphan did come to meet Fitzralph, and then left Ireland for the English, French and papal courts. Whether or not he journeyed to meet the sultan of Babylon is unknown, but his account of the revelations made at Lough Derg, the *Visiones Georgii*, was widely read and brought more fame to the Purgatory as a penitenital shrine.

The *Visiones*, as recorded by an amanuensis somewhere in southern France, belong to a venerable literary genre. The visions themselves were induced by fasting and by a mystique and ritual sobering even in a ritualistic age. But it does not tarnish the revelations to point out that they were carefully cultivated, or that, incidentally, they contained messages calculated to serve the interests of the merchants of Dundalk. The archbishop of Armagh was neither a mystic nor a simpleton, yet he traveled long hours to hear of the visions, and once he received the message, he obeyed it. His was the reaction of any intelligent medieval man, that revelatory messages were a matter for sober concern, an avenue of education and illumination.

For always beyond the distinctness and authority of churchmen lay the mysteries of the vision. Cleric and layman alike stood silent before the face of revelation. Churchmen might rule earthly reality, but visions were a reminder that this reality was a mere reflection of eternal truth, whose outlines were revealed to man only infrequently, when by a sudden grace a way of perceiving became one with the thing perceived, and the vision of this world became linked to the vision of the next.

Chapter four

THE IMAGE OF BELIEF

lways inseparable from the web of powers and concerns that made up the Western church in the middle ages was the devotion of medieval men and women. This devotion followed a rhythm of its own and did not respond in any direct way to the maturing of ecclesiastical institutions or to the political victories or defeats of the church. Powerful religious impulses swept across Europe at the turn of the twelfth century, then again in the mid-thirteenth and following the first appearance of the Black Death in 1348–49. During these years, devotional and ascetic practices reached a heightened intensity, and new and often extravagant forms of religious expression appeared. But even during times of lesser fervor, the lay religious imagination sustained a range of beliefs and practices which far exceeded the teachings of churchmen.

To understand the nature of popular belief it must be kept in mind that in the twelfth, thirteenth and fourteenth centuries the Christianization of Europe was by no means complete. Even the most superficial signs of conversion—collective baptism and reception of clerical ministry—were not accepted by the Slavs until the eleventh century or by other East German tribes until the twelfth. In the 1170's, Alexander III complained that the Finns, although nominally Christian, were making false professions and then harming the priests sent to minister to them.

In faraway Greenland, where even to tour the episcopal see took five years, shortages of goods and population hampered the most basic observances of Christian faith. The scarcity of wine led to a grant of papal permission to use beer for the mass; the scarcity of priests made all sacraments rare. Most bodies had to be interred without a Christian burial. A pole buried vertically along with the corpse marked the grave site; when a priest was obtained at last he pulled up the pole, pouring holy water on the body through the hole it made as he chanted the mass for the dead.

Further south, when Otto of Bamberg began the work of evangelizing western Pomerania in the 1120's (Vistulan Pomerania had been Christianized a few years earlier) he found there a Spanish bishop named Bernard who had come to seek martyrdom among the pagans; another Spaniard, Dominic de Guzman, originally intended to go as a missionary to the Cumans before Innocent III persuaded him of the importance of preaching to Western heretics. In time the order he founded—the Preaching Friars, or Dominicans—became a strong opponent of heterodox belief.

In the mid-thirteenth century a group of Franciscans formed a "holy militia to fight the powers of the air and obliterate the enemies of the Christian faith." Members of this Society of Pilgrims for Christ traveled through the lands of the "Ruthenians, Wallachians, Tartars, Saracens, Pagans, Greeks, Bulgarians and other Eastern and Northern peoples who do not believe," spreading Christianity and eradicating heresy. Yet at the end of the fourteenth century, nearly 150 years after the Society was founded, Benedict XI could still write of the "hard hearts of the infidels, and the vast lands and rude solitudes" that remained to be reached by Christian missionaries.

The missionary urges of the Dominicans and Franciscans were early signs of a more peaceful attitude toward non-Christians; in the past, pagans and heretics had been alternately evangelized and exterminated. When after 1056 the Slavs reverted to militant paganism—raiding neighboring Christian regions and mutilating or crucifying their inhabitants—Lothar of Saxony led his army in punitive reprisals against them, with no pretense of re-evangelization. As late as 1230 the Teutonic Knights led a crusade against the pagan Prussians, and the Patarines of northern Italy and the Cathars and Waldensians in many parts of southern Europe were the object of a number of better-known thirteenth-century crusades. Still further south, the whole of Iberian Christendom in this period was overshadowed by incessant holy war against the Moslems. Pascal II refused to allow Spanish penitents to join the first crusade, urging them to obtain grace and remission of their sins by joining their perpetual localized crusade.

It is understandable that Christian belief would be rudimentary in areas made remote by scarce population or difficult terrain. But even in regions with a venerable Christian tradition popular devotion was uneven in depth and frequency. An imperfect knowledge of doctrine tended to fade into the familiar climate of the enchanted world; cosmological, visionary and occult concepts merged with the popular perception of God and of the evidences of his power on earth. Local folklore and pre-Christian beliefs added another dimension to form a curious and heterodox faith.

Religious indifference too was to some extent a recurring problem everywhere, and self-interest frequently collided with the interests of faith. While some Western Christians prepared to fight in the Holy Land, others were selling arms, iron and wood to the Saracens, and building ships to their specifications.

Popular belief was fed from two sources within the church: parish priests and traveling preachers. Until the end of the middle ages parish priests represented the most familiar symbol of religious practice in the West. Although the concept of the cure of souls was not fully developed until the thirteenth century—the very time when priests were being superseded in popular esteem by the mendicant orders—the priest continued to be a significant agency of religious instruction, particularly in rural areas. How well were medieval priests equipped to inform popular faith?

Much has been written about the vice and appalling ignorance of medieval curates. Anecdotes about priests who read the gospels equally well from a lectionary held upside down or right side up because they had committed to memory the only scriptural passage they knew, or statistics about the numbers of illiterate or married clergy are familiar enough, but they tell us more about the legalistic attitudes of historians of religion than about the quality of parish instruction in the middle ages. It was often true that a priest's actual knowledge mattered less than what his parishioners *thought* he knew, and on this point at least they were not difficult to satisfy. Of course, the differences between a rural vicar in eleventh-century England and, say, a priest in *trecento* Florence make general statements about medieval clerics approximate at best.

It is generally agreed that despite the repeated prohibitions of reformers and of the canon law most parish priests had wives or concubines, and parish ministry was more often than not a matter of inheritance. Priests' sons, like the sons of peasants or knights, normally succeeded to their fathers' livings.

Like laymen, most clerics were married. The church's position on clerical marriage had from the beginning been ambiguous. Europe had never had a truly celibate clergy, and the harshly ascetic views of the Gregorian reformers were not echoed by later churchmen, many of whom questioned the wisdom of requiring that men in holy orders remain unmarried. Whole groups among the clergy claimed exemption from the law of celibacy; Swedish priests, for example, asserted that under papal privilege they were free of the prohibition against taking wives.

But a married priest had some difficulty supporting himself and his family on wages intended to maintain one man in ascetic circumstances. While some clerical livings were adequate, many were pitifully small, and what has until recently been unclear is that many priests relied on their wives' dowries or property to survive, since the livings from many parishes were impossibly meager. Not a few French parishes were exempt from royal taxation because their annual incomes were less than ten livres—an amount appreciably lower than the annual income of a day laborer. Although the richest living in England, Lindisfarne, brought in some £230 a year, others yielded as little as three shillings; the average parish income was about £10, half of which went to the priest. The superfluity of clergy in medieval England meant that even these small livings were often divided in half or quartered in order to benefice more clerics.

The problem of clerical livings was compounded by the normal practice of hiring a substitute to run the parish while another man enjoyed its revenue. The parish of Sainte-Catherine-hors-Dam brought the priest who held it an income of between five and six hundred florins a year, of which the vicar who ministered in it received only eighteen. The living of Coxyde, which went to the chapter of Saint-Bavon, amounted to about two hundred florins in a good year, but the curate who served it got only eighteen patards—a fraction of that amount.

It was these struggling vicars and not the comfortable higher clerks that represented the church to most medieval men and women. Few of them were priests; in England, most were subdeacons, elsewhere their ranks varied widely. Some parishes had no secular clergy at all, but were governed by monks. Others undoubtedly went for years without any form of spiritual service before the coming of the mendicants, whose mixture of solid learning and chilling and entertaining stories were the first true rural ministry in many parts of Europe.

Forced to earn a supplementary income, curates farmed or practiced a craft, and the pattern of their lives must have differed little enough from that of their parishioners. Priests sometimes lived communally or alongside professed monks in monasteries, but more often in rural areas they continued to live with relatives or with their wives and children.

In their behavior priests were virtually indistinguishable from the laymen in their care. Drunkenness was chronic among the rural clergy. In a handbook for parish clergy written by the Shropshire canon John Myrc, priests were explicitly warned against frequent inebriation. But if he should be drunk beyond speech, Myrc wrote, let the cleric avoid saying mass altogether, since it is difficult enough for a sober priest to perform the mass, and "How schulde thenne a droken mon/Do that the sobere unnethe [hardly] con?"

Where liturgical and theological training were concerned, the lower clergy were clearly ignorant to the point of absurdity. *Scientia sufficiens*—adequate learning—was the vague phrase used to describe the knowledge a priest needed to acquire. He had to be able to follow, however inexactly, the ritual of the mass, even though ignorant of the meaning of its texts. He had to know something of the other sacraments as well, although by the end of the thirteenth century friar priests took charge of penance, burial, and even marriage to an increasing extent, and in peasant communities pre-Christian marriage and burial customs existed which made his presence superfluous. The practice of the mass differed greatly from one parish to another. Its basic structure was established well before the Gregorian era, but ordinaries used by priests were not standardized, and local variations were common even in the eucharistic core of the ritual. Those canon Myrc called "priests of mean lore" lacked sufficient Latin even to pronounce crucial passages accurately.

Men whose knowledge of the belief and ritual of the church was so primitive could hardly have been expected to give profound

71

instruction to the faithful. Parishioners were taught—or were told to teach each other—to say the Credo, Pater Noster and Ave Maria; in some parishes those ignorant of these fundamental texts were fined. But most parish instruction stopped here, and most medieval Christians were not taught how to pray in their own language. (Where the clergy represented a conquering population, they were frequently unable to communicate with their parishioners at all; in fourteenth-century Cornwall the only priests who were able to hear confessions were itinerant Franciscans who had mastered the Cornish dialect.)

Partly because of these conditions, respect for priests declined steadily in the thirteenth and fourteenth centuries. Although some exceptional men were venerated, many were treated with grudging tolerance, riducule, or fear. G. G. Coulton found records of Italian nicknames for priests such as "Handsome," "Dry-the-Hay," and "Limping John." A trend toward less and less frequent communion, the effects of a renewed zeal for the apostolic life and an ineradicable contempt for the hypocrisy of the higher clergy all tended to alienate parishioners from the priests who served them.

Popular superstitions associated priests with death. Jacques de Vitry told of seeing men

> cross themselves immediately when they pass a priest, and say that to meet one is a bad sign. I know for a fact that one time when people were dying off by dozens in a certain French town the townspeople said among themselves, "This deadly pestilence can't end unless we throw our priest into the grave first, and then put in the corpse." So when the priest came up to the grave to bury the dead parishioner, the peasants and their wives snatched him, dressed as he was in his clerical robes, and threw him into the grave.[1]

Such things, Vitry noted, are the result of "devices of the devil and demonic tricks"; still in many parts of Europe it was considered bad luck to meet a priest, or to pass one by on the right side. In eleventh-century Denmark, priests were hounded by their flocks as bearers of bad weather, infections and "bodily plagues."

The condition of the clergy was not the concern of the church hierarchy alone. The people complained and even acted to prevent unqualified men from assuming spiritual office. In 1013 the people of Bruges refused to accept Gauzlin, a natural son of the king, Hugh Capet, as their bishop, and popular resentment against papal officials frequently led to violence as well. Legates, papal tax collectors and judges traveled at their peril, while inquisitors were never safe anywhere. Assassinations of inquisitors had become so frequent by the 1240's that the Dominicans petitioned the pope to free them from serving the inquisition in the future. Their request went unheeded, and the dangerous profession continued to take its toll. Peter of Ruffia, a Piedmontese Dominican who wrote learned refutations against the numerous Waldensian heretics of the Alpine valleys, was appointed inquisitor general of Piedmont in 1351, only to be killed in the Franciscan friary of the little town of Susa fourteen years later. His assassins were reputed to be heretics, but often in such cases the attackers were never identified with certainty, or were found to be ordinary laymen.

Popular criticism of churchmen took many forms; tavern songs and vernacular literature ridiculed the greed, lechery and hypocrisy of the clergy and counterbalanced the growth of vernacular hagiography and of popular cults. No cleric of the thirteenth or fourteenth century could anticipate a docile audience for his ministry or preaching. Sermon collections are full of anecdotes about pulpit criticism turned against preachers. "When you sin and say vulgar words and nobody corrects *you*," says a voice from the congregation to the preacher in one of these stories, "then the people have a saying, 'Let God and me alone!' "

Unfortunately, neither popular ridicule and hostility nor the external unsuitability of many parish priests gives a complete image of their religious influence. Neither can tell us much about their personal qualities of understanding, gentleness or pity. Doubtless some were devout and serious in their vocations, and helped to foster a sense of the holy without benefit of literacy. Learning and religious insight have in any case little direct correlation; many of the early lay Franciscans were illiterate or barely literate, yet their effect on popular piety was profound and enduring. The handbook of Canon Myrc was not the work of a learned man, but it revealed a large measure of sensitivity and practical wisdom in handling parishioners, especially where confession and penance were concerned. If a woman should hesitate from embarrassment to tell her sins, he advised, the priest should encourage her by confiding that his sins had been as blameable or even worse.

> Tell me boldely and make no scof . . .
> Wonde thow not for no schame
> Paraventur I have done the same.

(Such humility was probably all too appropriate in many cases; pastoral theology taught that a believer was not obliged to confess to a priest who had slept with any of the women of his parish.) Penance should be adjusted to the age and condition of the sinner, Myrc wrote, and the priest should consider whether or not the sinner was "in hys wyt"—in his right mind. Moderate penances were always preferable to harsh ones, since, if a man has too much laid on him, he will do none of it and be worse off than if he hadn't confessed at all. The priest Myrc described was altogether human, not marred by rigidity or aloofness and well aware that "mony men ful dyvers are."

While in many parts of France, England and the northern

Italian states parish life declined drastically in the later middle ages, it continued to flourish in areas remote from war or serious political unrest. In the Swiss cantons, where strong local traditions gave the priest a conspicuously important role in civic life, it was he who summoned and presided over the yearly parish assembly. Here the customs were recited and infractions were judged; among these customs were some entirely unrelated to clerical functions. One of the priest's duties was to reward with a cake the diligence of local shepherds on each of the great church feasts. Priests enjoyed a mixture of moral and civil jurisdictions, punishing adulterers, tax-evaders and those who avoided repairing their part of the church roof or bell tower.

The popular view of parish priests was doubtless affected by the diversity of their functions, as well as those of the church building and of the parish itself. Parishes served as both civil and religious entities; parish taxation was common, and parochial officials dispensed many of the charitable services taken over by secular government in modern times. Normally no stranger could marry or settle in a parish without a "certificate of Christianity" from the priest of his former parish. Church buildings too took on a wide range of secular functions; agreements were formally sealed, treaties ratified, families or cities reconciled in churches. In Italy, nobles and civic officials commonly held banquets in cathedrals, and oaths of all sorts—including political conspiracies—were solemnized on holy ground.

The purely religious character of parish functions became diffused; churches and their clergy took on an increasingly hetero-geneous appearance, in which secular and mundane concerns seemed to choke out matters of faith. Churches were used as granaries, marketplaces, arenas for gaming and fighting. Priests kept taverns, and brewed their ale in the church building. Fairs and pagan celebrations were held in churchyards and even before the altar; from the thirteenth century on ecclesiastical councils con-demned the singing, gambling and erotic dancing that frequently

75

went on in holy places. Such practices do not necessarily imply irreverence: only familiar abuse. But they helped to make parish ministry an unlikely source of devotional instruction, and made the preaching of itinerant mendicants even more welcome when it came.

Traveling preachers had been known in the West since antiquity but toward the end of the twelfth century their numbers increased and their messages took on a new urgency. Some, like Eon de l'Etoile, who called himself "Eum," simply sought to build a personal following by making bizarre and often blasphemous claims. According to Otto of Freising, Eum insisted that he was the one referred to in the formula that closed every prayer: "by him" (*per Eum*). Alongside these, millenarian preachers bearing a single cataclysmic message appeared frequently in the towns of northern Italy and the Rhineland. But the work of evangelizing and of refining the religious emotions of laymen was done by the apostolic preachers of the twelfth century and their spiritual heirs, the mendicants of the thirteenth and fourteenth.

So powerful were the themes of austerity, poverty and cultivation of Christlike virtues in the eleven hundreds that they overflowed the confines of orthodoxy. Both great preaching churchmen like Bernard of Clairvaux and heretical Waldensian and Petrobrusian preachers exalted the apostolic life. Cathar *perfecti*, who owned nothing and practiced the most rigid asceticism, persuaded many of the superiority of their beliefs by example alone, and Cathar preachers were among the strongest religious personalities of the twelfth century.

Two of the most effective popular preachers of this apostolic period were Arnold of Brescia and Francis of Assisi. Their messages were similar in many ways; both taught poverty and the imitation of Christ, and both enjoyed immense popular prestige. But their reception by the clergy differed so radically that one died an infamous heretic, the other a universally beloved saint.

Like Francis, Arnold embraced poverty in his own life, and in his fervor urged the clergy of Brescia to follow his example. From the first his anxiety for reform met with resistance and denunciations; despite the sincerity of his belief he became embittered and denounced the clergy in return. Advocating an end to the temporal jurisdiction of the church, his program took on an increasingly political character, and at the climax of his career he installed himself as head of a popular government in the papal city in 1146. With the enthusiastic support of many Romans he forced Eugenius III, who, he said, was "no longer the true *Apostolicus*," to leave the city. The pope, emperor and prefect of Rome conspired in Arnold's death, but he had in any case lost a large measure of his original support by the time imperial troops ended his republican experiment.

When Arnold of Brescia took over Rome, heresy was thought of as a localized disease to be purged largely by suppressive force. By Francis' time, few regions of continental Europe were entirely free of heresy, and even the mayor of Assisi was a Cathar. Although crusades were still called against heretics, and the papal inquisition was created in the thirteenth century to rout them through rigorous and often sinister examination, some churchmen were able to see in Francis' movement the seeds of an intense spiritual awakening that might prove effective against the dangers of heterodox belief. Although like Arnold he advocated renunciation of all temporal goods, Francis pointedly supported rather than criticized the secular clergy, and he and his followers received their support and protection. (It was not until later in the century that the implications of the poverty doctrine aroused the hostility of clerics and led them to attack the mendicants, in Bonaventure's words, "as violently as if we were heretics.")

Mendicant preachers created an entirely new kind of sermon,

one which deliberately brought the most remote components of secular life to bear on matters of faith. At the heart of the mendicant sermon were the *exempla*—frightening, amusing and often visionary anecdotes or brief allegories.

> "Now I imagine our whole life to be like a fair," one of these *exempla* began, "for as in a fair there is a great concourse of people, and great paraphernalia and trinkets, merchandise of various kinds and lots of booths, and yet in a short time it will all be taken away and removed elsewhere, and all the expense will have gone for nothing, unless one has been clever in buying or selling, and in the place itself nothing remains except more filth than elsewhere; so it is in this life. . . . Therefore we ought not to delay, but lead Christ to the tavern of contrition, and pledge him abundantly in the food and drink of tears."

This *exemplum* is from a Franciscan sermon collection. In a sermon another Minorite, Nicholas Philip, attacked pluralist clergy, who "labour to heap together more benefices, pensions and the like that some of them would seem to desire to be as another god." Like climbing monkeys, these rising prelates display their "disgusting posteriors to the derision of men."

Mendicant preachers were masters of startling effects: one Minorite to terrify his audience would suddenly pull out a skull from under his cloak. The obsession with death that became more and more pronounced in the fourteenth and fifteenth centuries has been linked to mendicant preaching; the *danse macabre* (from the Arabic *meqaber*, grave-digger) was a graphic imitation of a common theme of friar sermons. Some of these preachers carried large manuscript books of pictures which they would hold up to illustrate points of doctrine, and the Observant Franciscan Bernardino of Siena was associated with devotion to the name of Jesus, which he carried written on a banner and displayed whenever he preached.

Devotion to the name of Jesus was direct and literal, like much of mendicant preaching. The friars and other preachers who learned from them thought of themselves as popularizers of theological doctrine. A preacher, wrote sub-prior Rypon of Durham, is like a stomach that accepts the spiritual food, digests and prepares it, and then disperses it in usable form throughout the ecclesiastical body. In this way the doctrine of contrition was explained by one renowned preacher by means of a mundane analogy; just as a laundrymaid wrings out the last drop of water from the clothes, he taught, so a truly contrite man wrings tears from his heart. Bishop Grosseteste of Lincoln, a close friend of the English friars, used an *exemplum* to explain the functions of the senses, intellect and will. He compared man to a town,

> in which his bodily members are like the houses, his mouth, eyes and ears like the town gates, through which the populace enters and goes out. . . . The lord of this town is the Soul or Intellect, his lady the Will, which, according to Augustine is queen in the realm of the Soul. Memory is the hall or chamber in which guests are received. The chief sovereign is God Himself, who resides in the Reason, as a lord in the principal place of his township.[2]

A book of advice for preachers recommended explaining the concept of the trinity by comparing it to the water, ice and snow around an outdoor pulpit on a wintry day.

> Se the ensaumpul that I yow schowe
> Of water and ys and eke snowe;
> Here beth thre thynges, as ye may se,
> And yet the thre alle water be.

But instruction was only one aim of the itinerant preacher; it was his more important goal to reach and affect the emotions. Here the livelier atmosphere of graphic anecdotes gave way to prayer, meditation and even poetry. In the poems of friars William Herebert and John Grimestone, English Franciscans of the fourteenth century, the dialogue between God and the people could be represented both appealingly and simply. "My people," God says in one of these peoms, "what have I done to you, that you've led me to be killed?" In another Jesus speaks from his cradle. "I am iesu," he begins, "that cum to fith [fight] / Withouten seld and spere. . . . Undo thin herte, tel me thi though / Thi sennes [sins] grete an smale."

In about 1404 John Gregory, an Augustinian friar, preached a sermon on the text *"Per proprium sanguinem"* somewhere in southwestern England. His text was from the ninth chapter of Hebrews, "By his own blood he entered in," and his first illustrations showed that blood could heal and give strength. Good blood restores the sick to health, he wrote; mixed with mortar, blood makes stone walls impregnable. Laid to the root of a dry tree, blood restores it to life and makes it fruitful. And in a spiritual sense the same is true for man. Man becomes dry and barren through sin, but is redeemed to life through the blood of Jesus.

Having introduced these chief points of his sermon, Friar Gregory went on to reiterate them with examples drawn from history and popular legend and folklore. He reminded his listeners that when Constantine was struck with leprosy he was advised to bathe in the blood of a child, and that a common remedy for sickness was to anoint the victim with the blood of another man who had recovered from the same sickness. Man's greatest sickness is death; only the blood of one who died but triumphed over death can cure him of it. A story about King Vortigern drew out the analogy still further. Vortigern ordered a castle built for him, but as much as was built in one day fell down the next, and in desperation he called in wise men to advise him on what he should do. They told him to sprinkle on the mortar the blood of a child that had no earthly father, and the castle would stand. In the same way, wrote Friar Gregory, before the passion of Jesus all that men built up through good deeds was lost when they died and fell down into hell. But when the blood of one who had no earthly father, Christ, was added to their merits, that which they built up in good deeds stood standing for eternity.

After a particularized list of sicknesses of the blood, he introduced another long digression to show how blood gives courage. As the "great clerk" Pliny wrote in his book on the marvels of the world, the elephant has two main characteristics: he is lacking in feeling, which makes him tepid and listless in battle, and he has sufficient intelligence to be able to recognize and pay homage to kings. Man is like the elephant, insisted Friar Gregory, for he lacks the natural emotion of charity and does battle feebly against the devil, the world and the flesh. In this battle he falls wounded by the arrows of pride, anger, envy, and the other deadly sins. But just as the elephant is made courageous by the sight of blood, so man is roused to fight against sin through the blood of Jesus.

As the sermon drew to an end, the friar summarized what had gone before, then told a last story. At her marriage a great lord gave his daughter four rings, each engraved with certain words. On the first ring was engraved "I have loved thee; learn thou to love me"; on the second, "What did I, and how much? Why did I do this?" The third ring read "Thou art noble; never forsake thy nobility," and the fourth read "I am thy brother. Come to me, and fear not." Beyond these, the bride's husband gave her a seal with the inscription "Now thou art joined to me; turn never again from me."

The father, he explained, is God; the daughter, man's soul; the husband, the devil. The four rings are Christ's wounds, with which he speaks to man and exhorts him to return his love, to understand the purpose of his crucifixion, to be faithful to the high position he has gained through Jesus' sacrifice, and to approach Christ as a familiar brother rather than a fearsome stranger.

For man's soul is wedded to Christ through the Eucharist, and partakes of his blood, which is the key of paradise. Think on this, Friar Gregory concluded, and you may overcome all temptation. Hear this, and you will obtain the grace of a good life, and, when you go hence, joy everlasting.

Friar Gregory's sermon, whose basic structure is reflected in these passages, is complex in its arrangement and in its several concurrent levels of meaning. It wove together widely disparate material from the biblical and classical past, medical and agricultural lore, and the traditional stories collected into compendia for the use of preachers. Yet it was a persuasive whole, at once forceful, diverting and instructive. Despite its length, it blended without tedium the multiple worlds of folk knowledge, history and theology.

Friar Gregory's sermon was successful because it brought Christian truth within the bounds of the enchanted world. Recognizing the points of greatest congruence between Christian devotion and the far-ranging scope of medieval belief, the mendicant preachers spoke directly to the imagination as well as the understanding. At their best, they challenged the flexibility of perception in the same way as the narrative of the Mesopotamian monks. Their imagery, graphic anecdotes and visual props touched the visionary eagerness of the medieval audience. The result was a pervasive and unmistakable change in religious sentiment.

The response to this kind of popular preaching was spontaneous and extraordinary. Crowds of penitents accompanied preachers from town to town, and even noblewomen put on beggars' clothes and followed barefoot. As the sermons of itinerant preachers became more familiar, this degree of popular enthusiasm cooled, but the effect of their sermons on lay piety remained great. By the fourteenth century, popular preachers had helped to awaken and then to deepen the reverence and belief of medieval men and women. Faith had become a matter of inner conviction as well as of ritual; collective worship was augmented by personal devotion. By transforming the nature of popular belief, popular preaching helped to complete the Christianization of the Latin west.

One of the most convincing signs of this deepened piety lay in the increase in individual devotion in the later middle ages. The rosary came into general use in the thirteenth century, as did the Angelus—a ringing of bells at morning, noon and evening in token of devotion to Mary. The Angelus was only one of many signs of Marian reverence; in many European regions, Saturday was sacred to Mary, since she alone continued to believe in Jesus' resurrection on the day after his crucifixion, Holy Saturday.

Individual charity became less exceptional and more widespread. The chronicler Salimbene wrote that his mother took into her household each winter a poor peasant from the hills, and kept him as she did her own children until the harsh weather had passed; at the end of her life she joined the order of Poor Clares. As a young man the Irish St. Malachy's greatest concern was to bury dead paupers, according to his biographer Bernard of Clairvaux. And an observer from the Orient who came to the papal court in the mid-thirteenth century was astonished to watch the pope himself assemble all the members of his large household in Easter week and wash the feet of each one in imitation of Jesus, wiping them with a cloth he wrapped around his waist.

Among the wealthy, charity and devotional practices were even more spectacular. At the funeral of the affluent Florentine Nicolo degli Alberti in 1377, a contemporary chronicler wrote that five hundred poor people followed the bier, and these represented only some of the vast numbers he had helped anonymously during his lifetime. Strenuous acts of public penance or thanksgiving became more common. After the miraculous recovery of his son from a dangerous fever, Philip VI walked from the sickbed to the church of St. Denis, "a distance of four milestones and more, and not without great labor and trouble because a man of his station is not accustomed to such a strenuous task." He followed this with vigils, devotion to relics, and attendance at all divine offices, and ordered his household to follow his example.

Of course, a variety of motives lay behind such acts of public munificence or self-abasement—the piety of a great man or woman was expected to be as exalted as their rank. But extravagant devotion could be entirely sincere and disinterested. Early in the thirteenth century, Elizabeth of Hungary, countess of Thuringia, gave up everything she owned, and lived in poverty as a Franciscan tertiary, and a century later Philip de Majorca gave up his abundant patrimony to live as a wandering beghard.

Pilgrimages were another evidence of the flowering of lay religiosity. Few things satisfied the religious imagination of the medievals so completely as journeys to the shrines of distant saints. Pilgrims had been making the journey to the Holy Land for centuries, and pilgrimages to Rome were even more frequent; the Saxon kings Kenred, Buhred, Caedwalla and Ine were buried in Rome, and Bede wrote that in Ine's time many English men and women, noble and common, lay and cleric, traveled to the papal city. One appeal of the pilgrimage was its joining of the spiritual journey of man with physical travel to holy places. Another was the precise spiritual benefits it yielded. On martyrs' feast-days, one-third or one-fourth remission of penance could be obtained; on Holy Thursday, pilgrims "from beyond the seas" were granted three years' indulgence (or two years for those who had not come so far).

The benefits to be gained by coming to Rome were to increase many times before the close of the medieval period, but by then pilgrimage had ceased to be a matter of distant journeys alone. As the number of local saints burgeoned, local shrines flourished too—Canterbury in England, Tiegem in Flanders, Mont-Saint-Michel in France, Montserrat and, most venerable of all, Compostella in Spain. Entire towns or villages made collective pilgrimages. Day-long processions to nearby shrines covering ten to fifteen miles marked important crises or deliverances in the life of a community.

Pilgrimages were not only a common form of religious penance: they were frequently imposed as civil penalties as well. With a safe-conduct valid only along a certain prescribed pilgrimage route, an undesirable was out of the way but never beyond surveillance. Judicial pilgrimages were a convenient punishment for sorcerers, political conspirators, or ne'er-do-wells whose "useless existence" was judged a nuisance by the town. Involuntary pilgrims under sentence from inquisitorial courts and professional travelers who made their living carrying out vicarious pilgrimages also helped to swell the stream of pious travelers.

Because the number of these travelers was so large, itineraries and guidebooks of all sorts were drawn up to give them advice and enrich their journeys. One of the earliest of these, a handbook for Compostellan pilgrims written in the mid-twelfth century by a Frenchman from Poitou or Saintonge, suggested various routes and discussed the towns and regions along the way, commenting on the hospitality or irascibility of their inhabitants. The quality of the water in each place was carefully noted, and the author added a little lexicon of the Navarese patois as well: "God," "Mary," "bread," "wine," "master of the house," "mistress," "king" and "St. James" were only a few of the words he thought would be useful.

Pilgrimage narratives—accounts of actual or fanciful journeys to the Holy Land—became a popular form of literature in the fourteenth and fifteenth centuries. One such genuine account was the unusually detailed and candid narrative of Ogier VIII, lord of Anglure in Flanders. Ogier and his party left in July of 1413, intending to visit Jerusalem and the shrines of saints in Egypt and

Asia Minor. They traveled across northern Italy, then took ship at Venice and finally arrived in Jerusalem early in October. In the Holy City, Ogier was shown countless churches, relics and sacred grottoes. To some points of interest were attached legends of uncertain provenance: on one large stone, he was told, Jesus used to preach to his disciples while Mary sat close by on another and listened. In the Jordan valley, Ogier discovered what he called the "fruit of the earthly paradise," bananas, and these intrigued him almost as much as the Egyptian giraffes, crocodiles, and elephants whose trumpeting he found "blaring and terrifying to those who are not accustomed to it."

Cairo impressed him—"a city so amazingly large and full of people, Saracens and other peoples as well, that no one could believe it who hadn't seen it for himself." But the pyramids were even more marvelous, and his lengthy account of them contrasted sharply with the meager attention he paid to Christian antiquities.

After a trip up the Nile, marked by an attack of Saracen pirates, Ogier and his party came to the desert sanctuaries of St. Anthony at the end of November, then returned to Alexandria and set out for Europe again by sea. Several days out of port the ship lost its rudder, but after a long night of fear the pilgrims sailed into port at Limesso (modern Limassol) on Cyprus Christmas morning. Contrary winds delayed them in the Greek islands until the end of February, then left them stranded at Rhodes throughout the Lenten season waiting for another ship. Finally all the pilgrims on the island banded together to hire a Greek ship which eventually took them to Venice. At the end of May Ogier began the last leg of his return journey, back across northern Italy and through Switzerland, Burgundy and Champagne home to Anglure in late June.

The tone of Ogier's account was dispassionate, and the attention he gave to the religious history of the places he saw was superficial. Although he traveled for pious reasons, clearly the excitement and adventure of his journey overshadowed its spiritual meaning.

Doubtless many pilgrims felt a similar indifference, but there were some who found the sight of the great Christian shrines very moving indeed. A Russian pilgrim described the reaction of his companions on their first glimpse of Jerusalem:

> . . . each Christian felt an immense joy at the sight of the Holy City of Jerusalem, and all the faithful shed tears. No one could keep back his emotion when he saw that land he so ardently desired, and those sacred stones where Christ our God suffered his passion to take away our sins. And all hurried on foot toward Jerusalem. . . .[3]

Pilgrimages, charity, penance, personal piety: these were among the clearest signs of the internalization of Christian belief in the high middle ages. By the thirteenth century, popular piety formed a deep and permanent adjunct to the doctrine and ritual of the church. But it would be a mistake to view it from this perspective alone. Parish ministry and the sermons of itinerant preachers were able to guide and develop popular belief, but they could not control it. For beyond the power of the church, the stronger forces of the enchanted world continued to affect the religious and semi-religious practices of peasants and villagers, and medieval clerics tried without success to purge Christian belief of its venerable shadow.

Some of these practices were little more than elaborations of what was condoned or encouraged by the church. An old tradition taught that churches and churchyards offered sanctuary to fugitives and criminals. No one could be captured or punished who sought refuge within a chapel, a cemetery, or hospital, or who stood within a ring of sacred land that extended for forty paces around every religious structure. Earth from churchyards, building stones from ruined churches and even priests carrying the host offered protection.

Such precise localization of the divine presence encouraged belief in the miraculous properties of crosses, and from the eleventh century on these crosses multiplied in the fields and along the roads of western Europe. Market crosses marked the collection site for monastic tithes; boundary crosses indicated the limits of political jurisdiction. Preaching crosses were erected for the use of wandering preachers. "Weeping" crosses were monuments to penance; memorial crosses to bereavement. All these were a refuge for living offenders, and fought off the lingering stigma of death as well; victors in tournaments or judicial combats were obliged to erect a cross on the field where their rivals died.

Visual reverence for the eucharistic host increased importantly in the twelfth and thirteenth centuries. As the agency of salvation, it could benefit anyone who merely glimpsed it, and the practice of elevating the host during the mass to allow the faithful to profit from seeing it became customary after 1200. It was popularly believed that no one could go hungry or thirsty on a day when he had seen God's body. Greed would be foreign to him and all his "idle oaths and words" would be forgiven. Most important, he would be shielded from blindness and sudden death.

St. Christopher too warded off death, and his images and statues proliferated on bridges, at streetcorners, and on church walls. Once admired for their Christlike virtues, most saints in this period were given distinctive vocations as well, not from disrespect but out of a sense of intimate familiarity. Certain saints favored certain crafts— Peter was patron of bakers, Joseph of carpenters—while others cured certain diseases or protected property. St. Hubert cured rabies, St. Apolline healed diseased teeth; pigs were sacred to St. Anthony, while St. Medard kept the frost off the vines. In Flanders mock veneration was given to St. Arnold, patron of cuckolds.

In contrast to the careful judicial procedure by which the church collected the evidences of sanctity, the people assigned sainthood with unrestrained enthusiasm. Relics from antiquity were eagerly confused with Christian personages; the Virtues became angels, Hercules became Jesus, and many of the devout came to St.-Germain-des-Pres to kiss an ancient cameo of Germanicus and Agrippine, whom they took to be Mary and Joseph.

Saints were worshipped above all because they were thought to be efficacious, and this same attitude to the practical function of belief was at the root of many religious practices. Meals began with food that had been blessed in the church. Baptismal cloths, which were valuable in certain kinds of magic, had to be burned to prevent parishioners from stealing them for use in casting spells. Relics were frequently the object of theft. At Canterbury and St. Albans, watching chambers were built near the shrines containing Becket's remains where monk-guards kept vigil day and night. As we have seen, liturgical formulas and biblical passages were thought to ward off evil when carried in clothing or inscribed on amulets. That the clergy encouraged this belief seems likely; the jurist Agostino Trionfo chastised clerics who sold to their parishioners charms bearing the names of God and the saints.

Sanctified objects and places were appropriated to serve particular needs. After they had drunk wine and blood, newly reconciled families divided and ate a consecrated host as a sign of peace. Thinly disguised as Christian feasts, pre-Christian festivals at the vernal equinox or on the first of January were celebrated with dancing in churches or churchyards, often led by the priests themselves. Entire parishes sought escape from the fear of plague or famine in the delirious exhaustion of dance, and the repeated injunctions of church councils against dancing in churches proves the hardiness of the custom.

Church treasures were accorded magical properties. Like relics, ecclesiastical jewels could cure disease or ease the pains of childbirth. The beneficial effects of various gems were catalogued by medieval lapidaries, and Albertus Magnus devoted several treatises to the powers and virtues of precious stones. In addition to his duties as chronicler and master of the scriptorium, Matthew Paris was keeper of the jewels of the monastery of St. Albans, and wrote an account of the healing properties of each of the stones in his care.

Through beliefs of this kind, the acknowledged power of the supersensible was incorporated into the faith taught by the church. The wonder-working potency of sanctified objects was an extension of the perceived animation of all things. The localization of the divine—in the holy ground around crosses and cemeteries, in the host or altar ornaments, in holy words, in images of saints— satisfied the need to anchor the unseen miraculous to concrete places and things. Most important, the elaboration of new forms of visual reverence fed the visionary imagination of the medievals. The emphasis on seeing the eucharistic host and glimpsing the protecting saints made sight active in piety.

Church ornamentation in the later middle ages was a banquet of sight. Worshippers were surrounded by fantastic, demonic imagery. Creatures with distorted bodies or monstrous heads, devils in the shape of animated objects, Arabic and Indian motifs wound around the walls of churches. Satanic beings imposed themselves as forcefully as servants of the divine; grimacing trinities of evil faces mocked the triune God of orthodox belief.

The atmosphere of formal worship was not one of divine victory but of an uneasy truce between the powers of light and darkness. Here the dark side of the enchanted world—its fear of unknown yet powerful incorporeal beings—fused with the theology of evil. Together they underscored the sense of arbitrary tragedy that loomed so large in the medieval period.

Against this fatalism the theology of good offered little comfort or reassurance. It was the unsettling property of divine justice to be both inexorable and unpredictable in human terms. Even the most unselfish human acts might offend God's justice. Dante was rebuked for feeling pity for the misery of the sinners in hell when he ought to have concurred in the divine judgment against them.

At stillborn births midwives were wrong if in compassion they baptized a dead child in order to comfort the parents. Human sympathy could be both inappropriate and sinful when it interfered with divine justice.

Yet precisely because they were incomprehensible, divine judgments often seemed capricious. If blasphemers, usurers, suicides and excommunicated persons were refused Christian burial, and therefore excluded from paradise, so too were victims of misfortune: debtors, those killed in jousts, and those who had neglected to make a will. Medieval preachers emphasized the arbitrary nature of salvation; in one twelfth-century description of a visionary journey through hell, tormented sinners complained that though all men sin God chooses to save a few of them without regard to their good deeds or merits. However, the complaint was justified only in terms of human justice; the message of the work was that the devout must revere the mysterious and awesome ways of God.

This atmosphere of inexorable justice surrounded medieval believers. To escape it was impossible; no thought or act could be kept secret. You think you are alone in your crime, St. Bernard wrote, yet mere walls alone cannot keep out the horde of witnesses to your every deed. Good and bad angels will testify to your acts before the court of the Supreme Judge, who himself has seen your every move. "No one is safe," he insisted. "There are traps laid for you which you cannot escape." Nor were external acts alone blameworthy; although it moved forcefully against occult practices the chief end of the inquisition was to isolate crimes of thought: doubt and aberrant belief. Uncertainty was as fatal as error, and even in the private turnings of the intellect every man and woman risked mortal sin.

Astrology, as we have seen, was largely excluded from that risk. Denounced by some theologians as contrary to belief in free will and the omnipotence of God—among many others, the thirteenth-century Franciscan Alexander of Hales defined casting horoscopes as superstitious—astrology was in practice allowed to flourish. Augustine had written extensively against it in *De civitate Dei*, but specific condemnations of this kind were balanced by the accepted cosmology which made earthly events dependent on the movements of the stars. In his *De occultis*, Aquinas wrote that even Augustine admitted the power of the stars over corporeal bodies, and commended astrological calculations made to foretell the weather or strengthen medicinal cures while acknowledging that they were accomplished with the aid of demons.

Ordinary folk continued to cast the horoscopes of their children at birth, but in the end these and other attempts to cheat destiny—palmistry, augury, dream interpretations—only underscored the inevitability of bad fortune. With the recurrent waves of plague after 1348 the darkest currents in medieval piety flourished. Pilgrims sang *"ad mortem festinamus"*—"we hurry on toward death"—in the cemetery of Montserrat, and the dance of death moved closer to the center of popular religion.

> I go toward death, says the bishop, willing or not; I leave behind crozier, sandals and mitre.
>
> I go toward death, says the knight; I've come away victor from many a battle, but I have not learned to conquer death.
>
> I go toward death, says the logician; I taught others to close an argument skillfully, but now death has closed my arguments forever.[4]

In their recurring desperation medieval Europeans often turned on the clergy. In 1237, when Frederick II was besieging the Guelph city of Milan, Matthew Paris recorded that

> the citizens, raising their heel against God, became desperate, and distrusting God, suspended the crucifix in the church by its heels, and

ate flesh on the sixth day of the week in Lent, and many throughout Italy were sunk into this abyss of despair, reviling and blaspheming; they irreverently polluted the churches with filthiness unfit to be mentioned, defiled the altars and expelled the ecclesiastics and officials.[5]

Such blatant and thorough sacrilege would be astonishing in a medieval population if it were not so frequent. Bitter and brutal antagonism was an enduring feature of the relations between laymen and clergy particularly after 1200, and led to the proverb

Dum mare siccatur,
Et Demon ad astra levatur,
Tunc primo laicus
Clero fit fidus amicus.

(When the sea dries up
And the Demon [Lucifer] is raised
    to the stars again,
Only then will the layman
Become the clergy's faithful friend.)[6]

Impiety and anticlericalism were predictable results of the social dislocations of the Hundred Years' War and of popular revolts in England, France and the Low Countries; one of the leaders of the Flemish revolt of 1323–28 bragged that he had never been inside a church. Of course, this sort of antagonism grew out of the complex nature of the medieval church with its deep roots in property and political affairs. In Italy the church and the Guelph cause were inseparable, and when the citizens of Milan desecrated their altars they were reacting as much to a political as to a moral dilemma. But anticlericalism in Milan outlasted such periods of crisis, and was part of a broader change in the town life of the later middle ages.

93

Townsmen were becoming more and more impatient both with the idea and the fact of clerical privilege. For centuries men in holy orders had been exempt from taxation and legal prosecution; these rights seemed inappropriate in the more open and less traditional society of the medieval town. In the course of the thirteenth century, most northern Italian towns forced the clergy to pay taxes in despite of conciliar prohibitions, and town officials gained the right to sue them in the civil courts. In some extreme instances, laymen were allowed to dispossess or even attack clerics with virtual impunity, but this form of judicial reprisal was short-lived. In time a kind of truce was achieved in which town governments undeniably held the advantage. By limiting the amount that citizens could donate to religious or charitable bodies, and in some cases by forbidding the establishment of new monasteries near a town, church revenues were lowered and piety itself was restrained or channelled. In parts of France and Italy, radical anticlericalism became institutionalized in the *disvieto*, a kind of reverse excommunication in which the people ceased to make donations, boycotted the mass and other sacraments, and ignored the clergy even to the point of refusing them food.

But popular opposition to clerics ran deeper than the clash between an emerging town identity and the prestige of a venerable institution. A greater source of anticlericalism lay in its close links to heterodox religious enthusiasm, and to heresy.

Heterodoxy—belief that goes beyond or varies from orthodox doctrine—had always existed in the western church as the unavoidable result of partial or faulty knowledge of doctrine joined to the rich religious imagination of Latin and Germanic peoples. But where worship involves only the superficial observance of ritual it is unlikely for organized popular heterodoxy to develop; differing views emerge only when belief becomes a matter of inner conviction and meditation. By the mid-twelfth century the internalization of Christianity was sufficiently intense to promote the growth of alternative forms of belief. Thus the flowering of heterodox belief after 1150 was one dimension of a final stage in the Christianization of Europe. As such it was not a peripheral matter but one of central importance to popular faith.

For centuries heterodoxy had represented only vague or imperfect understanding of doctrine; as such it had been tolerated or ignored. By the twelfth century, however, many churchmen were convinced that simple misconceptions had given way to the intellectual poison of heresy—to what Bishop Grosseteste later defined as "opinion chosen by human sense, contrary to Holy Scripture, openly taught, pertinaciously defended." Although the distinction between confusion and willful error was never as clear as this definition made it, each served to strengthen the other and to weaken the claim of the medieval church to be the arbiter of faith.

The radical piety that appeared after 1150 was impatient with regularity and ritual; it saw priests as agents of an outworn and erroneous tradition and prelates as hypocrites and thieves. But it would be wrong to assume from this that the new piety turned away from Christianity itself. On the contrary, by rejecting the church it hoped to rediscover the pure core of biblical Christianity —the apostolic ideal—and to build a truer worship around it. With one exception—the Cathar church—western heresies arose not as substitutes for orthodox Christianity but as attempts to find and elaborate a truer orthodoxy of their own.

To think of heresy as a localized phenomenon with a limited number of adherents in two or three regions of southern Europe is misleading in the extreme. In addition to the vast numbers of Waldensians and Cathars throughout northern and central Italy and southern France, the Waldensians were well established in Toul, Metz and Liège. Trier had three Waldensian schools, and circles of heretics flourished in Bavaria, Bohemia and Moravia. Farther east, dualist Bogomils appeared and continued to gain strength in Byzantium in the late eleventh century.

Heresy flourished even where the church was strongest; the twelfth-century Cathars opened public schools in Rome itself, and were particularly strong in the Papal States, especially in the area around Viterbo. Writing in the early thirteenth century, Jacques de Vitry claimed that virtually every bourgeois commune in northern France had its fervent heretics. In the twelfth century heresy was a matter of public observation. Cathars gathered by the hundreds to support their spokesmen in debates against Catholic clerics or to decide matters of doctrine disputed among themselves. By the mid-thirteenth century all heterodox belief was the object of vigorous suppression and the heretics faded into a religious underground. Despite this there is sufficient evidence to show the persistence and extent of variant belief; only in England were heretics rare in this period.

The relatively few familiar names of these groups obscure the wide variety of heterodox beliefs; alongside Waldensians, *humiliati*, Patarines and Arnoldists, there were Menandrians, Arrianites, Origenists, Basiliadites, Carpogranites, Cherimanites, Nazarenes, Offitares and Atropornorfites. An inquisitor writing in the 1260's listed these and more than thirty other kinds of heresy in Italy alone. Some of the names he listed contain recognizable echoes of heresies that flourished in the early centuries of the church; churchmen customarily assimilated contemporary heretics to their counterparts in antiquity. However, although the names were confused the fact of variety remains, and the frequent disagreements between these groups tend to support an image of diversity.

In 1354 Bishop Grandisson of Exeter noted in his Register that a Cornish priest, Ralf de Tremur, was excommunicated for holding and preaching heretical doctrines. Ralf was a rigorous student of theology, and perhaps because his learning gave him a certain authority he persuaded a good many people of the truth of what he taught. He argued against transubstantiation and spoke unflatteringly about St. Peter and St. John, and, as a symbol of his opposition, took the holy wafer out of the church and burned it publicly.

For an individual to study and reason out the validity of what he believed was uncommon but not unheard-of in the middle ages. However, the great heretical movements did not grow out of such individual re-evaluations. For a long time historians of medieval doctrine believed that heresy was the product of class conflict. Doctrinal error was in this view a misleading cloak for social rebellion. More recent historical thinking has re-emphasized the purely religious element in these movements, but though they were not predominant medieval heresies did have both a nationalistic and an economic dimension. Where the church was an important political force heresy might become a rallying point for political opposition, as it certainly did among the Hussites in Bohemia and the Lollards in England. Throughout western Europe the wealth of the church overshadowed even that of the secular nobility; this was to many sufficient proof that the church of Rome could not be the bearer of the true faith, since true Christians had always been poor as well as oppressed. But whatever the depth of their political or economic motivation, all Western heretics had a common purpose: rediscovery of the apostolic life.

For centuries the early Christian values of poverty and asceticism had been preserved in Benedictine monasteries. Unlike the monks and nuns, however, the earliest Christians had been conspicuous for their preaching. Evangelism had been their customary work, and in failing to provide for this the monastic founders created an imperfect reflection of apostolic Christianity. Thus although they took some part in secular life the monasteries were in an important sense closed worlds which sought to preserve rather than to propagate the apostolic life. In the late eleventh and early twelfth centuries monasticism itself changed from within, and dozens of new orders were founded to create a more perfect framework for asceticism. A strong current of lay asceticism paralleled this, and, as we have seen, popular preachers for the first time sought to bring ascetic values into the lives of lay men and women. The very image of sanctity changed in this period. In the first feudal age, nearly all saints had been monks or other churchmen; after 1100 an increasing number of new saints were lay people, although few among these were merchants or laborers.

Eventually much of the enthusiasm for the apostolic life was channelled into the religious and secular orders of mendicants. Franciscan and Dominican tertiaries in particular—lay people who lived in the world but followed a modified religious rule—were able to satisfy their desire for a stricter life without leaving the world. But a large part of this enthusiasm found expression in heterodox doctrines. The *humiliati* dressed in undyed cloth and lived together in independent groups in poverty, supporting themselves by their own labor. The Waldensians preached barefoot—the women among them preaching as freely as the men, reviving a tradition of female priesthood suppressed with difficulty in the early centuries of the church. Many heretical groups not only preached but took over the clerical functions of baptizing and hearing confessions as well.

One side of the popular image of heresy comes through a letter attributed to Yvo of Narbonne, a cleric who had been in the household of the archbishop of Bordeaux. Accused of heresy, he wrote, he took counsel with the Patarines of Como in northern Italy, who protected him and confided to him their plans for growth. They sent scholars to the schools at Paris, they told him, to learn enough to support their beliefs more firmly; at the same time Patarine merchants were evangelizing laymen in the marketplaces.

These Patarines sent him to others at Milan, and from there he went to stay among "Cathar" communities in other Italian cities. In each case he was kept safe from detection, and the network of associated heretical groups extended even into Germany, where heretical beguines took him in. According to the letter, Yvo lived undetected in the heretical underground for years without fear of apprehension or discovery.

Whether or not the letter is genuine, or had a foundation in fact, it is significant for what it tells about one thirteenth-century image of heresy. To laymen who were not sympathetic to their teachings all heretics seemed very much the same. Despite their actual differences and bitter disagreements, to the lay observer they seemed a vast undifferentiated mass eager for mutual conspiracy and cooperation.

To an extent this view of heresy was valid where it concerned the Cathars, who were in many ways unique among Western heretics. In the twelfth century, while Latin crusaders were traveling eastward to recapture the holy places, Bogomil preachers came in small numbers into the West to build and strengthen the Cathar church. In time they helped to create a highly organized body of believers that extended southeastward from Béziers across the Po valley and down into Tuscany and the Romagna, with scattered groups in many other parts of Europe. At its height, the Cathar church held a council at St. Felix de Caraman in 1167, led by Nicetas, bishop of the Bogomil community in Constantinople. His presence symbolized and helped to ensure unity of Cathar belief; at the council he not only ordained the bishops of the Cathar church but reaffirmed the priority of dualism as the basis of Cathar teaching.

This strict dualism taught that two opposing principles were caught in an eternal struggle for predominance. As a result of an abortive attempt of the evil power to conquer the good, material creation appeared; like its author it was radically evil. Mankind

99

perpetuated this evil by generating children, eating flesh meat, and in fact by any method of prolonging human life. For this reason, the most rigorous of the Cathars, the *perfecti*, renounced every earthly contact and ended their lives through the slow starvation of the *endura*.

In brief summary Cathar belief sounds exotic and irreconcilably at odds with medieval Christianity. But in its mundane practices the Cathar church showed striking similarities to the Roman in both membership and religious use. In the *Alexiad*, Anna Comnena wrote that in Byzantium "a Bogomil looks gloomy and is covered up to the nose and walks with a stoop and mutters, but within he is an uncontrollable wolf." In the West, far from being eccentric outcasts dualist heretics often belonged to aristocratic families and were recruited from the wealthiest and most influential members of the community. In Languedoc, a number of Catholic prelates came from the Cathar or pro-Cathar nobility—Berengar, Catholic archbishop of Narbonne was the bastard son of the Cathar Raymond Berengar, count of Barcelona, and the prelates of Toulouse and Carcassonne had similar connections.

Cathar religion paralleled Roman practices at many points. Cathar penance, confession and a common ritual meal echoed the Roman sacraments. The only Cathar prayer was the Lord's Prayer, recited in unison; at the end of his first stage of instruction a Cathar initiate was given the privilege of repeating it. Most striking of all, the Cathar Bible was essentially the same as the Latin Vulgate.

Like most Western heretics, the Cathars were familiar with biblical texts in the vernacular, and committed large parts of them to memory. (The Waldensians too learned long biblical passages; a German chronicler wrote that he had seen one Waldensian peasant who had read the entire book of Job and several others who could recite the entirety of the Christian scriptures.) Few records of dualist liturgy have survived, but in a fragment of a Cathar baptismal ritual the language is strikingly academic. "Baptism," it reads in part, "is called washing or *supertinctio*. Whence it is understood that there are several kinds of washing. . . ." And the priest went on to enumerate with fine discrimination the various meanings of the term and of the sacrament itself.

That heretics relied on logic to confound their clerical and inquisitorial opponents is clear from the comments of the Dominican inquisitor Bernard Gui. Writing in the early fourteenth century, he noted that

> since modern heretics seek and strive to palliate their errors in secret, rather than to confess them openly, the learned men cannot prove them wrong through their knowledge of the scriptures, because they slip out by means of verbal trickeries and astute logical contrivances. And because of this, learned men are more often bested by them, and the heretics, glorying in this, are strengthened all the more, seeing that they can mock the learned thus, and then cleverly take refuge against them in sly tricks, stratagems and tortuous circumlocutions. . . . What is more, lay Christians take from this sort of incident matter for scandal, if once an inquisitorial process is begun it is broken off amid embarrassment, and they are in a sense weakened in their faith when they observe learned men being made sport of by rustics and villagers. For the laity believe that we have at hand explanations of dogma so lucid and obvious no one could argue against us without our being able instantly to convince him . . . and for this reason it is better not to dispute matters of faith with such astute heretics in the presence of laymen.[7]

Heresy did not arise out of ignorance; it was one more dimension of the spread of literacy.

The vast group of men and women of heterodox belief living according to the principles of the apostolic life and often more learned even than the clergy in biblical lore did not represent a temporary or aberrant phenomenon in medieval piety. Heretics were rarely easy to identify in the absence of a neat ecclesiastical censure; early in their development the heretical Pastoureaux were welcomed as "apostles of reform" by Blanche of Castille, and Peter Waldo, founder of the Waldensian sect, had two daughters who were nuns at the eminently orthodox abbey of Fontevrault.

Though subject to intermittent and sometimes savage persecution, heretics were never completely expunged. Waldensian communities survived in remote parts of the Italian Alps until the eighteenth century. Attacked by clerics and some laymen, heresy was looked on by thousands of others with tolerance or favor. In the fourteenth and fifteenth centuries doctrinal error ceased to be a major concern of many churchmen. As the religion of the church moved farther from the center of the medieval world view, indifference became an even more serious problem than heresy. The fact of excommunication provoked a more and more casual response; one English villager who had been under the ban of the church for seven years told a questioner that he didn't fear to be outside the Christian community and that "his labor would save him."

The church could guide but never entirely contain the faith of lay men and women. Popular piety had a rhythm and history of its own—a history which had at least as much to do with the visionary climate of medieval thought as with theology and ecclesiastical affairs. For religious belief was enriched by the same predispositions of sight and perception as belief about inanimate and incorporeal creation.

Concepts such as the trinity and the transformation of the eucharistic wafer and wine into Jesus' body and blood were easy to grasp for people accustomed to coevality and multiple identities. Intellectual vision made the mystery of the mass clear to Angela of Foligno, when she saw how God came into the sacrament, and understood how he could exist simultaneously on all the Christian altars of the world. But this same clarity of understanding came, according to Guibert de Nogent, to a young child watching the mass beside his mother. Seeing the priest take up the host the child turned to his mother and told her he saw the priest holding not the wafer but an infant in his arms, and then wrapping it in a napkin.

"Visions and wonders," Guibert remarked, "are borne through those who possess the gift of signs like water through canals." And the gift is given widely, he added: many possess it. Visions are not to be doubted or feared, but believed, as the prophecies of the dying are believed and heeded. God is to be sought through miraculous channels of this kind, and through natural wonders, just as he appeared to the Hebrews in whirlwinds and fire pillars. These prodigies, and the visionary glimpses that come through the eye of reason, were to be the food of earthly piety until men reached their ultimate reward. "For what else is paradise," Guibert wrote, "but the eternal vision of Christ?"

Chapter five

LAND AND RULE

n 1241, when the first rumors of the Mongol invasion of Russia and Hungary were reaching Europe, Frederick II wrote letters to his brother monarchs describing the imminent peril of the West. "Bursting forth from the abodes of Tartarus," he said, the Horde is even now battering like a sudden tempest at Germany, the "door of Christendom." Yet the day will come, he wrote, when Christendom will rise victorious against them,

when Germany, rising with rage and zeal to battle, and France, that mother and nurse of chivalry; the warlike and bold Spain, with fertile England, valorous in its men, and protected by its fleet; Almaine, full of impetuous warriors, the maritime Dacia; untameable Italy; Burgundy, that never knows peace; restless Apulia, with the piratical and unconquered islands of the Grecian, Adriatic and Tyrrhene seas . . . when bloody Ireland, with active Wales; Scotland, abounding in lakes, icy Norway, and every noble and renowned country lying under the royal star of the West, shall send forth their chosen ornaments preceded by the symbol of the life-giving cross. . . .[1]

As it happened the Mongols were kept by an accident of fortune from conquering Europe. But had they tested the will of the West to battle, they would surely not have encountered the close-ranked panoply Frederick described. For thirteenth-century Europe was not an ordered region but a geography of anomalies.

Theorists of medieval government liked to quote Aristotle on the need for unity in human affairs. "Things have no desire to be wrongly ordered," one of them wrote. "Inasmuch as a multitude of Princedoms is wrong, let there be one prince." This theoretical premise combined with the continuing idea of empire to shape a theory of government in which a network of feudal, civil and royal authorities culminated in the highest authority, that of the emperor himself.

Yet in spite of this theory medieval rulers everywhere exalted their own positions to overreach their place in the hierarchy of rule. Civic officials referred to themselves as barons or magnates, and feudal lords called themselves kings. In William I's time Normandy was "the monarchy of Normandy"; the duke of Aquitaine too referred to his domain as a monarchy, and exchanged ambassadors with other kings; the counts of Nevers, vassals of the French king, used the title "prince of the region." Reginald, king of the Isle of Man in the Irish Sea, in the twelfth century gave and received his kingdom from Innocent III as a fief, announcing that he would acknowledge no superior among secular men. In the same century the Spanish king Alfonso VII revived the old Leonese title of emperor.

Medieval government was shaped by the cognition of multi-dimensional reality. Like the body of Christ, plenary governmental authority was perceived to reside in many places at once. Each ruler had a multiple identity: as absolute head of his region, and as subordinate vassal to the heads of the larger regions of which it formed a part. Overlapping jurisdictions were perceived not as rival but as concurrent authorities, co-participants in a multiform pattern of rule.

For in actuality the boundaries of power were in the middle ages as flexible as those of perception itself. The practical result was a chaotic tangle of jurisdictions—a confusion in governmental affairs that defies systematic description.

Secular government in the twelfth, thirteenth and fourteenth centuries may be seen as a series of tenuously interlocking microcosms, under steady pressure on two fronts. On the one hand, every city, fief or kingdom sought to extend the limits of its sovereignty. On the other hand, every political unit was eager to gild its own majesty by associating itself with higher authorities. Nowhere was this more true than in the city of Rome.

The bishop of Rome was the spiritual leader of Christendom; the deacons and priests of the city's churches were the cardinals of the western church. Rome's traditional secular ruler, the emperor, claimed primacy over all the kings of Europe. Yet while proudly acknowledging (and profiting from) these distinctions ordinary Romans continually rebelled against both papal and imperial authority. Popular republican movements led by Arnold of Brescia, Cola di Rienzo and more obscure men continually asserted the autonomy of the city. Papal rule was not firmly re-established until 1278, and emperors who came to Rome to receive the "crown of the world" were often refused entrance. Frederick Barbarossa could not be crowned in St. Peter's until he barricaded the bridge over the Tiber under the fortress of St. Angelo. The most Rome-loving of all the emperors, Otto III, had to leave the city in the wake of the constant turmoil that followed his coronation. A hagiographer of St. Bernard put into Otto's mouth this wistful speech to the Roman people, supposedly made from the tower of his house on the Aventine:

Aren't you my Romans? For your sake I left my homeland and my loved ones as well; out of love for you I overthrew the Saxons and all the Germans of my own blood; for you I have conquered the far-flung corners of our Empire, so that your fathers might rule wherever they set foot, and so that your name and glory might be spread even to the uttermost. I have preferred you all; I have adopted you as my sons. . . .[2]

The commune of Rome formed a "little world" within the vast hegemonies of emperor and pope, but its claims of sovereignty troubled the tranquillity of both the larger entities. Other areas were troublesome because of the sheer complexity of their political arrangements. Still others were enclaves of exemption or privilege, freaks of history or local custom that set them apart from the normal course of rule.

Constantly at odds with the legal maxim *nulle terre sans seigneur* ("there is no land without its lord") was the equally powerful claim that all inherited lands were held independently unless it could be proved that they were held as fiefs. Allodial lands, whose owners were not bound into the hierarchy of feudal holdings, were scattered among fiefs in every region of Europe. In many areas outside the feudal heartland (northern France and England), allods were the norm. Even where the system of feudal holdings was strongest, proving lordship at suit was of necessity a frequent pastime of the nobility, and medieval law courts were filled with disputes over land tenure and use.

Often there was no documentary proof to establish true title to a holding. In England the Norman kings evolved the writ of *mort d'ancestor* to find the truth in this situation where fiefs were concerned. "Twelve free and lawful men" from the neighborhood were to swear whether the claimant's father held the disputed land on the day he died, and whether the claimant was in fact his nearest relative. "And in the meantime they shall view that land," the writ goes on, and then having satisfied their memory by sight their oaths are to be enrolled and judgment made by the sheriff or his justices. Frequently the buttress of memory was sought back through several generations. The judicial record of a dispute between the monastery of St. Nicholas of Angers and the canons of St. Maur tells how the canons complained that the monks of St. Nicholas were using part of a wooded stretch of land to which they claimed title. A church on the land dedicated to St. Lambert was theirs, they said, and to prove it they found a very old peasant who would swear that in his youth he had watched his own oxen plough that land, and had paid tithes to St. Lambert. The two parties determined to settle the dispute through the ordeal of cold water, with the abbot of St. Nicholas as judge. Because the old man was feeble, he brought a younger man to swear for him and to undergo the ordeal, but before it took place the old man had to identify the fief. He was loaded on an ass's back and led around the ancient boundary of the fief; where he pointed, sticks were put in the ground to mark off the limits his visual memory dictated. As it turned out, the ordeal proved him false, and the monks of St. Nicholas continued to make use of the wood as before.

In this case, memory alone was not sufficient to determine ownership: it had to be tested against the divine judgment of the ordeal by cold water. In the ordeal the animate unity of the natural world was invoked to cooperate in the discovery of truth. Water, once it was sworn to reject liars and criminals, would as a pure element refuse to take to itself a guilty man or woman. The procedure of the ordeal by water called for the accused to fast, then go to the church and swear on relics that he was innocent before taking communion. Blessing holy water, the priest next took some of it to the site of the ordeal, and gave it to the accused to drink. Then, turning to the pond or stream, he forswore it with this oath: "I adjure you, water, that you in no way accept this man if there be any fault in him . . . but make him swim on top of you, and let nothing be done against you, not any witchcraft by which he is able to hide himself." The accused stripped off his clothes, having kissed the gospel and the cross and having been asperged one last time with water. Then he was thrown into the pond. If he sank he was declared innocent of wrongdoing or falsehood.

In part because it was notoriously flawed as a judicial procedure, the ordeal of cold water was prohibited by some secular governments and later by the church. One of its principal uses had been to detect heretics, and with the coming of the Inquisition more sophisticated evidentiary methods made it obsolete. Ordeals in various forms continued to be used in some parts of Europe throughout the middle ages, however, and all the powers of the enchanted world were used to bend their outcome. Spells, charms and herbal draughts were employed to cripple or strengthen fighters in the ordeal by combat, and in the mid-thirteenth century Albertus Magnus included in his treatise on the wonders of the world recipes for curing burns contracted in the ordeal of hot water. In this ordeal the accused had to grasp a hot iron and walk with it, or reach into a pot of boiling water and bring out stones lying at the bottom of it; several days later when the bandages were removed from his hand the condition of his burns determined his guilt or innocence. To prevent harm, Albertus recommended a sulphur potion, or a medicinal salve made from egg whites and wild radishes, to be smeared over the hand twice and allowed to dry. "After this," he wrote, "you will be able bravely to undergo the fire without injury."

Visual memory and judgment by ordeal were uncertain guides to the just disposition of the medieval order even in the clearest of circumstances. But the conditions of medieval landholding were often not clear. For closely paralleling the multiform political authority of medieval Europe was its multiform geography.

Geographical areas were not then parcelled in a simple division among landowners. A principle of division was involved in the ownership of land, but what was divided was not the earth itself but the varying degrees of sovereignty that might be exerted over it, which were physically inseparable. Like political authority, landholding involved a chain of jurisdictions culminating in the one man or woman who had no superior. Where the feudal network was weak, ownership might rest in a local lord or governor. Where feudal ties were strong, the smallest fief was in theory linked to the most powerful feudatory in the region, or to the king. Ownership was thus not exclusive but inclusive; it was not defined by the unique rights of the immediate tenant but by the collective rights of all his superiors, tempered by dynastic and political anomalies generations into the past.

In these circumstances it is easy to see how a proprietary puzzle like that of imperial Flanders might arise. The lands that ran in a thin band along the eastern border of the county of Flanders and out into the North Sea west of Antwerp were until the mid-thirteenth century designated as the marquisat of Flanders. The marquis was an imperial vassal, and to distinguish his holdings from the county of Flanders the six small places were referred to collectively as imperial Flanders. But in fact each of the six had a unique juridical position and a complex history.

The first of them, the land between the Escaut and the Dendre known as "the county of Alost," was originally a part of Brabant, but the marquis of Flanders had taken it over sometime in the middle of the eleventh century; when the emperor recovered the territory later, the marquis became his vassal for Alost.

The tiny district of Overschelde, smaller than the land enclosed by the town walls of Ghent, extended out from the town between the two branches of the river. Marguerite, countess of Flanders in the 1250's, joined the Overschelde to Ghent and put it under the jurisdiction of the town elders. From then on it shared the political vicissitudes of the urban area, which repeatedly declared itself loyal to the French crown but was conquered by imperial forces in the second half of the century.

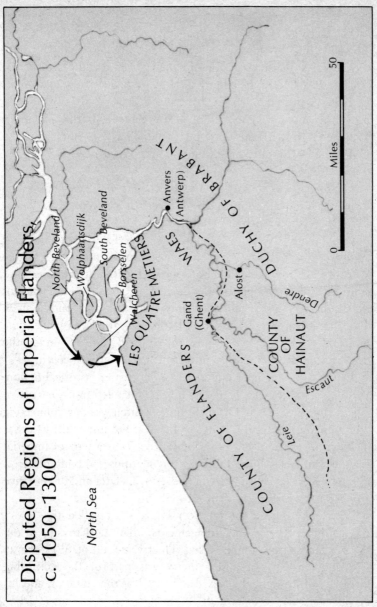

Disputed Regions of Imperial Flanders, c. 1050-1300

North Sea

North Beveland

Wolphaartsdijk

South Beveland

Borselen

Walcheren

LES QUATRE MÉTIERS

WAES

Anvers (Antwerp)

DUCHY OF BRABANT

Gand (Ghent)

Alost

Dendre

COUNTY OF HAINAUT

COUNTY OF FLANDERS

Escaut

Leie

Miles

The Zeeland islands of Walcheren, South and North Beveland, Borsselen and Wolphaartsdijk (not connected to Beveland until recent times) made up another fragment of imperial Flanders, but became attached to the county of Holland (a fief of the marquisat) in 1256. A precedent more than four centuries old was cited to prove the imperial rights: in 841, it was claimed, Lothar had given Walcheren to the Danish pirate Heriold. Thus it must have been a part of his patrimony, and as such should pass to the holder of the imperial crown.

The four towns of Axel, Hulst, Bonchande and Sassenade which formed a juridical group called De Vier Ambachten ("Les Quatre Métiers" to the French in Flanders) should from their geographical position alone have gone to France. (By the Treaty of Verdun, all lands to the west of the Escaut were to become part of the kingdom of the French.) But partly for ethnic reasons they continued to form a part of the diocese of Utrecht—and hence of the Lotharingian, or imperial, lands—into the high middle ages. The four towns were Frisian, not Flemish, and eventually came under the rule of the counts of Holland and so under the overlordship of the marquis, probably in the eleventh century.

A fifth component of imperial Flanders was a historical fiction. Because the chronicler Jean de Thilrode included in his history of Ghent the story that in Ottonian times a ditch was dug connecting "the imperial castle of Ghent" to the sea, the imperial castle was included in charters and other official deeds as a part of imperial Flanders. In fact, while a tenth-century marquis had built a fortress in the town, it was in ruins two hundred years later and did not give grounds for any imperial claims to Ghent.

The final piece in the puzzle was a district called the Waes, French under the Verdun arrangements, which Lothar, ruler of the West Franks, gave to his vassal Thierry, count of West Frisia (Holland) in 969. Because Thierry was part of the governing hierarchy of Lorraine, he was also a vassal of the emperor, and his dual loyalty lent the Waes an ambivalent status. The counts of Holland continued to claim the territory into the twelfth century, though it was administered for the counts of Flanders by the house of Alost. The record of the charters makes it plain that the Waes was French until at least 1252, when as emperor a descendant of Thierry of West Frisia, William of Holland, stated his definitive claim to the land, dispossessing Marguerite of Flanders and refusing to recognize her claim that she held the Waes from the French king.

Such in brief was the intricate legal geography of a relatively unimportant imperial fief. Its direction was determined as much by history as by abstract feudal relations, and its unity was strictly a matter of administrative convenience. Political groupings like imperial Flanders normally existed in a state of legal confusion until such time as their status was challenged. Clarification was not necessary to satisfactory local government, only to national ambitions. It was only the territorial expansion of the French monarchy that gave imperial Flanders a certain significance in the thirteenth century. By the fifteenth century its status had again grown tangled, and would not be fully clarified until in 1609 the northern provinces broke away from Spain.

Throughout Europe, vassals commonly had more than one lord, and fiefs geographically within one country might be subject to the ruler of another. Though subject to the king of France the counts of Champagne held three of their French fiefs from the German emperor; the French count of Toulouse held Provence from him as well. Complicating the situation east of the Escaut was the fact that the count of Flanders had as his lords not only the emperor but the French and English kings as well, and when Philip Augustus and Henry II were at war in the 1180's he was obliged to support both sides with knights.

Among the most intricate of medieval political territories was Burgundy, an area covering much of what is now southeastern

France and Switzerland. As the kingdom of Burgundy it became an imperial fief in the eleventh century, but was afterwards gradually taken over into the royal jurisdiction of France. The eastern cantons of Switzerland, known as "Little Burgundy," broke off from the rest and remained practically independent after the thirteenth century. The Free County (Franche-Comté) of Burgundy, the upper quarter of the territory, was an imperial fief joined to the jurisdiction of the French dukes of Burgundy in the fourteenth century. The duchy itself was a French fief and a province of France. There was also a landgraviate of Burgundy, an imperial administrative district called the "circle of Burgundy," and two vague geographical terms, Trans- and Cisjurane Burgundy, referring to districts north and east and south and west of the Jura Mountains.

In these circumstances it is hardly surprising that villagers were often confused about who their governors were and what powers they represented. Ancient landmarks used to mark off boundaries did not always correspond to the present order, and the rivers dividing land from land regularly changed their courses. Many fiefs lay across major frontiers. At least six French feudatories held lands on both sides of the Franco-German border, and the number of fiefs that crossed regional boundaries was legion.

There was no central court of record where uncertainties of this kind could be clarified. The papal chancery had documents touching the remoter parts of virtually all of Europe's ecclesiastical divisions, but its clerks were not infallible, and local custom or the best recollection of the oldest resident was often the most reliable index of legality in boundaries.

Language was no clue to jurisdiction. The common tongue did not change abruptly at a political perimeter; instead there was a gradual shifting of dialects that began dozens of miles before the frontier and was not complete until long after it was passed. Within linguistic communities enclaves of differing speech were common. Bretons spoke a Celtic dialect, and a Scandinavian variant was common around the Norman town of Bayeux. Two languages, English and Norman French, were heard throughout twelfth-century England, and although they later merged into one there were pockets of disparate speech in Cornwall, Wales and in the northern Marches until recent times.

This tangle of jurisdictions, boundaries and tongues meant that not only individuals but whole communities were at times bewildered about their political identities. But the complexity did not end here. For even at its most orderly, medieval georgraphy was spangled with exceptions—areas exempt from the normal pattern of jurisdiction. Outside the customary and feudal law vast tracts of land were ruled by the law of the forest—much of it cleared land, full of farms and villages. (In England, the entire county of Essex lay under forest law, as did much of Normandy.) Here panagers, supervisors and park-wardens traditionally abused their powers and ruled unrestrained in the king's or duke's name, cutting off whole populations from the political evolution going on around them. Nominally a part of the Papal States, the island of Sardinia was claimed in the thirteenth century by Frederick II, but continued in its practical independence as "a place of refuge for merchants, the comfort of the shipwrecked, and an asylum for exiles." Other sovereign entities grew up where pope and emperor contended for mastery; in the language of the fourteenth-century legist Bartolo, the great communes of Venice, Genoa, Milan and Florence were "collectivities recognizing no superior."

Differing patterns of settlement led to a great variety of exceptions in feudal Europe. The sulungs and yokes of Kent differed from the hides and yardlands of other English counties, and were equally divided among all the sons rather than being reserved to the eldest. In the honour of Richmond, knights' fees were paid by whole villages instead of individual sworn vassals, and other anomalies of tenure made the idea of personal service invalid.

Beyond the generalities of political and legal theorists the great political units of medieval Europe crumble into a mass of particulars. Regional and local governments varied widely in their customs, their procedures, and their systems of rule, even when they lay only a few dozen miles apart. Everywhere personal exceptions bent the law, and every government fell into periodic anarchy on the death of a ruler.

Government by fragmentation was the norm of medieval politics. Of the thousands of small parcels of land in the county of Nevers, for example, the count ruled only those that were not royal fiefs, or fiefs of another great lord, or allods ("free" lands, exempted entirely from the feudal chain of vassalage). From those under his jurisdiction, he claimed taxes in coin and goods from his tenants, a yearly tax from his serfs, income from court fines and tolls on rivers and markets. When a comital fief changed hands, the count gained a relief or alienation tax, and he retained the right to coin money, levy taxes on craftsmen and the goods they produced, and to demand hospitality from his vassals. In addition, the goods of bastards and strangers who died on his lands were his to claim, as were abandoned possessions and "things that wander away from their owners." In return for these benefits (which he shared with the bishop), the count sent between ten and twenty knights to the royal host, and defended the king's lands against his enemies at home.

The sixty-eight great fiefs of Normandy were divided between the duke (who for much of the medieval period was king in England) and the king of France. Ten of these were fiefs of the church; in addition, the dukes had alienated their income from the towns to churchmen, making them landlords of entire quarters of many Norman towns. Like the counts of Nevers, the Norman dukes enjoyed taxes and rights of toll and commerce, as well as reliefs and profits from coinage and justice. From many of their alienated rural lands, however, they claimed only a symbolic return—a pair of golden spurs, or a brace of fowl. The Norman dukes owned vineyards and pig farms as well as larger estates, and collected fees on wine transport and on the catch in herring, mackerel and other fish. All great fish which beached themselves on the Norman coast—whales were common in the English Channel in the middle ages—went to the profit of the duke, as did miscellaneous taxes in kind.

In Nevers and in Normandy the local rulers had two kinds of power: that which came to them as recognized arbiters of public authority, and that lent to them by their feudal overlords. Two systems of loyalties bound the free men of the medieval West. In one, vassals and overlords made contractual agreements in which each pledged to render services to the other. These were the links of *suzerainty*, or lordship, and they were at once more traditional and more tenuous than the national ties that grew increasingly strong in the thirteenth and fourteenth centuries. The other system revived in the *sovereignty* of the king the concept of public power lost after the breakdown of Roman authority in the ancient world. Suzerainty was based on personal promises, sovereignty on public authority. Suzerainty had explicit limits and defined obligations; sovereignty was absolute. It was the principle of sovereignty that in time gained the backing of the royal courts and of a rehabilitated civil law; it was suzerainty, though, that captured the medieval imagination and laid claim to the medieval vision of rule.

The two systems of loyalty yielded two classes of the ruled: vassals, men and women bound to their overlords by personal contracts of infeudation, and subjects, who were linked to their rulers by legal authority. Both arrangements evoked strong loyalties, but only one carried the social ideal of mutuality—the idea that government exists not for reasons of history or divine institution but because it is necessary for survival. For most of the early middle ages, governments were little more than mechanisms for survival; long after they became abstract institutions embodying public power the concept of mutuality continued to adhere to the office of king.

Much of the confusion of royal government grew out of these coexisting systems of rule. Having at hand two means of coercion, two constituencies, and two sources of power, the best medieval kings adapted their authority to meet each situation. The French king ruled in the lands of the count of Champagne by feudal right; he was the count's overlord. But in three of the fiefs of Champagne, the emperor was overlord. Here the French king ruled as sovereign, with rights grounded not in feudal loyalties but in tradition and past patterns of rule.

Where feudal loyalty was uncertain, medieval kings resorted to their public authority. Where sovereign rights were disputed, they fell back on their prerogatives as overlord. Royal armies showed this alternation in the principles of rule. The obligations of vassals provided the nucleus of a medieval army, but by the thirteenth century this nucleus was normally supplemented both by mercenaries and by publicly supported fighting men, recruited and paid by the king's subjects. The same was true of local armies; alongside his vassals the count of Nevers could call the tenants and serfs of the county to arms, since as subjects they were obliged to serve in the comital host. Given the fact that untrained footsoldiers were of little account in medieval battles, the manorial tenants of the Nivernais did not actually take the field: they did serve as ancillaries to the feudal host, however, as castle guards and fortress builders.

In every sphere of government the interplay between lordship and sovereignty was apparent, yet at its strongest medieval rule built on its suzerain character. It rested on personal relationships, rising in a living chain from man to man, and held together by oaths of honor.

Amid a host of official reciprocities it is easy to forget that friendship, not political rebellion, was among the greatest threats to orderly feudal rule in medieval Europe. Eager to find loyal servants not driven by personal or dynastic ambitions, twelfth-century kings sought advisers in men of low birth, and raised them to power over the heads of the great vassals of the realm. Thus the son of a London merchant, Thomas Becket, became chancellor and then archbishop in the court of Henry II; earlier in the century Roger of Salisbury rose from humbler origins to prominence at the court of Henry I.

Perhaps the most spectacular rise from obscurity to power came in the France of Louis VI, where the Garlande family threatened to take over every major post at the Capetian court. Two Garlande brothers, Paien and Anseau, became seneschals under Philip I, and sometime before 1118 another brother, a cleric named Étienne, became chancellor. When Anseau died the office of seneschal passed to another Garlande, William; meanwhile Gilbert de Garlande had become chief butler. By 1120, William's death left the key office of seneschal open to Étienne, who saw nothing extraordinary in combining command of the royal army with his religious duties. (In addition to the chancellorship, Étienne held benefices at Étampes, Orléans and Paris; he tried twice to become a bishop, but without success.)

Étienne de Garlande held as much power at the French court as any man since Charlemagne's time, and he owed it entirely to royal favor. Always at the king's side, as a contemporary wrote to Étienne, "both because of your office and for the sake of the friendship he bore you," Garlande drew on himself the suspicion and disapproval of churchmen, nobles, and Louis' queen, Adelaide of Maurienne. When in a final burst of self-aggrandizement he

119

tried to turn over the office of senseschal to his son-in-law, Louis stripped him of his offices and sent him away. Unrepentant, he entrenched himself outside the court and fought for three years for reinstatement. In the end, he not only came back to court as chancellor (Louis did not immediately revive the office of seneschal) but took flagrant vengeance on his opponents. Two of the clerics who opposed his position were assassinated by members of Étienne's household; though he was clearly implicated Louis took no action against him.

The power of Étienne de Garlande was directly traceable to the personal and arbitrary character of household government in twelfth-century courts. Though he rose higher than most Étienne was no different in his origins from the other petty feudatories of the Île-de-France Louis took to serve him; except for his impatient ambition he might in time have become a bishop, or even pope.

The nature of a medieval government in the twelfth century was still dependent on the men who staffed it. Offices were still created to suit the men who held them, and once a trusted official was found, more offices were heaped upon him. Jurisdictional areas were often designated by the name of the official in charge of them: not "the *bailliage* of Vermandois" but "the *bailliage* where Robert is *bailli*." Institutions were customarily changed by similarly personal means. When Simon de Montfort wanted to reform his chancery on the Roman model, he asked Innocent III to send one of his chancery officials to become head of Simon's clerks. Monasteries, too, were founded and reformed by importing individual monks, not regulations, from reformed houses.

This dependence on personal qualification and individual circumstance worked against uniformity, and made medieval government as particularized and circumstantial as medieval geography. Its contingent character was especially evident in the royal courts, where a protean group of familiar officials joined a fluid number of royal vassals to aid the king in the exercise of his rule. To the

120

traditional household offices of chancellor, chief justiciar and treasurer in England, seneschal, chancellor and dapifer in France was added the ever-changing membership of the royal council, an informal group made up of the vassals who were in the vicinity of the court. (In contrast to its solemn functions, the makeup of this body was almost entirely provisional.) Until the end of the twelfth century, many official functions were undifferentiated, and court officials were at times interchangeable.

The very substance of government was elusive: administration was what went on in the king's tent or chamber; law was what he dictated to his clerks; the treasury of the kingdom was the gold he kept under his bed. The king's political and legal functions lent themselves much more readily to an itinerant court than his role as paymaster and guardian of the treasure. King John's loss of the crown jewels is only the best known of many such losses. Though his contemporary Philip Augustus kept several money chests in different places as insurance against theft, he lost one himself at Frétéval.

Nor did his feudal suzerainty provide a medieval king with a firm substructure of rule. The feudal network gave only conditional assurances of personal loyalty, weakened through irregular application and continual dissipation of royal rights. For though theorists of medieval government have elevated it to a principle of rule, the feudal concept was little more than an attempt to rank free men in an orderly way and lock them into mutual obligations. The feudal relationship was perhaps the most conspicuous agency of order in medieval society, but this did not make it either systematic or effective.

In the winter of 1245, the English king Henry III was bivouacked near the sea in a remote area of north Wales with a small body of knights and a group of loyal Welsh from Cheshire and Shropshire.

Under constant danger from the hostile Welsh in the foothills, he supervised the fortification of a castle at Gannock while he and his men waited for provisions. Hungry and unprepared for the cold, they shivered in their light clothing and suffered in tents inadequate to keep out the snow and violent weather. "Cold and naked," wrote one of Henry's knights, "we spend our time in watching, fasting and prayer. We watch lest the Welsh attack us by night. We fast because we have not enough to eat, and a penny loaf now costs twenty times what it did. We pray that we may return home safely before long." Stranded, and without the means to retreat, the king and his men watched the little harbor that formed at high tide beside their camp for a supply ship. Along with the castle, the little inlet, at its fullest "about a crossbow-shot wide," was all that separated the king and his men from the Welsh, and navigation of its tidal currents was difficult.

At last an Irish provision ship came in sight, but was caught by the outgoing tide and ran aground at the mouth of the harbor, and stuck fast in the sand of the enemy bank. The mercenaries in Henry's pay went across in boats and succeeded in driving the Welsh away from the ship, pursuing them inland and then destroying houses, barns, and fields on their way back to the English encampment. In their eagerness for plunder they despoiled the Cistercian monastery of Aberconway, burning it to the ground and carrying off valuables of every kind, even to chalices and books. Burdened with these spoils the English force was attacked as it reached the shore, and in the ensuing fight many on both sides were cut down or drowned; hostages of high rank at first spared by the Welsh for the sake of their ransoms were also killed and dismembered. But the party that held the ship fought on, using its wooden walls as shields, and held out until the tide turned and floated the ship again.

By this time it was after nightfall, and once more the English sent boats across the little channel to rescue the last of their men.

They could not rescue the provisions, however, and the next day they had to watch as their opponents stripped the ship of its cargo and then set it ablaze. Seven casks of wine were all that they could salvage from its ruins. "While we have been here," the English knight wrote,

> we have often made armed raids in mortal danger to find food, both suffering and launching attacks. . . . There was so little food that many men and horses died of starvation; at one time there was no wine even for the king, and only one cask in the entire camp. At that time a measure of wheat cost 20 shillings, an ox three or four silver marks, and a hen eightpence. For want of these things horses and men grew thin, and many perished.[3]

But in a few months' time this futile expedition was over, and Henry had turned his attention to a disputed inheritance in the south of France.

That the king returned alive from this campaign was surely no miracle; to the last his survival would have been favored over that of his men. What is worth noting is not the climate of mortality but that any king should be so vulnerable to the dangers of exposure and starvation. To be sure, medieval kings and their families spent most of their lives out of doors, contending with the fatigues and uncertainties of travel. But Henry's ordeal was of a different kind. A poor strategist at best, he risked death in this Welsh campaign because like almost all medieval rulers his power to command was precarious, and had constantly to be reinvigorated by victories in the field.

Kingly power was normally bought at this price. For this reason, order in medieval government was usually the result of averted crises; peace was most often a breathing space between wars. Feudal government is best seen as an overly rational name given to a desperate and continuing compromise with anarchy.

123

Chapter six

THE POWER OF KINGS

In the thirtieth year of his reign Henry I of England saw a triple vision in his sleep. In a dream a crowd of serfs holding scythes and pitchforks gathered around him, angrily grinding their teeth and waving their weapons threateningly. The king woke in terror, leapt out of bed and took up his sword to attack the mob. He frightened off the guard that had been watching by his bed, but the angry serfs had vanished. Sleeping again, Henry saw a cohort of mail-clad knights with iron helmets bearing lances, spears and arrows and coming toward him as if to kill him. Even more terrified, he awoke again and struck out at the attackers with his sword, filling the palace with his cries for help. Finding himself alone, at last he slept again. This time a crowd of churchmen—archbishops, bishops, abbots, priors—stood around his bed, striking out at him with the points of their pastoral staves. The king woke a third time, but realizing that he was dreaming, he held his peace and the night passed without further alarms.

In the morning Henry's doctor, Grimsbald, asked him what had disturbed him, and finding that he had received visionary warnings Grimsbald told him what they meant, and advised the king to do penance for his sins and to be generous in his almsgiving.

Henry was an old man in his thirtieth year as king, and though he would live for five years more he undoubtedly took the visionary appearances to heart. The chronicler to whom Grimsbald confided the royal visions ascribed them to Henry's harsh taxes, but the king may have seen in them a warning of social and political rebellion or even assassination. Dream-portents had a venerable place in the fortunes of the Norman kings, and were not to be taken lightly. Before his birth William the Bastard's mother foresaw the Norman Conquest in a dream in which her intestines stretched out from Normandy across all England. And on the night before his sudden death in the New Forest William Rufus dreamed of massive bleeding. In his dream his surgeon bled him, and the stream of blood rose as high as heaven itself, blocking off the sun until the sky was dark.

Henry, who according to William of Malmesbury was a heavy sleeper and snored, was in any case afraid of night attacks. Some years earlier his chamberlain and other servants had conspired to assault him as he slept, and though he discovered the plot in time and dealt harshly with the conspirators he never again felt safe in his bed. He increased his night guard and changed his sleeping quarters often, and always kept a shield and sword within reach.

Henry I's uneasy rest was a hazard of calling for medieval kings. By whatever means power is measured—persuasive influence over the actions of others, license to break laws with impunity, ability to terrorize and overawe, physical invulnerability—the real power of kings in the middle ages was uneven and limited in its extent. Though kings ruled large geographical expanses their actual influence was at any given time confined to the area they and their effectual servants patrolled. Much of the time, the obedience of any group of subjects was determined less by their abstract loyalty to their king than by a judicious assessment of how far away his bailiff was.

This personal influence was weakened by the king's constant need to do battle or settle other pressing matters out of the country. Of the nearly forty-five years of Henry II and Richard I's reigns, for example, the king was in his kingdom less than a third of the time, and then stayed mainly in the southwest. Under these conditions it is easy to see how many of his perquisites would pass by default to local lords. Though he tried to restrict them, the French king Louis IX's feudatories freed serfs, created new titles of nobility, and, most important, increasingly took legislative authority into their own hands.

The extent of private jurisdiction in the two great monarchies of France and England was vast throughout most of the twelfth and thirteenth centuries. In twelfth-century England, most justice was either popular or feudal; both categories of law were administered by the lords of the region. All matters of property rights and use were in seigneurial hands, and given the wide authority of church law there was little justice left for the king to dispense. In feudal France, the king's laws applied only in his own domain. Elsewhere groups of lords joined in proclaiming regional laws, and every lord was judge on his own lands.

Complicating the restrictions of royal power was the continuing fact of royal penury. In an age when an average parish income might bring £10 a year, kings supported huge households on fluctuating sums ranging from a few thousand pounds to £30,000 or £40,000 or more from one spring to the next. The great French scholar of medieval monarchy, Charles Petit-Dutaillis, estimated that in 1170–71 Henry II received some £23,500 in revenue, of which he and his retinue consumed nearly a quarter for their own maintenance. Furthermore, in this year the taxes and other dues were unevenly collected; nearly half the royal income came from only four of the English counties. The kings of England were better off than their French counterparts, yet both depended heavily on incidental revenues for their economic survival. Reliefs (sums paid to the overlord when a flef changed hands), wardship (the royal right to administer and exploit an estate as guardian of its minor heir), fines, and the profits of justice all increased royal revenues by thousands of pounds every year. Among Philip Augustus' circumstantial feudal income were reliefs of 5,000 marks and 7,000 pounds Arras from the counts of Flanders and Boulogne; by the Treaty of Goulet in 1200 John of England paid him another 20,000 marks—a sum nearly equal to the entire income of John's father Henry II thirty years earlier.

These sums were, of course, increased still further by the king's right to demand of his vassals hospitality for himself and his court, but it seems certain they were never entirely adequate. Money was an important element in royal diplomacy, and every king needed ready cash. The Norman chronicler Wace told how when Henry I came into Normandy in 1105, hoping to take the duchy from his elder brother Robert, he brought with him bushels of gold and silver coins, carried in hogsheads loaded onto carts, and as he made his tour of the duchy he distributed it judiciously among the barons, castellans and knights whose allegiance he sought.

The cost of provisioning and, if need be, transporting an army in the field could be very great, and the scarcities that set in around a siege area compounded the expenses of battle. The mercenaries kings turned to more and more in the twelfth and thirteenth centuries were very costly, and even the knights who owed service in the feudal host had to be paid. There is no way to document these costs, but examples are suggestive. As we have seen, on the Welsh border in wartime an ox could be sold for the price of a curate's annual living, and a hen for a week's wages. On a larger scale, we know that when Philip Augustus took an army of some

650 knights and 1300 squires and their mounts and arms across by sea to the Holy Land, the sea passage alone cost nearly 6,000 silver marks.

More instructive than these comparisons is the realization that Western kings were paupers in contrast to the Arab rulers of the east. When in 1050 two aged princesses distantly related to the caliph of Egypt died, they left the caliph a treasure breathtaking in its splendor. In addition to several hundred pounds of emeralds, rubies and fine pearls, there were thousands of crystal vases, plates, inkstands and vessels of gold, 2,000 gold vases made to hold violets and 4,000 to hold other flowers, 38 barges, one of silver, a wealth of jeweled daggers, swords and lances, silken tents as large as castles, with gilded poles, hundreds of tapestries and intricate objects carved in semi-precious stones, and a mattress of solid gold. Compared with these riches, the treasure of the Angevins and Capetians was shabby indeed.

In view of the foregoing it is hard to escape the observation that medieval kings were in one sense little more than scavengers, with their eager need to profit from the vicissitudes of feudal tenures, their traditional right to beached ships and animals and other abandoned things, and their claims to the estates of bastards or strangers who died heirless on the royal domain. Agencies of accidental injury also went to the king; when a great timber fell from a building frame in Yarmouth and killed four carpenters, it was immediately hauled to the court of Edward I.

Court treachery was another force robbing medieval kings of their full weight of rule. A faithless servant could seriously weaken his royal master, repaying his generosity with betrayal and courting his political ruin. In the *Geste de Guillaume au court nez,* Count William warned his overlord:

> Traitors they are, and men of bad faith; swindlers and men of greed, who comfort you with lies alone, as you keep them by your side. True

enough, you've given them your lands and your money. If God's justice be not your undoing, their friendship will.[1]

Courtiers of all ranks were uncertain allies; even the most exalted of them had weaknesses which threatened to cloud their lord's rule. Writing to Becket, Arnulf of Lisieux described the mentality of his colleagues at the English court with their "disturbed ambition," their competitive natures and their perpetual jealousy. "Their minds squeezed in torment," he wrote, their constant aim is to improve their own situation by worsening that of others, and their usual weapon is hypocrisy. Desperate for praise, anguished by the attention paid to their rivals, they must nonetheless keep the semblance of gaiety (*hilaritas*); their good cheer and kind words were not to be trusted. "Fear the sudden laughter of the applauders," Arnulf advised Becket, "and the sweet songs of adulation."

But if medieval kings were weakened by shackled authority, shortage of money and false friends and servants, they had other sources of strength imposing enough to make these burdens seem mere inconveniences. First among these was the aura of majesty itself, which endowed kings with the powers of the enchanted world.

Since antiquity Western rulers had been set apart from ordinary men by the mysteries of coronation and sacring. Legends linked royal families to divine selection and approbation if not to divine ancestry, and medieval kings occupied a unique status, enjoying the multiple identity of laymen and cleric. To cite only one sign of this multiple identity, unlike laymen kings communicated at the mass in both bread and wine; normally communion in both kinds was reserved for clerics.

Myths surrounding the divinely sanctioned legitimacy of the

French royal house helped to sustain the Capetians through the military and financial crises of the eleventh and twelfth centuries. In the generations following the first crusade the figure of Charlemagne was so embellished by legend that his heroic dimensions dwarfed his descendants, the real kings who sat on the throne of France. In England, the Celtic chieftain Arthur took on a similar aura. Partly to counteract the stigma of Becket's murder, Henry II encouraged the monks of Glastonbury in their confident belief that they had found in their churchyard the tomb of Arthur and Guinevere. The remains of these famed ancestors were brought to a chapel Henry built in their honor, in 1191; observers remarked on Guinevere's amazing hair and the great size of Arthur's bones. Continuing discoveries of concrete, physical links to the Arthurian legend were a reminder that the Angevins were descended from a magic king; in 1278 Edward I had the tomb at Glastonbury reopened, and when two years later Arthur's crown was found there it was presented to Edward with elaborate ceremony.

In both England and France the majesty of the royal house was enriched by dynastic myth. At the same time, the mission of royalty itself was being redefined. In the twelfth, thirteenth and fourteenth centuries kings took on an image that far exceeded their functions as feudal suzerains.

In the *Couronnement Looys*, a poem describing the conflict between Charles the Great and his rebellious vassals, the aging king spoke about kingship to his son.

> "When God made kings," he told Louis, "it was in order to
>   exalt the people
> And not so they would set themselves up to pronounce false
>   judgments,
> Or indulge themselves in luxury, or do unending evil.
> Kings were not made to snatch fiefs from heirs of tender
>   years, or to steal from poor widows.

Rather the king's duty is to trample all injustice
    underfoot,
Yea, to throw it down and crush it utterly.
With poor folk you must be humble; you owe them aid
    and counsel.
Out of love of God you ought to give them their due
    justice and right.
But with the proud you must be as proud as they—
As proud as a leopard seizing his prey.
One of them makes war against you? Send your noble
    knights to France,
More than thirty thousand of them.
Where he is proudest, attack your enemy
Devastate his lands, pillage his holdings,
And, if you seize him and take him into your own hands,
Show no mercy, no pity! Chop him in pieces, burn him
    in the fire, drown him in the sea. . . ." [2]

Here the king is more than a feudal suzerain: he is a symbol of the
nation, an agent of ethical retribution, and an awesome force
whose barbarism serves the good of the people. This is an idea of
rulership far removed from the sophisticated political concepts of
antiquity, yet it is metafeudal—it endows the king with powers far
beyond those he holds as feudal overlord and obligates him to all
his subjects, not only those who are his vassals and their tenants.

This metafeudal image was most apparent in another phenomenon: the healing power of the royal touch. Agile manipulation
of the forces of the enchanted world was among the fearsome
marks of majesty. In the royal lines of France and England this
manipulation was concentrated in the ruler's ability to heal the
"king's evil," scrofula.

The idea that the Capetians and Angevins could heal this
disfiguring lymphatic inflammation—which was widespread among

medieval populations—grew into a routine royal activity by the thirteenth century. Healing became a normal function of kingship; Louis IX touched the sick every day after mass, and other rulers set aside at least one day in the week to minister to the invalids who traveled from all over Europe to be healed at their courts. Records of charitable donations made to scrofulites by the English kings allow estimates of the numbers who sought the royal touch; these records show that Edward I often touched and blessed a thousand victims in a single year, and did not cease when he traveled into France and Scotland. Edward III was much venerated as a healer, touching the sick daily and apparently achieving many cures. (Though it was extremely common, scrofula was not virulent and was subject to frequent remissions; according to the Moslem gentleman Usamah, a Frankish physician he met in the Holy Land knew a cure for it.)

Skepticism about the king's healing power prompted the theologian Bradwardine to attest to Edward's success. "Let whoever denies the Christian miracle," he wrote in the *De causa Dei*, "come and see with his own eyes. . . . No matter how insidious their disease, once victims were prayed over and touched by the king's hand, and blessed and signed with the cross, he cured them in Christ's name." And many swore that they had been cured, or had seen others who were, Bradwardine added, including large numbers from over the sea.

Whether or not all the cures were authentic it is undeniable that (at least) their own strong belief in the efficacy of the royal touch did relieve some scrofulites. By the thirteenth century touching had become a self-perpetuating miracle, at once drawing on the enchanted atmosphere of kingship and reinforcing it. Indeed it is hard to escape the notion that, given the thousands who came for cures, the fame of the two great Western monarchies may have been prompted as much by their healing gift as by their political or military prestige. It is certain that the miraculous properties of their kingship tended to proliferate, and to breed imitation. In England, rings made from coins the king offered on Good Friday were made into "cramp-rings" which cured muscular spasms and epilepsy, and by the fourteenth and fifteenth centuries kings elsewhere in Europe had begun to claim certain limited abilities to ease suffering and spread healing. Queens, though, were explicitly excluded from the royal gift. In France this was linked by theorists to the exclusion of women from the royal line itself, while in England queens were allowed to bless and distribute cramp-rings but not to touch for the king's evil.

It was perhaps in this dimension of his powers that a medieval king's identity was most convoluted. Though he was not formally within the church hierarchy, as a healer the king was within the circle of the miraculous. His powers not only approached but surpassed those of most clergy, and there was no clearer sign of this than the fact that monks and clerics afflicted with the king's evil came alongside laymen to be cured by the royal touch. Five years after his historic confrontation with Boniface VIII, the French king Philip IV touched three Franciscans and one Augustinian friar, and other scrofulites from the Papal States came to the French court seeking his blessing.

The question of the king's clerical identity was traditionally associated with his anointing. Following ancient custom, kings were anointed on the head; bishops received the same form of unction, while priests were anointed on the hands only. Twelfth-century liturgists anxious to preserve the special dignity of churchmen wrote in revised coronation rituals that kings would receive the chrism on the shoulder or hand only, but in practice the French and English kings continued to receive the holy oil on their heads, as did the Holy Roman Emperor in his crowning as German king. (As emperor he underwent a ceremony nearly identical with that used to create a subdeacon, and was spoken of as such by medieval writers.) But although the precise form of anointing was of

133

absorbing interest to both royal and papal propagandists, to focus attention on this technicality of unction is to lose sight of the broader issues which formed the popular image of monarchy.

The king's real challenge to the spiritual hierarchy lay not in the special form of his coronation but in the magical sanctity of his person. Kings were seen as wonder-workers capable of performing all kinds of prodigies. In twelfth-century Denmark the beauty of children and the abundance of harvests were ascribed to the royal touch, and in the not-too-distant past rulers had been deposed when the crops failed. Royal corpses were venerated as relics like the bodies of saints. Miracles were ascribed to Philip Augustus' corpse, and the thirteenth-century *Heimskringla* describes how the body of Halfdan the Black, king of Norway, was cut into four parts, each of which was buried under a mound in a separate part of the kingdom to ensure good harvests. In popular belief both infants born to a line of sorcerers and king's sons were said to bear at birth a mark setting them apart from other men—a *naevus*, often red in color and occurring commonly on the right shoulder. Clearly in the popular mind kings had long since passed into the category of the sacred.

To require of such beings competence in the mundane realities of administration would have seemed almost a sacrilege. And in fact, amid abundant criticism of medieval kings by their contemporaries the claim is seldom made that they were remiss in the day-to-day business of governing. In an age when the concept of public power was only slowly being rediscovered through the recovery of classical texts, royal governments were not expected to take responsibility for more than a very limited part of "the public good." But in one area kings were to become increasingly caught up in the trivia of rule. The rebirth of legal studies and their rapid expansion after the middle of the twelfth century gave kings their most effective weapon against the traditional restrictions of feudal suzerainty. In time the king's lawyers would surround sacred monarchy with the irrefutable bastion of legal primacy.

As royal servants lawyers had few peers, either for loyalty or effectiveness. They were rarely men of family or property; living by their wits they were no obvious threat to the organization of power in feudal society; and most important, they had no cause to serve beyond that of the king and his law. Lawyers had no broader institutional loyalty than their loyalty to their employer, and their intellectual obligations were equally narrow. Traditionally the divisions of medieval learning formed an interlocking hierarchy with theology the capstone and arbiter of the whole. But by the thirteenth century the study of the civil law was developing outside that hierarchy, within its own ethical parameters. "Does it follow," the thirteenth-century glossator Accursius asked, "that whoever desires to be a jurist or a jurisconsult must read theology? No, for everything [he needs] is found in the body of the law." By the end of the middle ages this combination of undivided loyalty, cleverness and relative intellectual freedom had made lawyers indispensable to kings. Every major court had dozens of men learned in the law to advise the ruler, act as his proctors or representatives, and draw up his legal documents and legislation. Kings keep lawyers, Matthew Paris remarked, as a huntsman keeps hounds.

To attempt to summarize in full the ways in which medieval pleaders, attorneys and other men of law strengthened the monarchy would be to detail much of the history of government after the twelfth century. One example must stand for the whole.

In Angevin England property relations were governed by feudal law, under which the vassal or property-holder had no rights of ownership, only rights of possession, and which allowed him to be dispossessed for a variety of reasons virtually without recourse. Feudal law was the law of privilege; that evolved by the king's justices was the law of equity. Over the generation of Henry II's rule the five pillars of Angevin land law were developed to challenge the imbalance in feudal law and eventually to replace it. Together with the grand assize, the assizes (or writs) of *utrum, novel disseisin, mort d'ancestor* and *darrein presentment* offered protection to lay and clerical vassals by offering them the right to purchase royal justice, and to bring disputes with their overlords into the king's courts. In succeeding reigns the king's lawyers and judges elaborated this procedure, evolving new laws and legal procedures to choke out the feudal courts and to make unlawful the customs by which feudal tenures were perpetuated, finally outlawing subinfeudation and encouraging nonfeudal tenures. Though it is overly simple it is generally true that by the opening of the fourteenth century the law of property in England was virtually synonymous with the common, or royal, law.

Here again, it must be noted, the king's dual authority would seem to have made him an ambivalent beneficiary of his lawyers' achievement. As chief landlord in England, his suzerain rights were weakened along with those of other lords. But he stood to gain far more in the strengthening of his sovereignty than he lost as feudal liege.

In their political and ecclesiastical relations, in their dynastic and financial negotiations, and in the cloudy area of their own unhindered rule medieval kings relied increasingly on the men of the new legal profession. To be sure, they were to learn soon enough that lawyers make uncertain allies, for the very flexibility that made them useful to kings could make them useful to the opponents of royalty as well. The law was a maze of contradictions, and could be made to serve a variety of interests. Maxims such as "what pleases the prince has the force of law" were offset by equally venerable dicta upholding popular over royal power. "The dictates of the prince which go against the public good are invalid," another maxim asserted, and it was lawyers who were among the first to recover the classical ideology of republicanism. Sacrosanct kings claiming to hold power by divine favor were reduced in this ideology to simple tenants of the popular will. "A prince who fails as a governor," wrote Manegold of Lautenbach, "may be driven away just as a farmer drives away an unfaithful swineherd."

But despite their inherent challenge to the image of divine kingship, lawyers not only girded sovereignty but restored the dignity of professionalism to law. Civil lawyers made a career of what had been a pastime or a tool of the nobility: the distribution of equity. And even though they did this imperfectly, often with little claim to impartiality or humility before the law, by their very existence they made possible a different image of the place of formal justice in human government. They helped to restore the concept feudalism had so long obscured: the idea of the transpersonality of the state. With their focus on mutuality and survival, feudal regimes all but lost sight of the abstraction of the state—the "public thing" of Roman law which transcended the collectivity of its citizens and the geography of its land area.

But even as they transformed medieval government, the men of law eagerly preserved its traditional appearances. Working to undermine the power of feudalism, they did not hesitate to assimilate its titles and honors. In his *Summa institutionum* the jurist Azo wrote that "Some knights are armed with weapons of war, others are without weapons, others are armed with letters and learning." To the armed nobles and the unarmed clergy were to be added the knights of the law. Glossators claimed knighthood for jurists, and as early as the 1180's doctors of law were demanding to be called lords. The great Bolognese lawyers were without exception accorded the dignity of lordship, and by a flattering misinterpretation of Justinian some jurists evolved the doctrine that any doctor of laws who taught for twenty years in a university earned the title of count.

Medieval society was tolerant of this kind of anachronism. Like much of medieval thought, it grew as much by agglomeration as by

137

substituting new ways for old. The best rulers managed to disguise change as a rediscovery from the past, and hoped they would not be accused of innovation. Successful rulership demanded that ubiquity, fearsomeness, and a small army of skillful lawyers and bureaucrats be added to the authenticating power of the miraculous. Without these, personal qualities alone were inadequate to sustain the burden of rule.

In about 1054 a child was born who should have been king of England. He was Robert, firstborn son of William, duke of Normandy and his wife Matilda, and from the beginning he was trained to succeed to his father's office and estates. He was called Curthose (*Curta Ocrea*, "Shortboots") and Gambaron ("Plumplegs") because of his short stature and round figure, but he was full of charm and courtly speech—a thing that set him apart from the Norman nobility far more effectively than his high birth. Before chivalry was fashionable, Robert was chivalrous, gracious toward friends and enemies alike, magnanimous to traitors, lavishly generous and with a gift for spontaneous brilliance on the battlefield. (In his blind courtesy he treated the treacherous Norman nobles as if they, too, were gentlemen of honor, courteously handing castles he had stormed back to their owners and repeatedly dismayed when his opponents did not keep their word.)

Robert Curthose was groomed and formally designated as heir to the English throne. As a child he had several tutors in letters and the knightly arts, and in the year of the conquest William summoned the Norman nobles and proclaimed in their presence that Robert was his chosen successor; they in turn pledged him their homage and fealty. Robert was then no more than twelve or thirteen years old, but when he was designated a second time he was no longer a child. Convinced he was near death, William on this occasion summoned the barons and required them to pledge their homage and fealty to Robert as heir to all William's lands, which now included the kingdom of England. Soon afterward a quarrel between the heir and his father led to bitterness. A rebel with an army of knights at his back, Robert met his father's forces (accompanied by those of William's second son William Rufus) at Gerberoi; in single combat with Curthose the king was unhorsed and wounded. That his army should be defeated at the hands of his son humiliated the conqueror. He cursed Robert and threatened to disinherit him. But before long they were reconciled, and after Gerberoi Robert was designated a third time as William's successor.

By the time William died in 1087, however, Robert was again out of favor and in exile, and on his deathbed William named William Rufus to succeed him as king, conceding to Robert his continental fiefs of Normandy and Maine.

For most of the next twenty years the men around him put pressure on Curthose to claim his rightful kingdom, first from Rufus and, after Rufus' assassination, from his second brother Henry. As conquered territory, England was in fact exempt from primogeniture, but Robert saw the matter as a point of honor and not of law. He was convinced that both Rufus and Henry were usurpers, and did not find either the conqueror's deathbed designation of Rufus or Henry's claim to pre-eminence of birth convincing. (While Robert was born a duke's son, Henry asserted, he himself was born *after* the conquest, to a king. A visionary prophecy seemed to confirm his claim.)

But outraged as he was at being deprived of his rightful patrimony, Robert clearly lacked the lust for conquest. His cause and his dukedom became the locus of rebellion for a generation, but with one exception Robert's army of invasion never materialized. In this curious incident, Robert and a growing number of followers crossed the Channel and marched unhindered to the seat of Norman royal government at Winchester. King Henry was genuinely afraid for his life, but somehow persuaded Robert to accept a money payment in lieu of a military contest (Robert was continually desperate for money), and the crisis was averted. Later, in striking another bargain with Henry to save the estates of a friend, Robert returned even the money. In 1106 he was captured at Tinchebrai in Normandy, and spent the final twenty-eight years of his life in captivity. The poets who made him a figure of romance claimed that in these bitter years he learned Welsh and wrote verse. Among the lines ascribed to him are these:

> Oak that hast grown up on the grounds
> Of the woody promontory fronting the contending waves
>   of the Severn sea;
> Woe! to him that is not old enough to die.[3]

Long before his capture in 1106 literary men had made Robert Curthose a romantic hero; the loyalist Norman chroniclers dismissed him as a self-indulgent rebel, pleasure-loving and soft. Setting aside these partisan images, it is not hard to see why Curthose failed as a would-be king. Unlike his father and brothers, he lacked the inclination to be everywhere at once. He was not ambitious, he had no political goals and could not conceive the painstaking network of bribes, political intrigue and calculated diplomacy necessary to round out battlefield victories in a feudal contest. He was utterly indifferent to record-keeping, as he was to meetings of his ducal court and the issuing of charters and other judicial acts. He did have a chancellor for his Norman lands, and a shambles of a chancery, but no orderly system of taxation and little if any feudal revenue.

He was prodigious in arms; his defeat of William at Gerberoi was only one of an imposing list of victories, and although he did not acquit himself with extraordinary distinction in the first crusade he left an aura of prowess behind him there. According to one literary historian, an entire epic cycle was written about Curthose in the Holy Land in the early twelfth century that has since been lost. Certainly an elaborate legend can be reconstructed from what remains: twelfth-century writers said that neither pagan nor Christian could unhorse Curthose, and that he was supreme leader of the crusade, excelling there all others at the Battle of Dorylaeum and killing Kerboga, the "Red Lion" and two Saracen kings in single combat. There was even a legendary justification for Robert's failure to become king in England. In the Holy Land, it was said, he was offered the crown of Jerusalem and refused it. In so doing he offended God and lost his rightful patrimony.

This literary vindication was neat, but grossly distorted. Robert was in fact neither a grim crusader nor a fire-eating combatant. He was the kind of fighter who loved the game of battle almost as much as the real thing. When he and Rufus were jointly besieging their brother Henry who had taken refuge in the peninsula of Mont-Saint-Michel, they held tournaments on the sand to while away the time. Robert performed well, but Rufus, who took the field only once, was immediately unhorsed by a simple knight. Rufus invariably preferred to buy off his enemies; Robert was given to conspicuous master strokes of arms. The "impregnable stronghold" of Saint-Ceneri he reduced without difficulty; another castle at Brionne that had taken the conqueror three years to besiege he took between about three in the afternoon and sunset.

But brilliance without consistency was inadequate to gain or keep a monarchy in Norman England. To help a friend Robert would sacrifice a fortune, yet he could not be counted on to take part in someone else's plans for his advancement. What was worse, he could not bring himself to follow up his victories with the ostentatious cruelty necessary to the image of majesty. After the retaking of Rouen during Rufus' first attempt to conquer Normandy, Robert was urged to execute the rebels who had sided with Rufus; he insisted that imprisonment was enough. Henry, who in this engagement was on Robert's side, urged his brother to be merciless and summarily dispatched the rebel leader by pushing him backwards through a window in the Tower of Rouen. Henry had himself been the beneficiary of Robert's chivalrous mercy. At the siege of Mont-Saint-Michel, when Rufus had cut off Henry's supply of fresh water, Robert ordered his soldiers to let a few of Henry's men slip through the lines to fill their waterskins; Wace records that he even sent Henry a tun of wine to refresh himself.

In an age when fear was the essence of rule these were not the acts of a fearsome lord. A century later, Richard Cœur de Lion would grow renowned and beloved for similar behavior, but by then the stories of the crusades had made the ideal of courtesy both familiar and enviable. Like Robert, Richard became a legendary hero during his lifetime, but because he had the backing of a stable and uncontested succession and an efficient bureaucracy, he was also king.

The foundation for Richard's untroubled accession lay in the exemplary career of his father, Henry II, unquestionably among the most successful of medieval kings. In his thirty-five-year reign, Henry was most conspicuous for his energy. "From morning until night," a contemporary wrote, "he never sits down except when he mounts his horse or takes a meal and he frequently rides in one day a journey four or five times the length of a normal day's ride." Everyone who came near him was struck by his restlessness; his closest advisers and his family were forced to adopt it as a way of life. If we follow the king's itinerary during a normal year of his reign, the causes of his success may grow clear.

In the first months of 1174 Henry wintered in Normandy, agreeing to a truce with his enemy Louis VII. While he was in his winter quarters he learned that on the Scots border Hugh, bishop of Durham, had also made a truce with the Scots king, but that Roger de Mowbray had fortified a castle on the island of Axholm without the king's permission. Ignoring this threat for the time being, and with ecclesiastical affairs temporarily quiescent—the new archbishop of Canterbury, Richard, finally received papal consecration in Rome in April—Henry took to the road with the first thaw, going into Anjou and then on to Poitiers to relieve Saintes, which was under attack by his son Richard's men. Returning to Anjou in May, he took Ancenis and devastated the lands around Saumur, building a castle at Ancenis to guard the advantages he had gained there.

Having heard in April that the Scots had broken the truce, news was brought in June that three hundred Flemish knights had been sent into England by the count of Flanders, and that they had sacked Norwich. Returning in haste to Normandy, Henry sent mercenaries of his own, Brabanters, into England in early July, then embarked himself, stopping only to hold council with his court at Bonneville. With him on the crossing were his son John and Princess Joan, and his prisoners Queen Eleanor, the young Queen Margaret, the earl of Chester, the earl and countess of Leicester, and possibly the wives of his sons Richard and Geoffrey. Landing at Southampton, he went to Winchester and on into Wiltshire, where he left Eleanor under the guard of Robert Malduit, then on to Gloucester, where he put Margaret and the others into custody in his castle at Devizes. By July 9 he was at Canterbury, where he stayed four days to do penance at Becket's tomb. On the fifth day he left after mass, riding to London where the news reached him that William, king of the Scots, had been captured by a party of his knights. A threat of invasion by Henry's eldest son, the young Henry, whose fleet had been thwarted off the coast of Flanders by foul weather, was abated for the present, but the king fell ill and spent the next several days in bed. On the 19th, though, he was up again and setting off to join the siege of Huntingdon 75 miles to the north, having in the meantime ordered fittings for a new warhorse and siege machines.

When Huntingdon fell on July 21, Henry went without pause to confront Hugh Bigod and his Flemings in his castle at Framling-ham, and at the news of his coming Hugh surrendered the castle to Henry, and the mercenaries were allowed to return home, leaving everything they owned behind in England. Another accident threatened to delay the king on the 25th of July, when a Templar's horse kicked him in the thigh, but by month's end he had gone into Northampton to deal with still another threat of rebellion. Over the preceding months, Hugh of Durham brought his nephew, the count of Bar, across the Channel with a fleet carrying forty knights and a force of Flemings. To guarantee his loyal intent, Henry required the bishop to renew his homage, and he agreed without protest, surrendering three castles to the king and sending his nephew back across the Channel.

By the first days of August six castles had been surrendered by four powerful northern feudatories, and to cap this reinvigoration of royal power in the north the captured king of the Scots was brought before Henry at Northampton, and a marriage alliance was sealed between the king's half-sister Emma and David ap Owen, prince of North Wales.

No sooner were these festivities complete than King Henry turned his attention to raising the large expeditionary force he planned to lead into Normandy. Taking the Brabanters he had had with him since coming into England less than five weeks earlier, he mustered in addition a large contingent of Welsh; together with his prisoners the Scots king and the rebellious earls, they made the crossing from Portsmouth and landed at Barfleur. Leaving the captives at Caen, Henry traveled on eastward along the coast, where he met with two ecclesiastics returning from Rome and informed himself about the state of the church. Satisfied with what he heard, he went on to Rouen, where Louis VII and the young Henry had put the town under siege. Between the tenth and fifteenth of August Henry set his Welsh mercenaries to capturing the provisions of the siege army, and forced Louis and his host to decamp by night and retreat into the Île-de-France.

Three weeks later Henry made peace with Louis at Gisors, then marched with his forces 250 miles south into Poitou to force Richard to submit on the 21st of September. At a town on the Poitevin coast he rewarded Richard de Lucy, a faithful supporter in the rebellion, with a formal grant, and in less than a week he met to make peace with his three sons at a town near Tours on the Loire. On the tenth of October the royal family was reunited at Falaise in Normandy (the prisoners were moved there from the donjon at Caen), where a formal peace was signed.

Later into the fall provisioning and travel grew increasingly difficult, and the king spent more and more of his time attending to administrative matters; from various castles in Normandy Henry issued charters to Norman and English monasteries and oversaw matters of forest justice and feudal claims. In December, he rounded out his year by coming to a satisfactory agreement with the Scots king, receiving Scotland from him as a fief. After releasing him, Henry spent Christmas at Argentan.

Even to read through this unrelenting round of journeys and crises is wearying; to follow the king must have been an act of loyal exhaustion. The conditions of medieval travel make the swiftness of the itinerary, which covered some 946 miles by land and sea, difficult enough to imagine, but the hardship of the journey was compounded when the travelers found nothing but wilderness at the end of the day's ride. "The fidelity of [the king's] followers," Peter of Blois wrote, "is subjected to severe tests, for they are frequently forced to wander through unknown forests for three or four miles after nightfall before they find lodging in squalid hovels."

That a king should demand this of his army is just within the bounds of reason; both soldiering and governing were outdoor vocations in this period. But that he should make the same demands of his family and court is harder to justify, even for those relatives and courtiers who were intermittently royal prisoners. Still more difficult to realize is that, in the few days or hours between journeys as well as in the course of his travels, Henry attended with expediency and care to the business of governing, overseeing justice, granting writs and charters, receiving revenues, and watching over a growing royal bureaucracy both on his vast continental lands and in his kingdom.

Ceaseless energy, vigilance on every frontier and in every feudal and sovereign relationship, suspicion even of intimates, and continual circummigration: these shaped the breathless pace of Henry's rule. Combined with his personal stamina and affinity for kingship, they guaranteed its success.

But in dwelling on the long reign of a robust king it is easy to forget what an intrinsically precarious institution kingship proved to be. Many rulers came to the throne as children, and had to spend the first years of their personal rule freeing themselves from the overburdening control of regents. A sizable group of rulers-designate died before their fathers—the well-known death of Henry I's heir in the disaster of the White Ship was matched in France when in 1130 the dauphin "was met by a pig, which, running against the legs of his horse in full gallop, caused [him] to fall off, break his neck, and die."

Even if they lived to manhood accident, disease and mental disturbance threatened to weaken kings. In the later years of his reign Philip Augustus was obsessed with the fear that Richard of England was trying to assassinate him; King John, whom his soldiers called "Soft Sword," was afflicted with a nervous disease that led to psychosis. Popular beliefs about kings accorded them a high degree of irrationality. The Emperor Henry V died in 1125, "but some allege," the chronicler Roger of Hoveden wrote,

> that having gone on a certain night to the Empress Matilda's bed as he customarily did, . . . when the lights were put out and the servants had gone to bed, the emperor, barefoot and dressed in woolen clothing, left behind the imperial vestments, his wife, and his kingdom, and was never seen again.[4]

Popular fantasies, legendary ancestors and the everpresent mysteries of enchanted kingship all tend to obscure the vulnerability of even the best-protected rulers. In actuality they were never really safe.

In the renewed fighting around Milan in 1159, during Frederick Barbarossa's second invasion of Italy, a stranger appeared in the emperor's camp, which was pitched on the steep banks of the Adda. He was tall and strong, but so foolish that no one feared him; his stupidity and fits entertained the soldiers, and so he was kept on as an object of ridicule. But one morning, when he saw the emperor leave his tent at daybreak and go to pray near his relics, the imbecile leapt on him and dragged him desperately toward the riverbank, intending to throw him over. Both men became entangled in the tent ropes, and Frederick's cries brought soldiers quickly to his rescue. He was not harmed, but he was lucky to escape with his life.

At first the would-be assassin was thought to be an agent of the Milanese, but was later found to be a simple madman. Either way he had for a moment held the future of the empire in his hands.

Chapter seven

THE FORCES OF DISORDER

In 1336 the parson of Huntingdon received the following letter:

Lionel, king of the rout raveners,* to our false and disloyal Richard of Snaweshill, greeting without affection.

We order you, on pain of your forfeitable goods, to oust him who holds the vicarage of Burton Agnes at your suffrance at once, and to allow the Abbot of St. Mary's to exercise his rights and have his nominee—who is more suitable for the post than you or any of your line—remain vicar.

And if you do not, we vow, first to the king of heaven and then to the king of England and our crown, that you will have the same fate as the Bishop of Exeter in Cheap.**

And you will be found, even if it be on Coney Street [in York]. And show this letter to your sovereign lord, and tell him to give up his false conspiracies and confederacies, and to let justice be done to the

* robbers' company.
** i.e., murder; Bishop Stapledon of Exeter was murdered there ten years earlier.

148

Abbot's nominee; otherwise by the vows made earlier he will suffer damage worth a thousand pounds by us and our men. And if you disregard our commands, we shall order our viscount in the north to distress you to the same extent.

Given at our Castle of the North Wind, in the Green Tower, in the first year of our reign.[1]

Little beyond this letter is known of the career of this "king of the robbers' company," but threatening messages in the form of parodies of royal writs were fairly common in the 1330's, and Lionel was part of a large and thriving criminal population. In Bristol in 1347 a "robber king" and his large force of armed followers held the town against the king's officers, commandeering ships and issuing proclamations while pillaging and murdering with impunity. A commission of royal judges sent to combat the mounting criminality solemnly declared that the armed bands had been waging open war against the king.

In the middle decades of the fourteenth century, parts of England were overrun with criminal bands whose members were drawn from both gentry and ordinary folk and whose powerful supporters employed them, fed them, and hid them from the judges and agents sent out by the court of king's bench. Like their employment, their numbers varied, but on major campaigns they grew to the size of armies. Testifying to events he had watched, the bishop of Exeter told how a great force of men arrayed like soldiers marched on his lands, breaking fences and gates before them and seizing hundreds of bullocks, cows and sheep and other things of value. The villagers fled in panic, thinking the plunderers were a foreign army of invaders foraging for food.

No road or public place was secure from the assaults of those who "rode armed publicly and secretly in manner of war by day and night." Roads were ordered cleared of hedges for 200 feet on either side, and roadside ditches filled in, to prevent ambushes.

149

Nevertheless, merchants and others were set upon in their shops as well as on the roads, and brigands on horseback rode straight through fair grounds at the height of fairs, overturning booths and stealing their contents and leaving behind them a burning town. Sometimes the assaults took the form of a private war between royal officials and the outlaws, with ordinary citizens only incidental victims of their struggle. Thus William Beckwith and his outlawed relatives and followers, some five hundred strong, held out against the king's justices in Lancaster for five years at the end of the fourteenth century, but for at least the last two they kept to the deep woods and did not molest men on the road or in their homes.

Beckwith's men were unusual in that they were almost exclusively servants, tradesmen and poor tenants who turned to outlawry. Most English criminal bands contained a sizable proportion of knights or knights' sons, and nearly every outlaw company had the support of powerful titled men.

The best documented of these bands grew around the six wayward sons of John de Folville, lord of Ashby-Folville in Leicestershire. (The seventh, who succeeded to his father's lands and eventually entered the local justice system as a keeper of the peace, had no part in their activities.) One of the six brothers, Richard Folville, was rector of a parish church; the others took solely to crime. The most infamous of the Folvilles, Eustace, was undoubtedly responsible for five murders (probably more) and a long list of thefts, assaults, rapes and extortion schemes. With several or all of his five outlawed brothers, Eustace murdered a baron of the Exchequer and a number of lesser men, kidnapped a royal judge, and was implicated in dozens of robberies and property damage suits over a period of nearly twenty years.

Associated with the Folvilles was another large criminal society, led by James Coterel and his lieutenant Roger le Sauvage. The Coterels (James and two brothers) had begun by robbing churches, and went on to join the Folvilles in their larger kidnap and extortion plots. As their fame spread, both bands gained recruits. Some were petty criminals already—John and William Bradburn, the counterfeiter and skilled informer William de Uston—but others came from a wide variety of situations: Robert Bernard was an Oxford master and chancery clerk who had been attached to Lichfield Cathedral, John Boson a minor landholder with a seat in the House of Commons, Roger de Wennesley a country gentleman sent by the court to arrest the criminals who joined them instead. Indeed as their numbers grew, more and more people were drawn into the vortex of criminality that surrounded the Folvilles and Coterels. The gangs became a locus of a large network of extra-legal relations which existed alongside the customs and institutions sanctioned by the law.

Thus among the early employers of the Folvilles were a canon of Sempringham and the cellarer of the Cistercian house of Hoverholm, who hired the outlaws for £20 to destroy a water mill and later sheltered them from discovery. Other employers included Sir William Aune, a Yorkshire constable, Sir Robert Ingram, mayor of Nottingham and sheriff of Nottinghamshire, the chapter of Lichfield Cathedral, and at least four royal bailiffs and seven members of parliament. In all, hundreds of people were cited as sometime abettors of the Folvilles and their collateral followers, but despite several determined forays by royal justices and their agents, most of the criminals avoided capture. Richard Folville was finally murdered outside his church by a local keeper of the peace, but the most notorious brother, Eustace, died a natural death in 1346, by which time he had become a prominent landed knight. The other brothers make their last appearance in the records as mercenaries in the pay of the king, bound for Flanders.

The ease with which outlaws were able to obtain pardons or ransom their crimes by joining the royal army helps to explain their fearlessness. Outlawed in 1326 for the murder of a baron of the

Exchequer, the Folvilles were pardoned at the beginning of Edward III's reign in 1327 to show the new king's magnanimity. A few years later, after the gang was outlawed again for murder, robbery and rape they were able to earn another pardon, issued generally to all who had helped to put down the rebellion of the earl of Lancaster. Following their boldest crime, the kidnap and ransom of the royal justice Richard Wylughby in 1332, Robert Folville was pardoned in exchange for "good services in the Scottish war." And it was as pardoned felons that Richard, Walter and Thomas Folville, with James and Nicholas Coterel, went with the king to Flanders in 1338.

Though they were not narrowly political in origin the crimes of the Folvilles and Coterels were certainly urged on by the political unrest in the early years of Edward III's reign. There is some evidence that the former enjoyed some favor with the courtiers of Mortimer, lover of the dowager queen and co-regent, and the latter were hired to devastate the manors of Henry of Lancaster, leader of the baronial opposition to Mortimer in the late 1320's. But they did not become outlaws as a direct result of the uncertain political situation. Rather they found that as enforcement of order grew more and more lax, and popular contempt for royal officials more and more pronounced, a rift opened in the social fabric, creating an extra-legal enclave within which criminality was both feared for its reinlessness and applauded for its open defiance of the agents of public order. In their haughtiest crime the Folvilles and Coterels waylaid Richard Wylughby, puisne justice of the court of King's Bench, while he was on a judicial commission in the southwest and held him until a ransom of 1300 marks was paid. Only one of the accessories to the crime was brought to justice, and the outlaws grew in public favor for punishing a hated judge who "sold the law like cows and oxen."

In their recurring crises the fragile governments of the middle ages were quick to lose the power of legal retribution they built up in times of stability. In these periods the pursuit of criminals and their trying and sentencing were all but suspended; the present impact of the king's justice lapsed, and those who lived outside the law grew in numbers and ambition.

In later fourteenth and fifteenth-century England the enclaves of impunity created by governmental crises eventually threatened to absorb the entire kingdom, and took on institutional form. Through the practices of maintenance (illegal coercion applied by a powerful man to influence the trial of a lesser associate), embracery (physical violence to prevent a jury from bringing an indictment) and the wearing of livery (uniforms of the private armies of magnates), a new system of personal protection, retribution and armed defense was superimposed on the existing social bonds. Those who sought to destroy it suddenly found that the very basis of power had shifted its ground, leaving them powerless. The royal court, the law courts and the parliament were riddled with magnates and their liveried retainers. Highly placed officials under the protection of the magnates could intercept petitions for reform, and bands of armed retainers could break open any court, council or parliamentary session and scatter the participants. Strangled in this new web of alliances, the traditional workings of government withered, while liveried retainers, mercenaries without a war, became the sole levers of power.

But few eras witnessed social disruption this acute. Maintenance represented crime on its grandest scale, with the high ambition to challenge the very foundations of public order. Less grandiose crimes—theft, rape, murder, committed against individuals by individuals—were commoner, and showed less fluctuation from decade to decade. Crimes of this sort were an expected hazard of

153

life, part of the unexceptional nameless violence that formed an important dimension of the medieval world view.

For along with their finely developed sense of order and of the ideal social hierarchy medieval people tolerated a degree of anarchy, violence and loss of life that is difficult for us to comprehend. Transcribing the plea rolls for 1221, the great legal historian Frederick Maitland found that in four Gloucester hundreds, forty murders were recorded, plus one suicide and three accidental deaths. Fully half the murders were committed by unknown persons who fled before their crimes were discovered; of those who were known, only one was captured, brought to trial, and hanged. (One other claimed the right of sanctuary and abjured the realm.) Murder was by far the commonest crime; in all, for 1221 the rolls list only eighteen thefts, three accusations of rape and fifteen cases of fraud, assault, and petty infractions.

What is striking in these judicial records is the variety and frequency of violent death: knife-murders, axe-murders, murders by bludgeoning with a stone; murder of a fetus through an assault on a pregnant woman (occasioning a legal debate over whether or not a woman may bring an appeal for the death of her unborn child); murders of close kin (murder of brother by brother, wife by husband, son by mother); murder of a man by his horse (whose value in coin was offered to the church as compensation). Two men are found slain by unknown assailants, the chaplain is drowned returning from a banquet, the reeve's servant dies from a fall, a serf falls from a horse and is killed—again the horse's value must be paid as compensation. A woman is brought into court and accused of concealing the unburied corpse of her husband who died of plague, but she herself dies soon afterward and the case is not pursued. Two pilgrims take shelter in the hundred of Holeford; overnight one kills the other and flees, and neither the victim nor his attacker can be identified.

There was nothing unique about the level of crime in thirteenth-century Gloucester. Plea roll entries for a single Norfolk hundred,

North Erpingham, over a twelve-month period two generations later list some fifty major crimes, with twelve men and women murdered by unknowns, five dying in fatal fights, and five more by suicide. Sixteen burglars were tried; one man was torn to pieces by horses for debasing the coin, the eleven others were hanged for various grave offenses. There are gang murders in these rolls too, and records of criminal families. In one of these families the leading offender is jailed in a wooden house; his young son tries to free him by setting fire to the house, but is trapped in the flames. The father escapes, only to be caught and executed.

The clearest and oldest detailed records of local crime in the twelfth and thirteenth centuries are English, but the pattern of disorder they reveal was closely paralleled in France and in the belt of feudal territories to the north and east. Urban crime in the cities of the northern lowlands and in the Italian peninsula showed a consistent plague of homicides for slight causes—disputes over the price of goods, personal insults, tavern fights—in addition to the continuing fatal menace of the blood feud. Here too the difficulty of apprehending criminals was made worse by the closeness of the fields and woodland; thieves, kidnappers, hired assassins in the towns slipped back into the anonymous countryside once their deeds were done, and profited from the rivalry between the fragmented local authorities. The gates of towns all over western Europe were locked at night against malefactors, and many had curfews, but as in England the inefficacy of the courts and the leniency of acquittals, pardons and sanctuary rights made custom and the law itself allies of the criminals. In many regions the prisons were emptied of all but the most notorious offenders on the great religious feasts. In fourteenth-century Siena, prisoners were freed in December and August of each year, and occasionally the total was as high as fifty or more.

Brigandage too was a universal menace in the medieval West. Some regions were so infested that no ruler claimed legal jurisdiction over them, and travelers' routes were strung between and around areas of known outlaw bands. But no matter how carefully these routes were planned, new threats arose constantly, and in a few years a peaceful region could fall prey to predatory bands. Under the abbot Fulk the Norman monastery of Saint-Pierre-sur-Dives was a peaceable and flourishing religious foundation. But on his death the abbey's overlord, Robert Curthose, sold it for 145 marks to a monk of St. Denis, who drove the monks away and built a castle on the grounds, selling the altar plate and vestments to pay a hired garrison. The swiftness of this transformation must have caught travelers by surprise, even though monastic violence was commonplace.

The mercenary "Great Companies" of the later middle ages swept through the towns and villages of Europe, stealing animals and valuables and often demanding money to spare the inhabitants. Italian cities paid thousands of florins to be rid of companies like that of Werner von Urslingen, who declared himself to be the "Enemy of God, Piety and Mercy." Seagoing mercenaries were an equally serious bane in coastal areas. Pirates controlled the harbors of Provence and Languedoc so thoroughly that no relief could be brought to these areas by sea in times of famine, and the slowness of overland transport greatly increased the risk of starvation in the port cities.

"Like the air," the Bolognese lawyer Jacques de Ravigny wrote, "the sea is possessed by no one, though used by all." The Mediterranean held a flourishing population of pirates who were alternately in their own and other men's employ, and who honored none but the laws and rituals of the sea. Genoese captains led the fleets of France, England, and the Empire, but most of them spent only part of their careers in the service of foreign governments, and nearly all were pirates at one time or another. Henricus Piscator, one of Frederick II's admirals of Sicily, was a Genoese nobleman who called himself count of Malta and joined the famed pirate Alamannus da Costa in his conquest of Sicily. Later Henricus took

Crete from the Venetians with his own ships and ruled the island for a time before undertaking to work for his native city. Eventually he consolidated his standing by marrying the daughter of the pirate and Sicilian admiral William Grassus, and in time became admiral himself.

The bounds of legality at sea were defined by medieval jurists in a way that was at once practical and equivocal: pirates' "rapine, invasions, depredations, prizes, reprisals, marques and other maleficent and illegal acts" were liable to punishment only if they were not sanctioned by legitimate authority. If a Genoese crew in the pay of the king of England sank a Scottish ship, the pirates aboard were immune from liability (though the king would almost certainly face reprisals from the Scots, or their French allies). But if the same Genoese crew raided another ship without license from any sovereign, the pirates would face death sentences, unless of course they bound themselves to rob and murder only in the name of the king or emperor from then on.

It was the tortured logic of medieval jurisprudence that a pledge of licensed violence for the future cancelled the stigma of unauthorized crime in the past. The result was to perpetuate crime by allowing its forms to proliferate, and to create that odd alternation of legality and illegality already traced in the careers of the Folvilles and Coterels. Like them, members of pirate families had respectable and even exalted status in their communities. The Alards, a seagoing family of Winchelsea, were at different times royal admirals, mayors of the town, and pirates.

But the fate and legal treatment of piracy were more heavily influenced than other forms of crime by the delicate issue of international affairs. Pirates' mobility and virtual impunity plus the absence of large and organized naval forces in the European states made them an invaluable weapon of kings. The issuing of letters of marque (royal or other licenses authorizing destruction or seizure of enemy goods as reprisal for earlier wrongs) was common by the

157

late twelfth century, and piracy was a constant instrument of diplomacy and warfare. The distinction between punitive and purely arbitrary and self-interested destruction was not an easy one to make, and letters of marque were often used as an excuse for far more extensive violence than diplomacy demanded. Where no letters of marque existed, they could be forged. Or the invaders could disguise their purpose by masquerading as harmless travelers. In 1288 a band of thieves dressed as monks entered the seaside town of Boston, and before the alarm could be raised they had set fire to much of the town and plundered the townspeople, so the chroniclers wrote, until molten gold flowed in streams from the hills to the sea.

Piracy, armed coercion, blatant and subtle violence were strong and constant forces in medieval life. The fourteenth-century Irish archbishop Richard Fitzralph, calculating his clergy's share in the spiritual commerce of the church, noted that in his diocese alone some two thousand "evildoers" came to his attention each year, many of whom sought and obtained (on slight repentance) pardon for their sins before God. And a recent student of medieval criminality in England, John Bellamy, concluded that "not one investigator has been able to indicate even a few years of effective policing" between 1285 and the end of the fifteenth century.

The inescapable evidence of disrule was reflected very faithfully in medieval historiography. Chronicles written thousands of miles apart evoke the same catastrophic view of history, a view which merged the ravages of criminality with the broader destruction of floods, droughts, famine, murrain and plague. Their accounts of human affairs, which often seem to leap from crime to hazard to disaster, were fully in harmony with their providential bias: crises and sudden death were necessary forms of divine retribution for sin, reminders of the transience of all earthly life. But none of these events were included solely to edify; they were seen as noteworthy elements in the human record, awesome burdens inseparable from the course of secular affairs. Just as it contained the lives and works of saintly men, so the *Miracles of Saint Benedict* preserved the memory of the epidemics, cyclones, invasions, wars, pillage, thefts and fraud that clouded the life of the monastery from the mid-ninth to the early twelfth century. And in the chronicle of the Russian city of Novgorod on the Volga, a city with a sizable European merchant population, the reciprocal devastation and slaughter of the border raids by Germans, Tartars and other invaders and the residents of "great Novgorod" consume the bulk of the narrative, with the rest unevenly divided between frequent accounts of recurrent natural disasters and their aftermath and less frequent notations of ecclesiastical affairs. Events such as these loomed as reference points in the flow of time, dividing year from year and often permanently altering the familiar pattern of society.

So often the events which medieval writers put in the foreground of their histories are those modern historians look past in their reading of these records. Yet to look past them is to overlook not only the real or exaggerated details of long-past tragedies but also the climate of insecurity they produced. Medieval people lived in expectation of misfortune and loss—an expectation made more pronounced by an accompanying conviction of helplessness. Within this frame of expectation, the present seemed vulnerable to innumerable hazards and the future uncertain at best, and even good fortune seemed fleeting and precarious.

The temper I mean to describe here is not one of unrelieved despair; rather it is an attitude to experience which greatly respects the power of unaccountable disaster, and is never free of its menace. It is neither optimism nor pessimism, but an ingrained awe in the familiar presence of bad fortune. At the heart of this attitude

159

was a deep awareness that disease, suffering and calamity were inexorable; once they struck, they would take their own course, unrestrained by men.

And in fact it is difficult to imagine the destructive power these forces had in the past. The threat and wreck of fire in medieval towns are particularly hard to conceive. Whether caused by lightning, accidents with cooking fires, candles or arsonists, fires begun in the densely built wooden structures of medieval towns spread rapidly from one street to the next and one quarter to the next. "The only plagues of London," wrote William Fitz Stephen in his description of the city in the late twelfth century, "are the immoderate drinking of fools and the frequency of fires."

The reaction of the populace was not to try to put such fires out but to salvage their possessions and flee, and indeed, the odds against the former were so great that flight was the only sensible reaction. Stone buildings were always sought out as safe refuges, yet even these usually had some wood in their construction, and did not offer any protection against smoke and heat. City chronicles record the frequency and extent of urban fires; over the three centuries covered by the Novgorod chronicle, the city was largely destroyed by fire several times (omitting fires started by invaders) with ten more devastating blazes obliterating extensive areas and twelve leveling one or more entire neighborhoods. Twenty-two lesser fires, destroying several streets, the entire marketplace or the commercial areas where the Scandinavians and other westerners lived and traded, were also recorded. But in their catalogues of destruction the chroniclers set down not only the streets and churches and suburbs affected, but the panic of the victims as well. During the great firestorm of 1340 that burned most of the city, the monastic scribe (who was not given to gratuitous rhetoric) wrote that

> so great and fierce was the fire, with storm and gale, that the people thought it was the end of the world; the fire went burning over the

water, and many people were drowned in the Volga; and the fire threw itself across the Volga to the other side and there by evening service time the whole of that side rapidly burned, from the Fedor stream into Slavno and up to the fields, . . . and whatever anyone brought out and laid either in the fields or in the gardens, or in the fosse or in boats or canoes, all was taken by the flames; and whatever else was brought out wicked men carried it off, who fear not God, nor expect the resurrection of the dead. . . .[2]

In a population largely ignorant of religious skepticism this prescience of the apocalypse must have been as devastating as the fire itself. Yet this was by no means a rare experience; major fires struck Novgorod on an average of once every seven years, often in the same year as floods, droughts, cattle diseases and plague. (The Black Death ravaged Novgorod only twelve years after the catastrophic fire of 1340.)

Though they shared with other medieval populations a pervasive undercurrent of apprehension, the citizens of Novgorod were not pessimists or cynics. Churchmen and nobles and merchants of the city continued to build several new wooden (and fewer stone) churches every year, and to rebuild the damaged neighborhoods around them, even though they must have known that much of what they built risked almost certain destruction within a generation. Pessimism and cynicism go beyond the hovering anticipation of disaster to deny the significance of good fortune as well. The medievals were not suspicious of good fortune, nor were they blind to it, they merely expected little of it, and were reconciled to the constant threat of cureless tragedy along with it.

The degree of criminality and other violence in medieval society was only one element contributing to this state of mind. One early researcher calculated that the insecurity of life under Edward III

161

was some eighteen times greater than in mid-Victorian England, but this statistic (based only on incomplete written records of fourteenth-century court convictions) must be compounded by factors that lie outside the realm of quantification. By and large, whatever their actual risk of harm Victorian Englishmen *felt* secure; however great their actual security, the subjects of Edward III did not.

Hints of this anxiety come to light at every social level. The flat assertion of the author of the *Dialogue of the Exchequer* in 1154 that "today the two nations [Saxons and Normans] are so mingled that one can barely tell apart who is of Norman, who of English blood" is often quoted as if it were more than one courtier's opinion (which in any case referred only to freemen of standing, not to serfs or peasant landholders), yet the reality may well have been far different. The chronicler Orderic Vitalis' tantalizing reference to the discovery in 1137 of an English conspiracy to kill the entire Norman population and bring in the Scots to rule suggests that racial harmony may not have been the norm, even if this particular conspiracy was mere rumor or fabrication. Henry I's dreams of pitchfork-waving Saxon peasants may have been linked to the same fear.

There was nothing in the institutional forces of social order to soothe this anxiety. It is not only that these forces were partisan, inefficient, understaffed and often corrupt—they were—but that they were in practice severely limited in their jurisdictions. Leaving aside the obvious weaknesses of regional feudal justice, even the most sophisticated national court systems were hamstrung by procedural limitations. The accusatory method of indictment meant that nameless strangers (who were responsible for a high percentage of medieval crime) could not be brought to account for their actions by the villagers they assaulted. Most housebreaking, with the theft and murder that often accompanied it, took place in stealth, by night (and was distinguished in law as more heinous than the daylight, public crime of homicide); in the absence of any agency of detection, and given the general indifference of medieval populations to crime in areas other than their own, apprehension of the anonymous murderers was very unlikely. Because of this, the majority of medieval lawbreakers never came into contact with the law or the courts at all.

Of those who were accused, few came to court to be tried unless they brought pardons with them (a fact which helps to account for the extraordinarily high percentage of acquittals). Those who did not appear joined the large company of men and women whom the law simply could not reach. The sentence of outlawry symbolized the inefficacy of medieval justice, as did the ritual of sanctuary, which used the concept of the refuge of holy places to sanction the impunity of crime. To take refuge on sacred ground ordinarily guaranteed an outlaw freedom from pursuit and passage to the nearest seaport, from which he was expected to abjure the realm.

Exile was a self-defeating solution to the unworkability of law, but at least it was a way of identifying and removing known offenders. More unsettling than the occupational lawlessness of known criminals, however, was the habitual lawlessness of otherwise harmless people. For many of these, acts done outside the law for profit were an intermittent supplement to regular income; their frequency reflected the rigor or laxity of law enforcement from one year to the next. Among the poor in the cities, chronic unemployment and criminality went hand in hand, and those who in the temperate seasons lived from outdoor work turned in the winters to crime. Even those exemplary in their obedience to law went willingly outside it when forced to avenge their honor by bloodshed, and in many parts of Europe legal systems continued to provide for remedies by violence. Civil wars, rebellions and most simple changes of government left in their wake a residue of honest men who chose not to rejoin honest society after order was restored, not to mention the hundreds of mercenaries forced to find another conflict or turn to outlawry. In the "plundering mentality" * of the fourteenth and fifteenth centuries many careers of law-abiding local officials showed intermittent gaps accountable only to flirtation with banditry or soldiering rounded out by free-lance crime.

Thus much of the criminal disorder of the medieval period was inseparable from the world of ordered society. For those outside the ranks of professional crime, obedience and lawlessness were less a matter of temperament than of expediency. Nor was this, to repeat, an indication of cynicism. It was merely that while lawful behavior was appropriate in some economic or political or ethical circumstances, in others it was not. And throughout the middle ages, traditions older than the written law of the royal courts or city magistrates lived on to clash with the legal systems which evolved in the twelfth and thirteenth centuries.

The underlying climate of insecurity in the medieval world was from time to time bolstered by crimes so dazzling in their scope that contemporaries compared them to the great clashes of church and state. Among the best documented of these spectacular feats was the burglary of the personal treasury of Edward I in the last days of April, 1303.

When the burglary occurred, the king was at York, near the Scots border. He had kept court there for nearly five years, with only occasional visits to his permanent administrative center at Westminster—a complex which included the royal palace, the Benedictine monastery, and the monastery church, Westminster Abbey. Partly because of the pressure on the northern frontier, there seem to have been few soldiers to guard the Exchequer treasure kept at the palace, and none to guard the Wardrobe

* The term is Bellamy's.

treasure, which for at least a decade had been kept in a sealed crypt in the basement of Westminster Abbey, adjacent to the room where the altar plate of the monks themselves was stored.

During the king's absence conditions in Westminster had worsened. A disastrous fire had made a shambles of the monastery, and with no effort at restoration in sight the life of the fifty monks had been disrupted for several years. When the deputy of the royal keeper, William of the Palace, moved his headquarters from the Fleet prison in London to the palace itself, he brought with him companions eager for good times at the king's expense. At least some of the Westminster monks seem to have joined the company of the palace as well, heedless of their feeble abbot, and by the time the burglar, Richard Pudlicott, met up with William of the Palace there were at least several dozen merrymakers ensconced in the royal lodgings.

Pudlicott, a former cleric turned wool trader and purveyor of butter and cheese, held a personal grievance against Edward I. While Pudlicott was in Flanders sometime earlier, his goods had been confiscated and he himself imprisoned by creditors of the king, as surety against Edward's repayment of war debts. He escaped from the prison, returned penniless to London, and eventually conceived—or was drawn into—the plot to rob the king's treasure.

There is little doubt that Pudlicott received a good deal of help and encouragement from the Westminster monks, particularly from Adam the sacrist, who had charge of the Abbey valuables and who probably furnished Pudlicott with the equipment he needed to break into the Wardrobe cache through the wall which separated it from the monks' treasure room. (Afterwards, William of the Palace testified that Adam and the sub-prior had masterminded the burglary, using Pudlicott to dispose of the treasure and as a decoy to divert suspicion. However, as a sizable share of the treasure was subsequently discovered under William's bed, his evidence is itself suspect; in the event, he and the sacrist were generally denounced by other witnesses as the chief authors of the crime.)

The identity of the instigator or instigators came to matter less and less, though, as more and more people became implicated. Once he had entered it, Pudlicott stayed several days in the Wardrobe crypt, emerging on April 26 with his share of the spoils. By this time accomplices living at the Fleet prison had also come to take their share, most of which was sold to London goldsmiths. Valuables dropped by the thieves in their clumsy getaway made common knowledge of the crime, as did other odd events; jewels and gold from the treasure were being sold in London on the open market, and to his astonishment a fisherman rowing on the Thames netted one of the king's golden cups.

Early in June word of the scandal reached the court at York, and the king ordered juries empanelled in every ward of London and every hundred throughout Middlesex and Surrey to name the thieves. Pudlicott, William of the Palace and the entire complement of Westminster monks were imprisoned, plus thirty-two others thought to be implicated along with them. The sacrist, the keeper, Pudlicott and three others were eventually hanged, but all the monks were released. The king remained in York for a time, but the Wardrobe treasure, most of which was recovered, was moved to the Tower for greater safety.

The scale and audacity of this burglary shocked monastic chroniclers, who likened it to the French knights' assault on Boniface VIII and the theft of his treasure six months later. But in fact the crime was not unique, and the loss it involved was minor. In Edward III's reign a gang led by one Adam the Leper stole the jewels of Queen Philippa, and burglaries greater in their profits were recorded. (Nine months before he attempted to penetrate the Wardrobe Pudlicott robbed the Westminster monks of their plate, apparently with impunity.) The net effect of the Wardrobe burglary was far more innocuous than the damage to the coinage from the £250,000 in "pollards and crockards"—worthless imitations of English pennies—which flooded England in the 1280's and 1290's. It is even questionable whether the thousands of pounds left unaccounted for by the mint officials of Edward I may not have exceeded the value of the unrecovered Wardrobe treasure.

Still, to rob the king was a symbolic enormity far more chilling than the loss of moneys at the mint, and it is this fascination with the symbolic triumph of the forces of disorder which is so prominent in medieval views of crime.

In the *Romance of Eustace the Monk*, the outlaw Eustace learns magic at Toledo under the tutelage of the devil, then uses it to turn the ordered life of a monastery upside down:

> Everything was put to confusion: the monks found themselves fasting when they should have been eating, going barefoot when they should have worn shoes, and swearing under their breath when they should have been reading the hours.[3]

In medieval folklore, crime was commonly associated with an upending of the expected order of things. The outlaws and the agents of public order exchanged places, with the outlaws taking the burden of restoring the justice perverted by corrupt officials. In "The Outlaw's Song of Trailbaston," a murderer swears to punish this corruption. "I will teach them [the royal judges] the game of trailbaston [brigandage]," he sings. "I will break their back and legs, *and it will be right.*" And indeed, until the very end of the middle ages the conduct of royal officials, judges and officers of the court was severely tainted with illegalities ranging from bribery to crude favoritism to dictating verdicts to jurors. Under Edward I, both chief justices were denounced for grave improprieties; one left

167

England under the same conditions as a common felon, while the other was disgraced and removed from office. Justice Wylughby, the man kidnapped earlier by the Folville gang, was indicted for bribery, and in 1350 Chief Justice Thorpe did not defend himself when charged with five counts of corruption, even though it meant a sentence of death by hanging. (Thorpe's sentence was later changed; he was released after only a year in prison, but much of his property was confiscated.) And again in 1365 Edward III had to arrest two judges for serious misconduct.

Abuses by officials surprised no one, but the contrast between corruptible villains in the guise of honest judges and popular heroes with the status of outlaws can only have increased the confusion between perceived justice and legal authority. And the reality was of course much more complex than a simple reversal of roles. Some proportion of judges and sheriffs and coroners were incorruptible, and many within the criminal population had no one's interest at heart beyond their own. If criminality was at times an instrument of public revenge, it was more often a mortal hazard. When ordinary people sheltered and fed criminals, they must have done so with a mixture of gratitude, admiration and dread.

Abrupt and startling changes in the status of criminals compounded this apprehension. During the Hundred Years' War, Charles the Bad of Navarre appointed the most pitiless of his mercenary captains, John Fotheringay, as marshal to administer his courts of military justice in Normandy. And in England, notorious outlaws were commonly set to capturing other criminals as part of the terms of their pardons. Thus two of the Coterel gang were sent out to catch a pair of local robbers, and John Coterel was authorized to apprehend a Leicestershire parson who had turned outlaw and bring him to justice. Others of the Coterel company were appointed to positions of trust almost as exalted as those of their prosecutors; Nicholas Coterel became bailiff of the queen, the group's accomplice Sir William Aune held another royal commission, and the informer Uston became an investigator for the court. Even the former Oxford master Robert Bernard returned to respectability, without losing his church living.

It was the ultimate irony of the saga of the Coterels and Folvilles that the keeper of the peace who finally captured and executed Richard Folville was not rewarded but publicly humiliated for his act. The keeper, Sir Robert Colville, apprehended Folville in his church at Teigh, brought him out forcibly, and beheaded him. As an agent of the king the keeper was well within his rights in killing Folville, who was an outlaw many times over—indeed he would have been culpable if he had spared him—yet because he broke the sanctuary of the church and because the outlaw he executed was also a priest, his action led to a chain of spiritual compensations that brought him greater disgrace than any his criminal victim ever endured.

To absolve themselves of their violation of sanctuary and clericide the keeper and those who were with him had to submit to being beaten with rods before the doors of every major church in the district, to the accompaniment of penitential psalms. Colville's personal sacrilege was so great that it could be remitted only by papal intervention. A letter of Clement VI ordered the bishop of Lincoln to grant absolution to Colville for the killing of a priest.

That Colville should be disgraced and humiliated for executing a known murderer in pursuance of his public duty is ironic in modern thinking only. In the medieval world it was no incongruity that a man might disturb one level of social order in attempting to preserve another. What made for this complication was the multiple identity of persons and places: Folville did not cease to be a cleric when he became a murderer, nor did a holy place lose its purity when used as a haven for wanted felons. To let a felon remain at large was no doubt an augmentation of evil. But there was a higher evil at risk: the violation of a locality inviolable by secular coercion.

Colville's offense is a touchstone for the multidimensional rights that clustered around the keeper, his victim, and above all, the parish church of Teigh. The weakest of these was the right of legal authority to capture criminals and bring them to justice. Beyond this was the right of the felon to seek sanctuary (a right widely thought to be invalid in the case of notorious offenders, which enfeebled Folville's claim to immunity).

Passing over the king's right to pardon wrongdoers and outlaws in all circumstances, and questions of the immunity arising from a felon's clerical status, the most far-reaching right at issue in this instance was that of a consecrated place to preserve all who stood within it from seizure or harm. In challenging this privilege, Colville had symbolically challenged all sanctuaries; in killing a priest he assaulted all priests. (In allowing several of his knights to break the sanctuary of Canterbury Cathedral and murder the archbishop, Becket, Henry II's culpability paralleled Colville's; his punishment was almost exactly the same.)

Given these complex layers of culpability and concurrent identity it is not surprising that some agents of the peace feared to act at all, and in desperation turned against the law in hopes of saving themselves from inescapable persecution. Hearing that a royal commission of oyer and terminer (a special judicial itinerary sent out to handle an unusual burst of criminality in a particular area) had been ordered, the constable of Rockingham Castle and keeper of the forest gathered a party of armed men and waylaid the commissioner. "You wish to destroy me," was his challenge, "but before I am destroyed I shall destroy all those who intend to destroy me, whatever their rank or estate may be."

The defiant figure of the constable of Rockingham comes close to the Romantic image of medieval disorder, but more prosaic forces undermined the smooth running of government and institutions

170

just as effectively. Of these, forgery was perhaps the most common, interference with the coinage the most potentially disruptive.

Forgery, in the middle ages the special crime of clergymen, became almost a matter of course in an age when well-kept records were an exception. Many forgeries were intended as faithful replacements of documents which had once existed; however, monks who acquired the habit of re-creating venerable records soon became accustomed to manufacturing new antiquities out of whole cloth, and forged charters, letters and similar documents came to play an important role in the history of most of the great religious establishments. In the early years of the Norman church in England, Lanfranc, archbishop of Canterbury, found it expedient to substantiate his primacy over the archbishop of York by means of forged records, even though his claim to headship of the church in England was sound enough without them.

Later forgers became more bold. Canonists at Oxford tried to prevent competition from masters of the Roman law by drawing up a bull banning the Romanists from teaching or holding benefices in areas ruled by feudal custom; they attributed it to Innocent IV, who was then pope. Crude and self-interested falsifications of this kind were certainly no rarity, but not all forgeries were lies. Some, like the competition between the universities of Paris (which traced its ancestry to Charlemagne) and Oxford (which claimed King Alfred as its founder) inhabited a middle ground between fantasy and self-delusion. Often the myths of forgers had less to do with reality or fabrication than with what was thought to be an appropriate past for a venerable institution. In view of its excellence, Cambridge forgers thought it entirely plausible that the university's beginnings lay in the age of King Arthur.

Periodically counterfeiters, clippers and dishonest officials impeded the circulation of adequate supplies of sound money. In France, where until the close of the medieval period the king controlled only the coinage of his own region, local feudatories coined their own money and varied the proportion of base metal to silver or copper as well. England had a single coinage (though foreign gold coins circulated freely), but continually lost revenue to the greed of mint officials. Within one ten-year period under Edward I, every Master of the Money was either jailed for theft or left the country richer by thousands of pounds of the king's silver. At least one of these officials grew wealthy lending out the royal money, and the worst of the group, John Porcher, owed the treasury £3500 (a sum as large as the annual revenue from a small shire) before his term of office ended.

Beyond the quagmire of the mint were the false moneyers, whose activities ranged from counterfeiting to entrepreneurship on a large scale. In Scarborough in the 1340's, a husband and wife operated a sort of counterfeiting factory, which not only turned out false money but false vessels and utensils, and supplied imitation silver and gold (which they made from copper, brass and quicksilver) to other moneyers as well.

But the endemic disorder that tangled medieval life went deeper than weak government, corruption, social conflict, or criminality. It was linked to a pervasive acceptance of physical violence as a norm in the relations between individuals and groups. This habituation to violence was not limited to the professional combativeness of the knightly class, but was spread generally throughout medieval society.

As abbot of Clairvaux, Blessed Gerard of Fossanova had spiritual care of the thousands of monks in abbeys affiliated with the mother house. On a visitation to the abbey of Igny in the diocese of Rennes, he corrected the behavior of one of these monks, Hugh of Bazoches. On the same day, after lauds, Hugh waylaid the abbot and stabbed him to death. A few years later, while Gerard's successor was visiting the abbey of Trois-Fontaines, a monk of that house named Simon assassinated the abbot. Commissioners or other higher authorities who came to inspect the conduct of the monks frequently met with assaults which often led to tragedy. When Steven of Lexington, abbot of Stanley in England, was sent into Ireland on a reforming mission he narrowly avoided an ambush set for him by monks at Kilcoolyard Nenay; shortly after he left, the abbot of Fermoy and a monk of Inislounagh in Lismore were set upon and killed. Representatives of the Cistercian Chapter General sent to oversee the convent at Düsseren near Cologne were beaten back by a party of the nuns, armed with swords and stones. And the entire population of another Cistercian abbey, headed by their abbot, drowned a visitor sent by the Chapter General in the late fifteenth century.

The statutes periodically revised by the heads of monastic and religious orders were written in expectation of assaults made by members of the order against each other and against outsiders. Prohibitions of sword fighting and carrying arms appeared first in the mendicant rules early in their history, and in the great Farinerian Constitutions of the Franciscans—a legal watershed for the order—friars were forbidden to assault each other with stones or other missiles, or to mutilate laymen, or to hire assassins to take vengeance against their enemies. The vitriolic opponent of the mendicant orders, John Wyclif, wrote that prospective friars who presented themselves at the convent armed with clubs would be assured of reverent acceptance. He greatly exaggerated the truth, but by the fourteenth century violent conflict had undeniably become commonplace among the mendicants.

The eventuality of clerical violence was, of course, abundantly provided for in church law generally. The late thirteenth-century episcopal provisions of Siena spelled out punishments for church-men implicated in riots and assaults, as well as those guilty of sexual offenses and of plotting against the state. Medieval records yield abundant examples of criminous priests, such as the renegade cleric of Ferrara who shortly after he was elevated to his priestly status became a bigamist, rapist and mass murderer.

The bad behavior of renegade churchmen who formed a part of the wayfaring population of medieval Europe has long been recognized. But until recently the extent of physical conflict within clerical communities has not been brought to light. Abbots were the most common victims of fatal assault; at least fifteen Cistercian abbots were killed by hostile monks or lay brethren between the opening of the thirteenth century and the close of the fifteenth, and many others survived attacks intended to be fatal. Quite a few poisonings are recorded, along with other forms of intimidation. At Belakut Abbey in Hungary the monks imprisoned and tortured their abbot in order to force him to give up his seal. And in 1243 the monks and lay brethren of Hovedö in Norway marooned the prior, sacristan and sub-cantor on a sea island and left them there to starve.

Even when the majority of the community was peaceful, a single individual could disrupt the convent; at Saint-Antoine, a nun called Xanta Tumet joined the community, having been transferred from another house for disciplinary reasons. Before long, she and a companion nun, Jeanne de Louvain, had brought a band of armed accomplices into the monastery and threatened the lives of the abbess and other nuns. Order was restored, and Xanta was severely punished, but before long she had outwitted the convent authorities and opened the house to another group of brigands.

Occasionally abbots assaulted their monks, or quarreled among themselves. Pierre de Châtillon, former abbot of Pontifroid in eastern France, struck the abbot of Cîteaux in the face with a sword which he hid beneath his habit; later he admitted planning to kill the abbot of Morimond as well. For this offense Châtillon was condemned to perpetual imprisonment in chains, but if his victim had been a layman his sentence might have been much less severe. Perpetual imprisonment was the normal punishment for murder of another religious, but murder of a layman resulted only in expulsion from the monastery; furthermore, the murderer could be admitted into another convent, provided he or she accepted the lowest status of all the religious.

Status was a more conspicuous issue among the Cistercians than other monastic orders. Unlike the Benedictines, who brought in laborers and servants to do the agricultural and domestic work of the monastery, the Cistercians tilled their own fields. But this led to a division within their ranks, with one group of monks living the full religious life and devoting itself to study and prayer, and the other—usually much more numerous—observing only a minimum of the *opus Dei* and forming a separate community of illiterate laborers. Members of the latter group, called *conversi*, bound themselves to the vows of poverty, chastity and obedience yet lived isolated from their fellows. *Conversi* had their own sleeping and eating quarters, and even their own choir and altar in the monastery church, and this clear difference in their status seems to have led to friction and defiance. In 1230 a rebellious *conversus* at Heilsbron in Bavaria ran at his abbot with a stick and then a knife, leaving him severely wounded; a monk who came to the abbot's defense was killed. A similar incident occurred at Baudeloo in Flanders, and at Eberbach the *conversi* of the convent revolted *en masse*, and before order could be restored, the abbot was dead.

Convent violence, especially among the Cistercians, is to some extent traceable to the lawless climate of the underpopulated areas and frontiers favored by the order as sites for its foundations. But every order was plagued with mortal hostilities, and it would be misleading to ascribe them to the monastic situation itself. Rather they were a faithful reflection of the tameless contentiousness of the era, and of the bruising discord which soured most relationships.

The rector of a Lincolnshire church developed a grudge against a member of his parish. On his order, another cleric and a group of laymen attacked the man and held him down while the rector drew a knife and cut off his upper lip (a usual form of mutilation for certain classes of criminals). The rector was fined—it was thought too trivial an incident for referral to the church court—and the matter ended.

The hostilities between the clerical partisans of Canterbury and York were of much the same kind, though on a larger scale. Clergy from the two rival archdioceses came to a solemn council at Westminster, and convened in the presence of Henry II and the cardinal Hugezun, with the suffragans and monks "arrayed against one another like hostile armies about to join battle." At issue was the symbolic privilege of sitting on the cardinal's right—a sign of status of the kind traditionally contested between the two archbishops. The archbishop of Canterbury stepped up to take the place of honor; the archbishop of York got in his way, and began to recite the precedents in his favor. When Canterbury went on undismayed, York took hold of his pallium to stop him. At this point the bishop of Ely, who was standing near them both, grasped York so roughly that his mitre fell from his head and broke. Then Canterbury's retainers rushed at York and beat him so severely that his recovery took several years.

It was a short step from personal injury to all-out warfare, and warlike clashes between groups of clergy often paralleled those of the knightly aristocracy in their ferocity. A quarrel erupted between the clerks of St. Stephen's in Prague and the Franciscans of the city over a burial fine. The friars refused to pay, and the priests of the cathedral pronounced their excommunication in the presence of the entire parish. In response the Minorities armed themselves and their followers, stormed the cathedral, and fought the priests to the death as the congregation looked on. Despite attempts to expel the friars from Bohemia as a result of this atrocity, the Franciscan conservator persuaded the bishop and his staff to forgive the outrage and restore smooth relations between the two groups. Settlements of this kind are deceptive; in the absence of a persuasive arbiter, violence tended to evaporate yet remain in the atmosphere, ready to explode again on the next slight pretext.

The same was true of the perennial bloodshed between towns and great monasteries, in which reparations were rarely sizable enough to satisfy the injuries, and the leading issues in the dispute were often left in question. Of the destructive tumult that broke out between the citizens of Norwich and the cathedral priory in 1272—during which mercenaries hired by the monks climbed the belfry to fire catapults on the heads of the townsmen and later pillaged the town, and most of the monastery buildings were gutted—the only enduring symbol of reconciliation was a golden pyx bought with the judicial fine levied on the town by Henry III. And when the abbey of Bury St. Edmunds was virtually leveled by the burgesses of Bury in 1327, the enormous fine of £140,000 levied on the town was remitted by the king's order, even though the looters had removed everything of value and had lived off the monastery for ten months, terrorizing the monks, before burning it to the ground.

When it was not simply ineffectual, legal punishment for wrongdoing of this kind normally took the form of counter-violence. It did not restore order; its effect was usually to multiply existing anxiety, fear, and tension, and so to perpetuate discord and disorder. Punitive justice was characteristically wholesale, and brutal. Under Henry I all the chief coiners were brought to Winchester, castrated, and deprived of their right hands. Mass executions and prominent displays of the heads and corpses of criminals were customary deterrents; after the burglar Richard Pudlicott was hanged, his body was pared and his skin hung on a door of one of the Westminster buildings as a warning to future malefactors.

The prospects for bearable detention, much less for leniency, under English law must have seemed very bleak to the outlaws rounded up by the sheriff of Yorkshire in the 1270's, many of whom chose to be beheaded at once rather than be tried "according to the law and custom of the realm." Some who were convicted found ways of lightening their torment. A Nottingham woman implicated in her husband's death endured imprisonment for forty days without food or water, and so impressed her captors that they attributed the miracle to divine intervention and freed her. Criminal confinement was generally less painful for the rich and well connected; Henry Taperel, a fourteenth-century provost of Paris, was accused of providing poor prisoners to die in the place of wealthy ones in return for a fee.

The apparatus of medieval law did not eliminate disorder, but behind the fallibility of human justice stood a force whose power of deterrence cannot be traced through court rolls or the records of mundane violence: the abiding vision of divine retribution. In the saga of the outlaw Hereward, the robber and his band sack and burn a town and monastery, heedless of any form of legal revenge. Hereward abandons his career in terror, though, when he sees a vision of St. Peter, frowning above him in his omniscience, and carrying the huge key to hell.

Keeping order in the middle ages meant little more than combatting anarchy. Yet the anarchy of the medieval countryside was not an orderless chaos. To be sure, in large areas of western Europe society functioned without external governmental coercion. In these conditions, survival often depended on the mutual defense of blood relatives, on the presence of reliable physical defenses, and on maintaining the illusion of invulnerability. Guarantees of personal loyalty often outweighed the empty protection of law, and the ligatures of fidelity grew more tangled with each generation.

To the simple oath of feudal allegiance in time were added the special oaths taken by the "sworn knights" of the king; the bonds of fidelity were cemented by the exchanging of warranties and sureties—oaths by guarantors who vowed to step in and take the lord's or vassal's place if he defaulted. Pledges of money or goods were made in support of loyalty oaths, and the taking of hostages normally sealed truces and other diplomatic negotiations. But these were negative forces; complementing them were forms of positive coercion whose influence has often been underestimated in the reconstruction of the past. Among noblemen, the preservation of honor was a curb to some forms of violence, and a strong support of the concept of social rank. Ideas about the limits of conventional behavior establish a natural mean for conduct in all societies; in the village communities these ideas exerted a continuing pressure whose importance is only now beginning to be understood. Fear of disapproval or exclusion may have been more potent deterrents to anti-social behavior than fear of legal punishment. And paradoxically, it may have been the very ineffectuality of government that kept the popular urge to remedy disorder strong.

For throughout the high middle ages, popular movements arose to counteract the turbulence of private war and criminality, bad government and injustice. Knights in Poitou, under the leadership of Richard of Aquitaine, formed an association called the *pacifiques* to wipe out brigandage and restore quiet. Small groups periodically swore among themselves to enforce the truce of God, the temporary antidote to private war intermittently in effect since the late eleventh century. The taste for violence remained strong among feudatories, but there grew up alongside it the habit of seeking arbitration in private quarrels with neighboring lords or ecclesiastics called in to make a judgment as an alternative to combat.

Local records reveal the close scrutiny of officials by villagers, and their intolerance of petty tyranny and corruption. "The villagers say," reads the roll for the village of Wiston in 1316,

> that the beadle, John Waryn, is not fit to remain beadle because he accepted a bribe to quit a certain man of his homage, and has vexed and burdened others with more homage than customary, to the harm and complaint of the greater part of the whole village.[4]

Where enforcement was lax, village reeves were fined for failing to admonish the guilty, and the degree of self-enforcement of village by-laws seems often to have been very high.

The aristocratic and ecclesiastical focus of many medieval documents belies the significance of these humbler forces. But evidence of many kinds points to the silent workings of popular justice. When Richard Plantagenet came to Anse in the county of Bigorre, he found there the count of Bigorre, whom the citizens of the town had imprisoned for his misconduct and were holding for Richard's arrival. The count was released, and ransomed himself, and the feudal norm was re-established. In Normandy in the early twelfth century, Hélie de la Flèche captured and imprisoned the bishop of Le Mans, Hoël, in hopes of strengthening his claim to the county of Maine. The people of Le Mans rose in protest. Crosses and statues of saints were thrown down, brambles were heaped before the doors of churches as a sign of mourning, the bells were silenced, and no masses were said. So powerful was this demonstration that Hélie relented. Bishop Hoël was freed.

Chapter eight

THE VISION OF WOMEN

In the 1140's the abbot of Rievaulx set down the unusual events that took place at the Gilbertine convent of Watton in Yorkshire. He had been a witness to some of them, and he recorded them, he wrote, believing that misfortunes could edify as surely as miracles. The story concerned an oblate brought in childhood to the priory by Archbishop Henry of York. She was only four years old when she came to Watton, and Ailred noted nothing of her parentage or condition. By the time she reached girlhood it was clear that she had no monastic vocation. She showed neither love of religion nor respect for the order, and showed moreover "an impudent eye, immodest speech and a lustful walk." The nuns tried to correct her but their words had no effect; beatings failed as well. In time she turned her lascivious thoughts to secular men, and even to monks.

One day it happened that brothers from the men's house (Gilbertine priories in England were invariably double monasteries, with convents of both nuns and monks) had to come into the women's cloister to make repairs. Out of curiosity the misfit nun—Ailred did not record her name—watched them work, and her attention rested on the handsomest of them. Their eyes met and they caressed with a look; at once, Ailred wrote, "the winding serpent slithered his way into both their breasts, and gladdened the vitals of the man." Sweet speech broke the silence between them, and in time, their feeling melting into one, they "sowed the garden of love."

Afterwards they met when they could, secretly and at night. The sound of stones on the convent roof was their agreed-on signal, and they met in a hidden place outside the convent walls. Despite their elaborate precautions, neither her sisters nor the clerics who guarded the convent were at first aware of the girl's rendezvous. Unhappy girl, Ailred wrote, nothing could dissuade you from your evil. Reverent thoughts were shut out by the filth in your blind heart, and you were lost. "Shut your ears, o virgins of Christ, and open your eyes. She goes out a virgin of Christ, and returns an adulteress!"

Eventually the sisters became suspicious when they heard pebbles falling on the roof night after night, and their first thoughts were of the irreverent girl. The sudden flight of her lover from the monastery aggravated their suspicions, and calling the girl before them the "wiser matrons" forced her to confess the whole story. What she told them stupefied them at first, but then "their zeal blazed forth from their very bones, and, looking round at one another, they beat their hands together in anguish and rushed upon her." Snatching the veil from her head, some said she should be burnt, others that she should be skinned, and still others that she should be bound to a stake and roasted over the coals. She was beaten and thrown into the convent prison, fettered and chained.

But imagine, Ailred went on, what a lamentation arose when day after day her womb swelled larger and larger. Then all the nuns felt her shame as if it were their own, as if the eyes of ridicule were turned against them, and the teeth of betrayal. They wept alone and together, and in their frustration they attacked the girl once again. But when their passion subsided a little, they met together to decide her fate. Afraid to expel her for fear her death from want and exposure would be on their hands, still they could not keep her, for her screams in childbirth would reveal her shameful condition. Finally one of them suggested that "the adulterous whore with the pregnant belly" be given to the execrable author of her wickedness. To expedite this the girl herself told her sisters where to find her lover, who would be at their meeting place that night, and concluded stoically, "Let the will of heaven be done."

Monks from the adjoining house were brought in to hear the story then, and together with the nuns they planned the capture of the renegade monk. When he appeared later expecting to meet his beloved—now "a secular not only in habit but in his thoughts"— he met instead a monk disguised as the girl, and as he went up to him the others sprang at him from the bushes and "applied the bitter antidote of their clubs, and put out his amorous fire."

By the time the captive was brought before the nuns, they had abandoned their original plan. No longer intending to send him away with the girl, they asked the monks to leave him in the convent for a while, on the pretext of forcing him to confess his crimes. Left alone with him, they threw him to the floor and pinned him down. Pulling out the cause of all his crimes for all to see, they thrust a knife into his unwilling hands and forced him to castrate himself. In a final act of revenge one of the sisters snatched up the bloody remains of his manhood and threw them in his mistress' mouth.

Like the sword of Levi, or the zeal of Phineas, through these fearless virgins chastity has triumphed and the injury to Christ has been avenged, Ailred wrote. I praise not their deed but their zeal, not their shedding of blood but their emulation of the saints. What might they do to preserve their chastity, when they have done so much to avenge it?

The story of the nun of Watton—which has been retold here as nearly as possible in Ailred's language—says more than any abstract description about the view of women in the middle ages. Although most of the principal characters in Ailred's account were women, and women in a monastic order at that, there was little in their behavior that we would call feminine or religious. But as so often happens it is our meanings that are at fault and not the words themselves. Twelfth-century femininity included heartless cruelty; twelfth-century religiosity embraced barbarity. This incident may not have been typical of convent life, but it was not unique either. Abelard had made love to Heloïse in the refectory of a convent, and like the wretched sister at Watton Heloïse had become pregnant while living among sisters vowed to chastity. Abelard was castrated for his lustful crimes (although Heloïse was avenged by her relatives, not by the nuns of Argenteuil) and later, after he had taken orders himself, Abelard feared for his life as abbot of St. Gildas. Abelard's account of his misfortunes was written a decade before the events at Watton, and the tale of his affair with Heloïse was well known in England. It is conceivable that these famous events influenced the Gilbertine sisters in their revenge, but neither castration nor convent violence were uncommon in the twelfth century, and there is no reason to assume inspiration from the famous scandal.

Ailred's story has been retold less for its sensationalism than because it draws together so clearly the themes that formed the vision of medieval women: misogyny, female docility, female savagery, an exaggerated emphasis on virginity and an exaggerated abhorrence of sexual sins. All of the women in the story are evil; all of them are described as caricatures of vice rather than as real people. Ailred was a humanist and classical scholar who wrote with insight and subtlety on other themes, but in his account the nuns of Watton became one-dimensional and repellent. The wayward young nun was condemned for being independent and unsubmissive; her sisters were equally ungovernable in their pitiless fury.

Their anxiety about their common chastity was equaled only by their loathing for fleshly sin, and Ailred commended both.

The young girl's rebellion against convent life, the attraction of the lovers, the elemental passions of the nuns—all were seen from a peculiar angle of vision. Disobedience, lustful temptation and vengeance were dominant in all the actors, and the evil results of what they did were as inevitable as their motives were clear.

But the attitudes reflected in this account were not Ailred's alone, nor were they the invention of medieval thinkers; they were an integral part of the patristic heritage. They appeared in the third, fourth and fifth centuries in response to the ethics of late antiquity and to the needs of the early church, and they were given lasting formulations in the works of Cyprian, Augustine, and, above all, Jerome.

Early Christian doctrines of marriage, sexuality and the status of women were formed in the dark years between the anarchy of the third century and the definitive barbarian triumphs of the fifth. The gradual Christianization of the empire begun by Constantine helped to establish the administrative structure of the church, but heresies still prospered in the world of late Roman society, and troubled the meditations of ascetic Christian theologians.

Gnosticism was among the most dangerous of these heresies, and caused the greatest confusion over the appropriate position of women in the church. The gnostics believed that the created world was inferior to the spiritual reality it imperfectly reflected. Matter was evil; therefore to create a material being was to create evil, and in consequence procreation was condemned. Many gnostic sects wanted to do away with women's maternal functions entirely, and saw marriage as the devil's work. "Marrying and reproducing," they wrote, "are said to be instigated by Satan."

This view was widely held even outside gnostic circles. An ambiguous passage in I Corinthians had said that Christians were to be saved "by the works of women," and some took this to be an anti-procreative verse. In his *Stromata*, the second-century bishop of Alexandria, Clement, attributed these words to Jesus: "I am come to abolish the works of women."

Closely connected to the abandonment of childbearing was the idea that women ought to preach, baptize, and prophesy alongside men. There were abundant biblical precedents for this: the daughters of Philip prophesied and preached, Phoebe, Prisca, and other women were important leaders in the early church, and the frequent mention of such women as Theonoë, Stratonice, Eubulla and Artemilla in the Christian apocrypha made it clear that the Jewish idea of excluding women from the ministry was not dominant in the first centuries of Christianity. Legends ascribed important roles to the wives of the apostles—by her martyrdom Peter's wife was said to have eclipsed him—and Clement wrote that they went with their husbands as fellow missionaries. The largest number of women preachers, however, were found among the gnostics, and it was a gnostic sect, Montanism, that promoted their ministry most effectively. Two of the chief Montanist leaders were women, and the group had female bishops as well as priestesses. The most startling Montanist beliefs came in a vision Priscilla received while she was asleep on the holy mountain at Pepuza. In her dream, Jesus came to her "in the form of a woman clad in a bright garment" and slept by her side. The vision of the female Christ was perpetuated in Montanist liturgies and in their reverence for Eve, whose sin had brought on the miracle of the Incarnation. (Many early sects exalted women in their worship: the Collyridians, originally a Thracian sect, distributed bread from temporary altars which was sacrificed "to the name of Mary," and other groups maintained they had received their doctrine through Mary. The sensualist Carpocratians even claimed descent from Salome.)

Gnostic sects probably gave a higher status to women than other groups, but women were a major influence in many early heresies. There were important women leaders among the Donatists, and the letters and chronicles of churchmen tell of individual women whose ministry was not associated with any group in particular, but who were effective as itinerant religious leaders. Women were not expressly prohibited from the priesthood until 352, and although in the early fifth century Epiphanios maintained that they had never risen above the rank of deaconesses, the Apostolic Constitutions contained a formula for the ordination of women. The shock and distaste of male clerics at female sacerdotalism revealed a growing prejudice against female ministry, and the churchmen who attacked women who preached and celebrated mass accused them of being instruments of the devil. Exorcism was to be the common remedy for women who assumed religious duties soon to be reserved to men alone.

When the first anchorites escaped to the Eastern deserts in the wake of the Decian persecutions, many among them were women. The ascetic feats they accomplished paralleled those of the male desert saints, and they showed the same aversion to comfort, palatable food and baths. But because the idea of female sanctity was improbable at best, many of these holy women had to dress as men in order to avoid discovery and condemnation. Early accounts of the desert fathers show their fear and hatred of women very clearly. In the *Life of Saint Pachomius* the biographer told of a young monk who ran wildly up to the saint and confessed that a woman had somehow gotten into his cell, seduced him by trickery, and vanished. Without waiting for an answer the tormented monk tore off across the desert until he came to a village and then destroyed himself by jumping into a furnace.

Temptation often came in female form, and the hermits and monks of the desert competed to see who had lived longest without the mischance of seeing a woman. Because of this the blessings of the desert saints were often denied to women, no matter how

187

earnest their needs. A young Roman girl was said to have made a pilgrimage from Italy to Alexandria to be blessed by Saint Arsenius. Despite his refusals she forced her way in to see him, and enduring his utter rejection of her, begged him to remember her and pray for her. "Remember you!" he cried out, "it will be the prayer of my life that I may forget you!"

The misogyny of the anchorites is so well known that it distorts our view of relationships between men and women in the early centuries. Within the eremitical movement itself a form of religious marriage united men and women anchorites, and religious groups experimented with new definitions of sex roles.

Throughout the eastern part of the empire, the institution called syneisactism involved large numbers of holy men and women in "spiritual marriage." Some scholars have argued that the women living in these arrangements were little more than housekeepers, but there is good evidence to support the view that they were equal partners with the men in evangelism and eucharistic ministry. Though an occasional scandal indicates that some syneisacts broke their vows of abstinence, most seem to have found this life of mutual chastity congenial and even inspiring, and despite dozens of prohibitions by church councils of the early middle ages, syneisactism lasted until the spread of cenobitical monasticism made it superfluous.

Among laymen, asceticism could exist without rigid separation of the sexes and without misogyny. Among the Abeloïtes, all members of the group were married and lived continently; each couple adopted a boy and girl, who grew up to imitate their situation. In the 340's, a council held at Gangra to condemn the fanatical anti-matrimonial teachings of one Eustathius recorded the existence of another group which attempted to obliterate distinctions of inferiority or superiority between men and women. The women in the group cut their hair—long hair symbolized their lower status—and wore the same clothes as the men. That women were the spiritual guides of these Christians is instructive, but their aim seems to have been to promote equality rather than female dominance.

But these groups were condemned along with syneisacts, and it was the misogynist tradition that the church revered. Like the gnostic exaltation of women, syneisactism and other communal experiments were to remain a forgotten backwater of church history, while the antifeminism of the desert saints and church Fathers still rang through the monasteries and universities centuries later.

To Jerome, Ambrose, Augustine and even earlier writers such as Tertullian and Cyprian, the choice between the syneisacts' unprecedented regard for women and the ascetics' wary distaste for them was an easy one. They found little in the behavior of contemporary Roman women to alter the misogynist ideas they absorbed from the Latin classics; giving every appearance of independence, these women openly exploited the laws of marriage and inheritance (laws which punished adultery but tolerated prostitution) and combined sexual license with callous destruction of their unborn children. Roman mores were after all worlds apart from the lives of most Christian theologians. Puritans who lived in monastic isolation themselves, the Fathers were inclined by experience to antifeminism, and faced with the paradox of exalted Christian women and debased Roman ones, they hit on what was to become an enduring formula: they loved virgins but hated women. "Per mulierem culpa successit, per virginem salus evenit," they wrote—"Sin came through a woman, but salvation through a virgin."

The mass of women, in this view, deserved all the abuse antifeminists had poured out against them for centuries. Morally and physically weaker than men, they were at best a dangerous distraction, at worst the gateway to hell. By contrast, the few women who preserved their virginity were above criticism, and worthy of unusual veneration. Denial of the flesh was all the more remarkable in creatures so prone to lust and incapable of self-restraint. Among the best-loved of the early female saints were those who combined both sides of women's nature in a single life. From the Magdalene on, the repentant harlot had been a popular saintly image, not least because it reinforced the idea that holiness was not a natural inclination in women.

Patristic exaggeration of virginity was already strong in the writings of Tertullian, and after his conversion to Montanism he claimed that the chief sanctity was that of the virgin, and was willing to exclude "exceptional" women from the conventional restrictions against speaking in the church. Another third-century writer, Cyprian, made of virginity the distinctive mark of Christian holiness, and with Cyprian virginity ceased to be a matter of private observance and became a highly public virtue. Continence of the flesh was accompanied by a spiritual purity that was obvious to all. "Anyone who sees a virgin," he wrote, "cannot be mistaken about what he sees."

In the works of Cyprian and his later contemporary Ambrose, virginity became the province of a small group of superior Christians, and the term they used to describe it—*integritas*, wholeness or intactness—strongly connoted *female* virginity. They created the idea that Christian women were divided into those who lived normal lives (which for most women meant married lives) and those whose chastity made them unmistakably superior.

Of course, these writers advocated virginity for all Christians, men as well as women, and it would be wrong to assume that only women were exhorted to chastity. But male virginity was never stressed in the same way as female virginity, and when the second-century theologian Origen castrated himself out of devotion to sexual purity he was severely punished by the Alexandrian church, and excluded from the priesthood. By a venerable tradition, priests had to be "whole" men, but here wholeness was linked to sexual potency rather than to abstinence. By contrast, an entire genre of theological literature was addressed exclusively to young women, urging them to guard their chastity inviolate.

Here it must be remembered that while men had at least three sexual alternatives, in the thinking of churchmen, women had only two. Men could either marry, become ascetics, or live as bachelors. Women could choose only between marriage and the semi-cloistered life of a consecrated virgin. The idea of spinsterhood was foreign to the thinking of patristic theologians; they assumed that any woman who did not choose virginity would marry.

This reasoning could only reinforce the long-established concept that marriage was a poor second to a life of chastity. Tarnished by intercourse, the married state represented the triumph of lust over piety, flesh over spirit. Commenting on the Pauline text "Better it is to marry than to burn with vain desire," Tertullian had argued that the "good" in marriage is really only a lesser sort of evil. Paul's logic was no stronger, he insisted, than the argument that it was better to lose one eye than two. The development of monasticism discredited marriage still further, until by the middle of the fourth century an eastern bishop, Eustathius of Sebastia, maintained the extreme view that married people could not be saved, and attracted a large following to his opinion. So influential was this doctrine that two church councils were needed to check its spread, and in the vehement debate that followed several controversialists appeared who defended the opposite viewpoint.

One of these, Jovinian, was a married monk who denied the special efficacy of virginity. Jovinian spoke out in favor of marriage for priests as well as laymen, and challenged the pope in Rome and the prestigious (and married) Ambrose in his episcopal see of Milan. Synods in both cities drove Jovinian out, but in 412 he returned to Rome and harangued his many followers in open meetings. By this time Jovinian had brought down on himself the venerable irritation of Jerome, and in punishment for his blasphemy (he denied the virgin birth of Jesus) he was scourged with a leaden thong and exiled to the rock of Boa on the Dalmatian coast. His followers were deported too, but not before one of them, Vigilantius, had carried his doctrines into Gaul and Spain.

It was while the beliefs of Eusthatius, Jovinian and Vigilantius were being debated that the most influential of the Fathers developed their doctrines on marriage and the status of women. Augustine, bishop of Hippo in Africa, knew the danger of falling into the Manichean error of condemning all procreation, but his own youthful marriage had acquainted him with the power of sexual desire as well. He compromised; he linked marriage to sin, but only to venial sin. "A permanent union for the sake of slaking incontinence," he wrote, marriage was redeemed by the desire for children and by its sacramental character.

Though they disagreed on doctrine Augustine conceded that Jovinian was a sincere and virtuous man. Jerome conceded Jovinian nothing, and it was in Jerome's lengthy treatise *Against Jovinian* that the most influential and enduring patristic statements on marriage and women are to be found.

From the outset, it was clear that Jerome wedded praise of virgins to distaste for women. Even the pagans of antiquity, he wrote, recognized that womanhood and virtue are mutually exclusive most of the time. While they approved of the few heroines who remained chaste, or who killed themselves to preserve their honor, classical writers knew that most wives were ill-tempered and vicious and that marriage made a man unfit for a life of philosophy or religion. The Christian revelation only made these truths more plain. "In view of the purity of the body of Christ," Jerome argued, "all sexual intercourse is unclean."

Jerome's ideas on female education and behavior are evident in his vast correspondence. Many of his correspondents were women —fully half of his theological letters were written to nuns or pious matrons—and he liked to write little biographies of women whose conduct he admired. One of these was the young widow Blesilla, whose sudden and extraordinary asceticism led to tragic results, and was for a time a subject for scandal in Rome.

The daughter of Jerome's pious correspondent Paula, Blesilla was widowed after only seven months of marriage, and with Jerome as her spiritual adviser she then began a regime of extreme austerity and self-denial. "Mourning the loss of her virginity more than the death of her husband," Blesilla's "steps tottered with weakness, her face pale and quivering, her slender neck scarcely holding up her head," Jerome wrote in a letter to Paula. Her fasting brought on a fever, and within three months of her conversion Blesilla was dead.

Probably because of her high social standing her story was well known in the capital, and popular resentment against the monks and against Jerome in particular was very great. At her funeral, mourners whispered to one another that she had been killed by fasting, and asked "How long must we refrain from driving these detestable monks out of Rome? Why don't we stone them or hurl them into the Tiber?" To the Romans, Blesilla was a victim of the exaggerated cult of austerity; to Jerome, she was a Christian heroine. But even as he praised her, he assigned her a rank in the female hierarchy, a rank that was determined by her physical purity alone. "As a childless widow she will occupy a middle place between Paula, the mother of children, and Eustochium the virgin," Jerome wrote. And he added, "In my writings she will never die."

Of course, Jerome admired more colorful women as well. His portrait of Marcella, an erudite widow whose life of austere scholarship paralleled Jerome's own, exalted her learning and courage. (Marcella was indeed remarkable. She drove the Origenist heretics out of Rome single-handed, and faced the Visigothic invaders in 410 without flinching.) But Jerome was careful to note that Marcella deserved praise because she never overstepped the proper bounds of female conduct, and never assumed authority that might "inflict a wrong upon the male sex."

Jerome's recommendations for the education of girls, given in a famous letter he wrote to one Gaudentius, described behavior that was much closer to Blesilla's than to Marcella's. The letter actually outlined a plan for the training of a child who had been dedicated to a life of virginity, but medieval thinkers used it as a standard of education for all girls, whether they were to marry or not, and for centuries it was to serve as a commonplace of medieval writings on female education. Many of Jerome's guidelines were negative; the young girl must know nothing of boys, and must be taught to dread playing with them; she must never learn the meaning of obscene words, and must avoid leaving her room. As an adolescent she was never to look at young men, never to hear sensual songs, and was to confide only in a "sober, grave and industrious" chaperone. The direction of her education he summed up in a single phrase: "Let her know nothing of the past, let her shun the present, and let her long for the future."

By the time Jerome wrote, the course of Christian history had changed the Christian image of women from its apostolic form. Condemnations of heterodox groups in which women had been prominent as leaders and ministers meant that women would remain subordinate in the community of believers. The sacerdotal movement had put barriers not only between the clergy and laity, but between the clergy and women; no woman could legitimately enter clerical orders, and a group of important councils had ruled that all clerics above the rank of deacon must remain chaste. Finally, a disproportionate admiration for virginity established the view that unlike men, women were to be judged according to their sexual status, with virgins high above married women in holiness and virtue. Jerome's writings restated all these ideas, and added to them the chief arguments of classical misogyny. In his synthesis the patristic view of women received its most magisterial formulation. Augustine would write about marriage and sexuality with greater humanity than Jerome, and Chrysostom with greater intolerance, but neither would be read with more admiration by medieval thinkers.

These patristic doctrines reached the lives of ordinary Christians through the penitentials, and from there they passed into the canon law. Penitentials were written to guide priests in hearing confessions and assigning penance. Compiled for use in monasteries, the penance books catalogued sins from the viewpoint of an ascetic community. Sexual sins were given an understandable prominence in these compilations, and the punishments they merited were heavy. These punishments may have been appropriate for monks, but when applied to lay men and women they attached a stigma to sexual sins that was out of proportion to other forms of wrongdoing. In combination with Old Testament dictates and with popular superstition, the morality of the penitentials led to a distorted view of marriage and of female sexuality.

A large number of penitential cautions and prohibitions clustered around menstrual blood and its harmful effects. Hebrew law condemned couples who made love during menstruation, and many early medieval writers described the diseased or misshapen children born of unions during the proscribed times. It was commonly believed that leprosy or epilepsy cursed children conceived amid the pollution of menstrual blood, and because of its association with witchcraft Isidore of Seville wrote that the poison of the menstrual flow withered flowers and aborted the fertility of the fields.

Fearing this contamination, churchmen were anxious to keep women away from the sacred objects of worship. At the Council of Chalcedon women were forbidden to approach the altar, and were allowed to grasp the host only through a veil. Other councils ordered women to be on their guard lest they carelessly befoul the church, and in the east no woman could enter a church while in an unclean state.

Closely related to the pollutions of menstrual blood were those which clung to a woman after the birth of a child, particularly a female child. Gregory the Great repeated the Hebrew formula that a woman must wait thirty-three days after the birth of a son and sixty-six days after the birth of a daughter before she could enter the church and receive the sacrament, and indeed the physical trauma of childbirth was accompanied by the spiritual trauma of virtual exclusion from the Christian community. As she neared her full term a pregnant woman was encouraged to take communion, both because the likelihood of death was high and because from the onset of labor until her churching, she would bear the double stigma of unclean blood and the "filth of sin" (sordes peccati) without the consolations of the church. (The filth or "bodily uncleanness"—immunditia corporis—was the sinful residue of the lust of conception.)

By custom the child was favored over the mother at birth; a fifteenth-century pastoral handbook instructed midwives to save the infant's life at the expense of the mother's, "for that is a charitable deed." Many women survived the ordeal of annual childbirth: it would be misleading to generalize from random examples, but among the eleventh- and twelfth-century Norman nobility large families of twelve to fifteen children born to a single wife were not uncommon, although a high proportion of the children died in infancy. But death in childbirth was a common hazard for medieval women, and not the least of its terrors was the prospect of unconsecrated burial.

Because in popular belief the blood of the afterbirth was thought to attract demons, a woman who died before she had been purified after giving birth was refused burial in consecrated ground, and denied admission to paradise. Even a pregnant corpse was excluded from the churchyard, since in the opinion of many theologians the unbaptized child in the mother's womb invalidated her claim to Christian burial. Humane churchmen urged acceptance of these corpses, but without complete success, and even in areas where a consecrated grave was found for a woman unlucky enough to die while carrying a child, the burial was often done without dignity, in secret, and in a lonely corner of the churchyard.

Motherhood entailed spiritual risks for medieval women, yet marriage without children lay outside the expectations of medieval society. Both contraception and abortion were denounced in the penitentials, and although both were probably widely practiced they brought heavy penances. Intercourse without procreation had been unthinkable to patristic writers, both because it seemed to inhibit nature and because it made sexual pleasure rather than the generation of children the primary object of marital sex.

Even so, intercourse was surrounded with guilt and enmeshed in a tangle of restrictions. Lovemaking was not permitted on Sundays, Wednesdays or Fridays, or on any church feast; the penitentials forbade it during Advent, Lent and on rogation days, and it was of course prohibited during pregnancy and after childbirth, and while either spouse was fulfilling a vow of penance. By the fourteenth century sexual relations were explicitly outlawed during some 220 days out of the year, and there was no lack of influences urging voluntary abstinence beyond this. Lovemaking made a couple unclean, and unworthy to take the sacrament. Consequently Gratian advised husbands to keep themselves chaste for three or four or even eight days before accepting the Eucharist, and wives were urged by itinerant preachers to try to control their husbands' lust. (In medieval discussions of sexual sins, it was normally assumed that the husband controlled lovemaking and that the wife only sinned if she willingly consented.) The natural arbiter of marital purity, the wife was encouraged to resist "unnatural" sex "even to death."

197

These views contrasted oddly with the popular mythology of lust in which women were often seen as temptresses overcome by their sexual appetites, and indeed the polarized imagery of women's nature that characterized patristic writings was very much in evidence in later centuries. Mutually contradictory models of female behavior were to be found in the writings of theologians, poets and preachers. The Christian virago flourished alongside the nagging wife, the temptress alongside the ascetic virgin. Only in their degree of caricature did these images meet on common ground.

One reason for this was the continuing reverence for the writings of the Fathers. The letters and treatises of Jerome, Ambrose, Augustine and Gregory were approached by medieval thinkers not as theological antiques but as living texts to be read and reread by every learned man and woman. In a real sense the sentiments of patristic writers were rewritten afresh with every generation, for as we have seen, medieval thought was agglomerative, and medieval writers savored quotations.

Jerome's *Adversus Jovinianus* had a multiple rebirth in the twelfth century. Widely quoted by the Gregorian reformers and in the early canonists' collections, the antifeminist arguments of Jerome were repeated by Abelard and by his students in their commentaries on the *Sentences*. Gilbert Foliot, Peter of Blois and John of Salisbury all incorporated Jeromian borrowings into their works, although John tempered his with backhanded counter-arguments in praise of women. But it was in a pseudonymous treatise of Walter Map that the views of Jerome were revived with greatest force and virulence.

The *Dissuasio Valerii* (Valerius' Dissuasion against Marriage) was a merciless satire, irrefutable because of its outrageous exaggeration. "Friend," Map wrote under his antique soubriquet, "no matter what they intend, with a woman the result is always the same. When she wants to do harm—and that is nearly always the case—she never fails. If by chance she should want to do good, she still succeeds in doing harm." Jerome had said that with an extreme effort a few women could become exemplars of virtue. "Valerius" denied this. Women cause evil, he insisted, by their very presence; a virtuous woman is as rare as the phoenix. "A few women have brought back from the field of battle the banner of modesty—the Sabines, Lucretia, Penelope. But friend, no Lucretia ever existed, nor Penelope nor the Sabines. Fear them all."

The *Dissuasio* was put into the mouth of an ancient author partly to deflect criticism and partly to take advantage of the contemporary taste for classical works. (Some took "Valerius" to be Valerius Maximus.) The work proved to be immensely popular; five commentaries on it were produced in the twelfth century alone, and before long Map acknowledged it as his own by including it in his longer work *On the Frivolities of Courtiers*. The *Dissuasio* repeated many of Jerome's unflattering commonplaces about women and turned the flattering ones sour. Despising marriage, Map had little love for the alternatives, and even found something nasty to say about parthenogenesis. The subtle, mocking tone of the treatise is in evidence in this little story:

> Weeping, Pacuvius confided to Arrius, "My friend, I have an unlucky tree at home. My first wife hung herself from it, and my second wife as well. Now I've just lost my third in the same way." "I'm amazed to find you crying in the midst of such good fortune," Arrius answered. "Think of the money that tree has saved you! Friend, give me a slip of it so I can plant one in my garden." [1]

"Good reader," Map added, "take care that you aren't forced to beg for a slip of that tree, for you won't be able to find one."

The misogyny of Walter Map combined the most telling elements of classical and patristic writings against women with anecdotes and proverbs from popular folklore. Most writings

199

against women occupied more formal and well-defined literary genres. Building on models provided by Juvenal, Cicero and Ovid, the classicist writers of the twelfth century revived the antique genres of satire, and used them in both Latin and the vernaculars. Within the two broad divisions of diatribes against marriage and Ovidian ridicule of women's sensuality, more specific thematic genres developed. In the *pastourelle*, a shepherd-girl argued with a courtier over the preservation of her virtue. The twin forms of the "husband's lament" (*chanson de mal marié*) and the "wife's lament" (*chanson de mal mariée*) battled over which spouse had the worst lot. Women did not get the worst of the argument every time—some "defenses" succeeded—but few of these poems had anything good to say about marriage, and any condemnation of marriage was an implicit condemnation of women.

These poems elaborated the traditional range of feminine vices—stubbornness, arrogance, overweening lust, jealousy, vanity, faithlessness and shrewish competitiveness. Here they paralleled a view of women which was well developed in troubadour poetry. "Women," wrote the Provençal poet Marcabru,

> are tricksters and know how to cheat and lie; wherefore they make
> their husbands support other men's children. May God never forgive
> him who wishes to honor and serve these passionate and impassioned
> whores who are worse than I can tell you.[2]

There were a good many antifeminist satirists among the troubadours, and their attitudes toward the women they loved were shot through with ambivalence. Like the patristic writers, they found admirable women particularly precious because there were so few of them, and their peculiar sexual code—which called for unrestrained eroticism up to the threshold of intercourse and not beyond—was intended to heighten their own pleasure and not to show respect for the beloved.

Much of the medieval literature that exalted women had its misogynist counterpart. If the troubadours balanced their amorous poems with attacks on the declining number of worthy women ("never have there been so many deceitful women since the serpent drew down the branch"), the archtheorist of courtly love, Andreas Capellanus, wrote a book against love at the end of his life. It was a convention of medieval letters to imitate Ovid's *Ars amatoria* and *Remedia amoris*; Chaucer and Boccaccio counteracted their anti-feminist arguments with the *Legend of Good Women* and the work *On Famous Women*. At the summit of this genre, of course, were the two parts of the *Roman de la rose*, which had no peer in its simultaneous praise and blame of women. Both parts of the *Roman* met with success, and both were the object of controversy.

The literary debate over the vices and virtues of women in time became an academic debate, and the *querelle des femmes* occupied some outstanding fifteenth-century thinkers, including the ambivalent feminist Christine de Pisan.

But like the literary works that preceded them the writings in this quarrel have the flavor of intellectual abstraction rather than of reality. The horizons of the argument were finite, and the choice of examples and authorities was narrow. Even when put into the Bernardine language of the spurious "Letter of Blessed Bernard to Abbot Codrille," the limited vocabulary of literary misogyny grew dull and dissolved into a string of classical tags. "Listen to what the philosopher Secundus told the Emperor Hadrian," wrote the anonymous author of the letter, trying to make the commonest of all antifeminist descriptions sound fresh: "Woman is man's confusion—an insatiable beast, a continual care, the dwelling of turbulence, an impediment to chastity, a man's destruction, the channel of adultery; she is the enslaving of a man, and his heaviest weight of all."

In the *Morte de Garin*, Blancheflor goes to her husband, Emperor
Pepin, and asks him to help the Lorrainers.

> The King hears her; . . .
> He raises his fist and strikes her in the nose
> Four drops of blood issue from it . . .
> And the lady says: "Thank you so much,
>   my lord!
> If it pleases you, you may do it again." [3]

The contrast between the mundane brutality of the romance and
the disembodied rhetoric of the *querelle des femmes* is broad and
telling. Literary antifeminism can thrive on tradition alone; it need
not reflect actual behavior. But there is no gratuitous misogyny in
the *chansons de geste*, and the full range of male-female relations
in the feudal period is evident there, as in the friars' sermons.
When Friar Guillaume exhorted wives to tolerate their husbands'
beatings and other cruelty "since these can not help but add to
your merits and increase the size of your eventual reward," he was
not repeating a literary commonplace.

  Misogyny has been treated in various ways by medievalists.
Literary scholars have argued that attacks on women were part of a
narrow debate that went no farther than the polemics themselves.
When Chaucer satirized women he was "attempting neither to
abolish a code nor to transform a sex," one commentator has
written. His antifeminism was part of "a very courtly game, which
fits excellently into medieval pomp and ceremony, themselves only
half-serious . . ." Attacks are always more amusing than defenses,
and making fun of a thing indicates acceptance of it. D. W.
Robertson, a scholar unusually sensitive to the design of medieval
thought, still sees only one side of medieval misogyny. The writers
of the middle ages, he has said, "condemn women not because

there is anything intrinsically evil about women, but because women may easily be regarded as a source of fleshly rather than spiritual satisfaction."

To make antifeminism into an allegory of the fight against fleshly desires is to ignore the abundant evidence of physical mistreatment of women and the popular beliefs about their innate inferiority to men. On every level of medieval credence—from proverbs to theological arguments—the myth of feminine weakness and vice was perpetuated, and no woman was free of its stigma.

Crucial to this myth was the continued growth in the early feudal age of the concept of the Christian virago. The Stoic idea Jerome had echoed—of the strong and courageous woman, able to fight and to stand up to men—merged with Germanic ideas about women's bravery and fighting ability. But the synthesis of the two created a hybrid and artificial image. Rather of Verona evoked it in his ninth-century *Praeloquia*:

> Are you a woman? Seek then zealously to turn the mildness inherent in your name [*mulier*] to the virtue of submissive obedience rather than to the vice of dissolution. For in the beginning the woman was called *virago*—that is, strong and manly [from *vir*, man]. . . . A man in mind, a woman in body, seek to conquer the spirit of mindless vice and pleasure . . .[4]

In this curious passage the strength women had in the past is contrasted with their present weakness. What virtue a woman might attain she had to borrow from male characteristics; self-discipline and reason were seen as masculine, self-indulgence and sensuality, feminine. Only by becoming a man in her mind could a woman control her unruly and sinful body.

For Rather a virtuous woman was a sort of hermaphrodite with the intellect of a man and the physiology of a woman, and since this union was precarious and rare, few virtuous women were likely to exist. This version of the virago concept helped to reinforce the enduring patristic doctrine that admirable women were rare; to these were added the restrictions and incapacities of feudal and canon law.

In general, married women were not allowed to inherit or bequeath land, or to appear in court on their own behalf. Indeed their legal personalities were not so much repressed as nonexistent, for under much of medieval law a woman was her husband's property, like his plate and his horses. In England, a man could not sue his wife for infidelity because he would in effect be suing himself. (He could sue her lover, but the suit would claim property damage, not adultery.) Canon lawyers set out in detail the subordinate position of women. "Man is the head of woman," Gratian wrote, and repeated the passage from the pseudo-Augustine which argued that whereas Adam was made in God's image, Eve was made from Adam, and thus women were not made in the likeness of God in the same sense as men were.

Writers of the next generation were to find an even more persuasive justification for the superiority of men. Aristotle's writings on the generation of animals defined a female as a "misbegotten male"—a biological imperfection useful only in reproduction. The male seed ordinarily breeds other males, Aristotle taught, other perfect beings. But should the sperm be flawed, or affected by accident or climate, a female is formed instead. This inherent imperfection was closely linked to the intellectual inferiority of women; "woman is naturally subject to man," Aquinas wrote, "because in man the discretion of reason predominates."

The Aristotelian argument passed into law, theology and even literature. Boccaccio called woman "an imperfect animal, obsessed with a thousand revolting and abominable passions," and by the time he wrote the case against women had grown weighty and complex; from poetry and popular myth it expanded to embrace the chief categories of medieval learning, and few thinkers failed to repeat and elaborate the stock arguments of the misogynistic corpus.

Given this overwhelming antifeminist brief it would be odd not to find at least a thin strand of pro-feminist sentiment. Writing to Heloïse and the nuns of the Paraclete, Abelard tried to restore to them a sense of the worth of their sex.

> What has been so necessary to our redemption, he wrote, and to the salvation of the whole world as the female sex which brought forth for us the Saviour himself? The singularity of which honor the woman who first ventured to intrude upon Saint Hilarion opposed to his marvelling, saying: "Wherefore turn away thine eyes? Wherefore shun mine entreaty? Look not upon me as a woman but as one that is wretched. This sex gave birth to the Saviour." What glory can be compared to this, which that sex won in the Mother of the Lord? The redeemer might, had he wished, have assumed his body from a man, as he chose to form the first woman from a man. But this singular grace of his humility he transferred to the honour of the weaker sex. He could also have been born of another and a more worthy part of the woman's body than are the rest of men, who are born of that same vilest portion wherein they are conceived. But, to the incomparable honour of the weaker body, he far more highly consecrated its genitals by his birth than he had done those of the male by circumcision.[5]

Though he was writing to nuns, Abelard's praise was for all women. Unlike the patristic writers, who had reserved their approval for women vowed to chastity, Abelard located the source of women's worth in the very sexuality the Fathers had condemned. Praise of women was not entirely foreign to vernacular literature either; along with their misogyny many romances commended the *"preudefame"* and declared that "a good woman illumines an entire kingdom." The English *Southern Passion* explicitly blamed those who criticized women in songs and books when blameless women are a commonplace of everyday experience, and lamented that a woman who strays from virtue is censured a thousand times more roundly than a sinful man.

But the most influential effort to rehabilitate women came from the vernacular preachers whose sermons informed the popular theology of the medieval West after the middle of the thirteenth century. In their sermons for the first time marriage was exalted as a desirable condition and a source of spiritual blessing, and a large number of arguments were advanced in behalf of this teaching. Instituted in paradise, before the fall of mankind, marriage was to be recommended for its antiquity as well as because it was an agency of concord in human affairs. In support of married life mendicant preachers quoted the text from Ecclesiastes, "Blessed is the man who has a good woman," and even adopted the curious if venerable logic that marriage was good because it often resulted in daughters, and hence increased the number of virgins.

Another of the reasons commonly given for the excellence of the married state was that Mary had chosen to become a wife; here as in many other areas of moral theology her life was called up as an example for all women to follow. But this advocacy of marriage was based in a current of thought far broader than Mariology, a way of conceiving women's lives that constituted a direct challenge to the patristic view of marriage as a *pis aller*. Several important mendicant theologians spoke of the "order" of married persons, and compared it advantageously to the religious orders of the thirteenth and fourteenth centuries. The Dominican Henry of Provins wrote that

> the *ordo* of marriage is one whose statutes are not just from yesterday; it has existed for as long as humanity itself. Ours and the Franciscan Order have only recently been established; all the other religious Orders belong to the era that began with the incarnation. But the

order of marriage is as old as the world itself. Moreover, our Order was the work of a simple mortal, a Spaniard, just as that of the Friars Minor was the work of a Lombard; it was God himself who instituted the order of marriage at the foundation of the world.[6]

Rehabilitating marriage could have gone far to rehabilitate ideas about women, but traditional antifeminist opinions were always stronger and more telling than philogyny. Abelard's exaltation of women was accompanied by the old disparagement that "inasmuch as the female sex is naturally weaker, so is its virtue more acceptable to God and more worthy of honor," and preachers who looked favorably on marriage in the abstract were more cynical when it came to judging actual unions. "Out of every thousand marriages," the great preacher Bernardino of Siena insisted, "I believe 999 are the devil's."

When the experience of individual medieval women is examined, it is immediately apparent that in countless ways the realities of their lives were at odds with the abstract restrictions of theology, law, literature and folklore. The apparent contradictions are heightened when the biographies are those of noblewomen or others who belonged to the literate minority, and medieval women's history has often been written as if it could be reconstructed from these contrasts. In this model, the power, achievements or relative freedom of a few medieval women were taken as proof that the rest were similarly unhampered by theoretical restraints.

But this assumption is misleading, on two counts. First, the historiographical bias that entered women's history with the feminist movement imposed restrictions of its own, defining women's past according to narrow modern concepts of limitation or liberty. But during most of the middle ages these categories had little meaning; in fact they obscure more important changes that affected women. And second, the few surviving biographies cannot without distortion be taken to stand for the incalculably varied experience of medieval women as a whole.

It now appears that, however much we may come to know of about the vision of medieval women, we will never have more than fragments of information about their real condition. Like the Jews, women were excluded from most of public life, and what concerned them was thought to be both atypical and unworthy of record. Yet the most far-reaching themes in women's history may very well be those which seem on the surface to have least to do with the whole of medieval society. The *Frauenbewegung*, or "women's movement" of the thirteenth and fourteenth centuries, the revival of female ministry and evangelism, the enclaves of female guilds and of women's medical learning have seemed to both medieval and modern historians to form closed worlds, outside the mainstream. But much of the substance of woman's history lies within these separate worlds, and although relatively little is known about them, they can shed light not only on the experience of medieval women but on medieval society as a whole.

The best-known of these separate domains is the one the nineteenth-century historian Karl Bücher called the *Frauenfrage*, or "woman question." Whatever their conscious and unconscious motives, beginning in the early years of the thirteenth century large numbers of women in northern Europe chose to live together in the self-supporting houses called beguinages. The life they shared was anomalous in its form; beguines imposed on themselves a regimen grounded in piety and religious observance, but they generally took no vows and spent their productive time making cloth. Since Bücher's time historians have argued over the precise nature of the beguines, some arguing that they were the product of a growing urban class-consciousness or of demographic shifts, others insisting on their essentially religious character. Neither interpretation attributes the phenomenal growth of the beguinages to the fact that they offered women the first respectable alternative to binding monastic vows or marriage. The beguine was a new creature: a woman who lived in a pious community but was free to leave it at any time, a woman whose life was balanced between religious devotion and profitable labor, a woman who was not directly answerable to any man, and who, within her community, was entirely self-determined and entirely self-supporting.

Furthermore, the beguine movement may be seen as only one part of a broader change in the behavior and expectations of women that began in the twelfth century. They entered fervently into the revival of asceticism associated with the Premonstratensians and Cistercians early in the 1100's. Accounts of women followers of Norbert of Xanten, founder of the Premonstratensians, told how "their behavior was even more strenuous and strict than the men's," while the women among the Cistercians

> voluntarily assumed the order of Citeaux, passionately, yea freely. And putting aside their linen garments, dressed only in woolen tunics, . . . they not only did women's work but also labored in the fields, clearing woods, pulling thorns and brambles, and, working assiduously with their hands, in silence they strove for their bread.[7]

In their enthusiasm a growing number of women defied the antique law of the church which, in the fourth century, had decreed that "no woman, no matter how learned or holy, may presume to teach men assembled together," and not only preached but assumed priestly functions. A continuing stream of denunciations of women preachers reached a climax early in the thirteenth century, when Honorius III ordered the bishops of Valencia and Burgos to refuse the pulpit to abbesses, and the Dominican Humbert of Romans insisted that women must not be allowed to preach because of their inferior intelligence and status, their weakness for luxury, and because of the stigma of Eve, whose words had sealed the fate of mankind.

Although complaints about women priests were made throughout the middle ages, in the twelfth and thirteenth centuries they were often linked to accusations of heresy, and it is clear that women were active and vocal participants in the heterodox groups of that age. A Premonstratensian abbot writing against the Waldensians devoted a lengthy chapter to the scandal that women among them were allowed to preach, arguing that if the scriptures enjoined silence on women and subjection to their husbands, it was all the more inappropriate for them to preach to other men. Abundant evidence shows that among the Cathars, women commonly attained the highest spiritual station, becoming *perfectae* and administering the Cathar sacraments and preaching. Others joined together to live communally, working to support themselves, and entire convents of *perfectae* flourished in the south of France.

The similarity of these heretical women to the northern European beguines was noted by contemporaries, and led to denunciations and persecutions of both groups. But in reality the orthodox beguines of Flanders and the heretical women who lived communally in southern France may have been part of a monolithic change in the lives of medieval women, a renewed impetus toward participation and leadership in public life which found its readiest expression in the burgeoning religious movements of the twelfth and thirteenth centuries. And by facilitating new forms of economic organization and increasing the numbers of adherents to new religio-social doctrines, alterations in women's behavior were not only significant in themselves but in that they helped to determine the direction of medieval society in its entirety.

In the end any attempt to define the view of women resolves itself into an attempt to re-create the psychological climate within which most women lived out their lives. While many of the determinants of this climate are known, others remain to be discovered before the outlines of women's history become clear. Until then the historian must listen for the infrequent sound of women's voices in chronicles and other records. "I am but a woman," wrote a German nun in the eighth century whose name has not been preserved, "weak on account of the frailty of my sex, neither supported by the prerogatives of wisdom nor sustained by the consciousness of great power, yet impelled by earnestness of purpose . . ."

What unites these voices most consistently is a shared conviction of their place in the hierarchy of creation, below men and angels and yet above the lower animals. This condition they accepted as uniquely and appropriately their own, and the more learned they were the more eloquently they defined their role.

> For woman is weak, and looks to man that she may gain strength from him, as the moon receives its strength from the sun; wherefore is she subject to the man, and ought always to be prepared to serve him. . . .
>
> For when God looked upon man he was well pleased, for man was made in his image and likeness. . . . But at her creation woman partook of a mixture of the two [man and God]; she is a different creature, created through another than God, . . . The woman is therefore the creation of the man . . . and the man signifies the divinity, the woman the humanity, of the Son of God. The man therefore presides over the tribunal of the world, ruling all creatures, while the woman is under his mastery, and subject to him.[8]

The woman who wrote these words, Hildegard of Bingen, was among the most learned figures of the twelfth century, yet she saw no reason to question the status she described. The circumstances of Eve's creation, and her grave sin, proved the inferiority of all women, and attempts to redeem them were effectively opposed. For when it came to women, medieval perception lost its flexibility. From the age of the Montanists on, attempts to shape a countervision of women were drowned out or suppressed.

211

In the Dominican *Annals of Colmar*, the chronicler recorded that

> A virgin came from England, fair to look on and eloquent in speech, who said that she was the Holy Spirit, made incarnate for the redemption of women. And she baptized women in the name of the Father, the Son and herself.

What obstacles the Englishwoman who believed she was the Holy Spirit encountered during her ministry to redeem women are not recorded. But after her death her corpse was exhumed and burnt, and at least two of the women who believed in her died at the stake.

Chapter nine

EPILOGUE: A WEB OF VERITIES

Sometime in the second half of the fourteenth century an episcopal staff was made in England, probably for William of Wykeham, bishop of Winchester. The knop of the staff was elaborately formed with figures, architectural designs, tracery and enamels. Above a gallery was a miniature sculptured copy of Waltham Cross, probably made by a London goldsmith, and on top of this sat a little Gothic church, with rose windows and towers. Angels and saints filled the arched niches of the design, and in the crook was a figure of the bishop himself in profile, kneeling in prayer.

Like many representative medieval works of art, the crozier synthesized the vision of the craftsmen who made it. They determined the relative proportions of the carved figures to the architectural motifs, and although by now it was a commonplace of iconography they determined to include the miniaturized church. It was they who decided to mix the market cross with the church, biblical and angelic personages with the ordinary man carved in the crook. The multidimensional imagery, the overall symmetry and balance of the proportions were their work, and they bound all in a self-contained unity of design.

213

However their styles and personal experience differed, the goldsmiths and enamellers who made Bishop Wykeham's crozier shared a basic unity of vision. In the same way the medieval Europeans of the twelfth, thirteenth and fourteenth centuries held a common vision: a shared perceptual base, common predispositions of sight, and an agreed-on concept of reality. This vision was dynamic. It was in a sense re-formed with each new generation, and it varied in depth and detail from one individual to the next and from one decade to the next. But beyond differences of eras and regions the unchanging horizons of the medieval vision are discernible.

At their furthest bounds was the fuller reality of the enchanted world. Medieval men and women blended the evidence of their senses with firm convictions about the presence and power of unseen creation. Their concept of the real embraced much that we would now call imaginary; planes of truth we perceive as distinct and clashing they saw as concurrent parts of a harmonious whole.

To accommodate this understanding they engaged in a continuous vigil with the visible world, believing that from time to time it yielded evidence of the more powerful realm of the invisible. This vigil was continuously rewarded by messages, warnings, clarifications and revelations communicated to the visionary imagination. Most important, it was encouraged by the enduring belief that spiritual understanding was linked to visual acuity—that man's perception of God would ultimately come through the purification of his sight.

The union between seeing and knowing was reinforced by theology and mystical writings, and was part of the common fund of knowledge of educated men. Hugo Metellus, the classicizing canon of Toul, wrote of it in a letter which is a long paraphrase of Augustine. Cheerfully acknowledging the limitations of his own understanding, Metellus took courage from the great theologian he was citing. "How can I know God, if I do not even know myself?" he asked, but then added that "following Augustine, and with

Augustine . . . I, who am of no moment among the swans, may yet bawl out songs like a goose."

Human eyes cannot in their earthly state see God, Metellus wrote, since God has neither a body nor a physical location. But they may be trained to see him in things which do have substance and locality, just as whiteness is perceived through white objects and the sun is perceived in the brightness of the air. God was visible to human sight through Jesus, whose divinity was evident in a "remarkable external brightness":

> For if in Christ's face there appeared a marvellous glory and terrible brightness, which frightened the buyers and sellers and sent them fleeing from the temple, so much more will ineffable brightness blaze forth from Christ's glorified body which God will show to man.[1]

The same visual sensitivity that allowed human eyes to recognize the divinity in Jesus would ultimately be called on to receive in paradise the vision of God. But vision was crucial not only to piety but to all earthly affairs. Metaphors of sight run through every part of medieval life. If Nicholas of Cusa saw God as an all-seeing eye, Henry II's justiciar Ralph de Glanville was also called "the king's eye." And Adelard of Bath described astronomy allegorically as a maiden, "surrounded by shining splendor, her body all eyes."

The visionary mentality of medieval men and women is inescapable. It filled chronicles and popular works; it illumined the writings of scholars and poets. And it gave rise to a unique literary genre: the vision narrative.

In the mid-twelfth century an Irish knight named Tundale confided a vision he had experienced to a monk who wrote it out for him and called it "Tundale's Book on the Pains of Purgatory and Hell and the Joys of Paradise." The punishments of many kinds of sinners as well as the "fields of happiness and fountain of

215

life" provided for the blessed were revealed to him while he lay in a deathlike sleep. Then suddenly at his funeral the signs of life returned, and he asked for the communion wafer and wine. When he had eaten and drunk he began to praise God, "who had shown him so many trials and evils and then revived him to bring him back from the abyss." And immediately he gave away all he had to the poor, and vowed to bear the cross of penance for the rest of his life. All that he saw he later told to his monastic amanuensis, who transcribed from his account a complete journey through the landscape of heaven and hell.

It was an angel who guided Tundale's frightened soul through the shadowy terror of the valley of the murderers and traitors, along the narrow pass over the great sulphurous mountain, half ice and half fire, where vicious souls were impaled on demonic tridents, and across the slender bridge over the abyss where the souls of the proud were eternally humiliated in torment. Passing a huge beast with flaming eyes whose groaning belly held a thousand sufferers, once misers on earth, Tundale came to a whole herd of beasts like great towers, lowing terrifyingly and feeding on the souls of thieves. Gluttons and fornicators—both seculars and religious—followed, until the angel announced that all those they had seen were still awaiting divine judgment. They had been in purgatory, and were about to descend into hell.

Immediately they plunged into a cold horror, and an unbearably foul odor surrounded them in the blackness. The anguish of hell's tormented souls made even the angel despair; demons and the prince of darkness himself joined in punishing here those whom God had forsaken, and some who despite their good intent had been negligent in charity.

But then they came to the high gate of heaven, which opened on a fair field, pleasing and full of light and the smell of flowers, and saw the crowd of souls who dwelt there, knowing no night and drinking forever from the fountain of life. Beyond these were the faithful spouses, then the martyrs and those vowed to continence. Their faces splendid as the sun at mid-day, these had golden hair and jeweled crowns, and stood just below the monks and nuns in order of holiness. On the highest levels were the builders and defenders of the church, the virgin Mary, and the nine orders of angels; and last of all in a burst of ecstatic patriotism Tundale glimpsed the patron of Ireland, St. Patrick.

Tundale's spiritual cosmology was informed by a definable world view—an all-encompassing web of interlocking truths that accounted for all existence. It wove the Neoplatonic view of created beings and Christian teleology into a complex visionary synthesis. This synthesis included both corporeal and noncorporeal beings, occupying appropriate planes in a vast retributive scheme. The familiar design of earthly geography—its mountains, lakes and meadows—formed the backdrop for this drama; Christian morality dictated its scenario.

What Tundale saw was nothing less than a visual distillation of ultimate truth, played out in a dimension outside time. Yet this distillation was not in fact independent either of time or of earthly affairs. It was intimately linked to the chain of human lifetimes that stretched backward to Adam and forward to earth's last man. The events of hell and purgatory were the final sum of all earthly sin; those of paradise the essence of all earthly virtue. No corner of history was omitted from this overarching logic; judged against it, the present too took on new meanings.

Tundale's vision was one representation of the medieval design of reality. But that design had multiple identities, and could be expressed in a variety of ways. An "Apology" added to Tundale's account by a later medieval writer made this clear:

> If anyone should object about the foregoing narrative, judging it to be ridiculous, and if he should argue that it is hardly probable that there are corporeal punishments or beasts or mountains or bridges in hell,

217

or other things described there, let him be reminded that even in the scriptures the pains of hell are described by corporeal similes. . . . Let it therefore not disturb you that both spiritual and corporeal things are mixed in the foregoing work; for just as corporeal things are compared to physical sight, so spiritual things are compared to the understanding of the soul which has cast off the body.

Therefore once he returned to his body, the things seen by the knight's soul—the spiritual torments and the terrors of punishment he endured—could not except through corporeal similes be explained to men who use their physical senses.[2]

Only by an effort of the imagination can we who perceive a controlled, atomistic and one-dimensional world step into the chaotic, holistic and multidimensional reality of the middle ages. Though there are signs of change the mid-twentieth century still believes in the one-dimensional perception we call "objective reality." We assume that the single plane of sensate awareness is the seat of truth; for us truth is bound up with sensory reality. But our idea of reality is of a fleeting and transitory thing—the confusion of experience a person accumulates in his lifetime, and that dies with him. Our concept of truth is bound not only to sensation but to mortality.

In the middle ages truth was defined differently. It was not wedded to temporal existence, to the world of individual variables. To a medieval man or woman the world of sensation was only one part of a much vaster pattern of unchanging and immortal reality that stretched out far beyond the boundaries of known time. Day-to-day experience occupied a finite plane in this infinite scheme; it was only a pause between two eternities. The visionary imagination linked the finite with the infinite, and the imminent possibility of such a link made medieval people watchful for visions.

Visions, a visionary worldview, and distinctive habits of mental

and corporeal sight were norms of medieval life. But to acknowledge that their sensory universe was different from ours is only the
first step toward a deeper discovery: that of the profound strange-
ness of the past. For what keeps us most in ignorance of history is
the fact that we know too much about it that is wrong. It is the
assumption that basic human experience does not vary from one
age to another, and that the twelfth century shared a common
perceptual vocabulary with the twentieth. To approach the mani-
fold reality of the middle ages is to realize that this judgment is
flawed to the point of serious distortion. Understanding the past
means first discarding these inaccuracies as well as others built up
through literary and cinematic stereotypes. It means trying to
re-create a holistic view of existence that has not been generally
held for four centuries. Most important, it means recapturing a
perception of ideas and events in terms of an all-encompassing
design.

To live in medieval Europe was to appreciate that the events of
ordinary experience were linked irremediably to the past and the
future, and that beliefs and judgments were inseparable from a vast
network of complementary ideas. Strictly speaking, no one in the
middle ages sought to discover truth, but merely to illuminate the
obscurer parts of a web of verities whose general outlines were
already clear. Here the educated and the illiterate were on
common ground. Both looked at experience from the viewpoint of
someone putting together a jigsaw puzzle in which each piece bore
clues to its place in the whole. Both allowed the shape of what had
already been formed to determine the usefulness of the odd pieces.
The educated person's puzzle was more diverse, intellectually as
well as intuitively ordered; that of the uneducated was simpler and
more subjective. But their vision of the shape of truth was one.

Notes

CHAPTER ONE

1. Macrobius, *Commentary on the Dream of Scipio*, tr. William H. Stahl, Records of Civilization, XLVIII (New York, 1952), 143.
2. *Ibid.*, p. 145, citing *Iliad* 8,19.
3. A. J. Grant, "Twelve Medieval Ghost Stories," *Yorkshire Archaeological Journal*, XXVII (1923–24), 365–366.
4. *In Isiam*, Lib. xi, ch. 40.
5. *Differentiae*, 2,41.
6. William Durand of Mende, *Rationale divinorum officiorum*, tr. John Neale and Benjamin Webb, 3rd ed. (London, 1906), p. 17.
7. Roger Bacon, *Opus majus*, tr. Robert Belle Burke (Philadelphia, 1928), I, 410, 418.

CHAPTER TWO

1. *Matthew Paris' English History*, tr. J. A. Giles, 3 vols. (London, 1852–54), III, 61.
2. Giraldus Cambrensis, *The Itinerary of Archbishop Baldwin through Wales*, tr. Sir Richard Moore (London, 1806), pp. 32–33.
3. *The Chronicle of John of Worcester*, ed. J. R. H. Weaver, Anecdota Oxoniensa, Medieval and Modern Series, 4th Series, part 13 (Oxford, 1908), p. 31.

4. *The Conquest of Lisbon*, ed. and tr. Charles W. David, Records of Civilization, XXIV (New York, 1936), 89–91.

5. Peter the Venerable, *De miraculis*, ed. J.-P. Migne, *Patrologia Latina*, 189 (Paris, 1890), col. 939.

6. Macrobius, *op. cit.*, p. 118.

7. George B. Parks, *The English Traveller in Italy*, Storie e Letteratura, XLVI (Rome, 1954), 210.

8. *Selected Letters of Pope Innocent III concerning England*, ed. C. R. Cheney and W. H. Semple (London and New York, 1953), p. 29.

9. H. L. Ward, *Catalogue of Romances in the Department of Manuscripts in the British Museum* (London, 1893), II, 493.

10. Eadmer, *Vita sancti Anselmi*, ed. and tr. Richard Southern (London and New York, 1962), pp. 12–13.

11. Roger Bacon, *Opus majus*, tr. Burke, II, 580.

12. Nicholas of Cusa, *Vision of God*, tr. Emma Gurney Salter (London & Toronto, 1928), pp. 106 ff.

13. Angela of Foligno, *Le Livre des visions et instructions*, tr. Ernest Hello (Paris, 1914), pp. 148–149.

CHAPTER THREE

1. *Epistolae Hugonis Metelli*, ed. C. Hugo, *Sacra antiquitatis monumenta* (Saint Dié, 1731), II, 312.

2. *The Letters of Arnulf of Lisieux*, ed. Frank Barlow, Camden Society, 3rd Series, XLI (London, 1939), 21–22.

3. Matthew Paris, I, 143.

4. *Selected Letters of Pope Innocent III*, pp. 17 ff.

5. Aubrey Gwynn, S. J., "Archbishop Fitzralph and George of Hungary," *Studies, An Irish Quarterly Review*, XXIV (1935), 569.

CHAPTER FOUR

1. Jacques de Vitry, *Exempla*, ed. F. Crane (London, 1890), p. 112.

2. C. R. Owst, *Literature and Pulpit in Medieval England* (New York, 1933), pp. 29–30.

3. *Itinéraires russes en Orient*, ed. and tr. Sofia Khitrovo (Paris, 1889; reprint Osnabrück, 1966), pp. 11–12.

NOTES

4. Emile Mâle, "L'Art français de la fin du moyen âge: l'idée de la mort et la danse macabre," *Revue des deux mondes*, XXXII (1906), 658.

5. Matthew Paris, I, 66.

6. Georges de Lagarde, *La Naissance de l'esprit laïque au déclin du moyen âge*, 3rd ed. (Louvain, 1956), I, 202.

7. Bernard Gui, *Practica inquisitionis heretice pravitatis*, trans. in Carolly Erickson, *The Records of Medieval Europe* (Garden City, 1971), pp. 278–279.

CHAPTER FIVE

1. Matthew Paris, III, 347.

2. James Bryce, *The Holy Roman Empire*, 3rd ed. (London, 1871), 305–306.

3. Matthew Paris, II, 110–112.

CHAPTER SIX

1. Léon Gautier, "L'idée politique dans les chansons de geste," *Revue des questions historiques*, VII (1869), 101.

2. *Ibid.*, p. 88.

3. Charles W. David, *Robert Curthose, Duke of Normandy*, Harvard Historical Studies, XXV (Cambridge, Mass., 1920), 188.

4. *Annals of Roger of Hoveden*, tr. H. T. Riley, 2 vols. (London, 1853), I, 218.

CHAPTER SEVEN

1. E. L. G. Stones, "The Folvilles of Ashby-Folville, Leicestershire, and Their Associates in Crime, 1326–1341," *Transactions of the Royal Historical Society*, 5th Series, VII (1957), 135.

2. *Chronicle of Novgorod*, tr. Neville Forbes and Robert Mitchell, Camden Society, 3rd Series, XXV (London, 1914), 134.

3. Quoted in M. H. Keen, *The Outlaws of Medieval Legend* (London, 1961), pp. 55–56.

4. J. A. Raftis, *Tenure and Mobility: Studies in the Social History of the Medieval English Village*, Studies and Texts, VIII (Toronto, 1964), 96 n.

CHAPTER EIGHT

1. *Dissuasio*, ed. Wright, p. 151.
2. Quoted in A. J. Denomy, "Fin'Amors: The Pure Love of the Troubadours, Its Amorality, and Possible Source," *Mediaeval Studies*, VII (1945), 144.
3. Quoted in Léon Gautier, *La Chevalerie* (Paris, 1884), p. 350.
4. Rather of Verona, *Praeloquia*, ed. J.-P. Migne, *Patrologia Latina*, 136, 191.
5. *The Letters of Abelard and Heloise*, tr. C. K. Scott Moncrieff (New York, 1926), pp. 159–160.
6. LaMarche, *La Chaire française*, 2nd ed. (Paris, 1886), p. 429.
7. Guibert de Nogent, *De laude S. Mariae*, ed. J.-P. Migne, *Patrologia Latina*, 156 (Paris, 1880), 1001–1002.
8. Hildegard of Bingen, *Liber divinorum operibus simplicis hominis*, ed. J.-P. Migne, *Patrologia Latina*, 197 (Paris, 1882), 885.

CHAPTER NINE

1. *Epistolae Hugonis Metelli*, p. 403.
2. *Visio Tnudali*, ed. Oskar Schade (Halle, 1869), p. 23.

Suggestions for further reading

The following list has two purposes. First, it credits source texts and interpretive works quoted or extensively used in the preparation of this book. And second, it serves as a guide for students who may want to pursue further the themes discussed here. Where available, English translations of primary sources are cited. Many non-English titles have been omitted from the list of secondary works.

PRIMARY SOURCES

Alan of Lille. *The Anticlaudian.* Tr. by William H. Cornog. Philadelphia: University of Pennsylvania Press, 1930.

————. *The Complaint of Nature.* Tr. by Douglas Moffat. Yale Studies in English, XXXVI. New York: Holt, 1908.

Alexander III. *Epistolae.* In *Patrologia Latina,* 200. Ed. by J.-P. Migne. Paris: Garnier Frères, 1855. cols. 70–151.

Anderson, M. O. *A Scottish Chronicle Known as the "Chronicle of Holyrood."* Scottish History Society, 3rd Series, XXX. Edinburgh: University Press, 1938.

Angela of Foligno. *Le Livre des visions et instructions.* Tr. by Ernest Hello. Paris: A. Tralin, 1914.

Arnulf of Lisieux. *Letters of Arnulf of Lisieux.* Ed. by Frank Barlow. Camden Society, 3rd Series, XLI. London: Offices of the Royal Society, 1939.

Atthill, William, ed. *Documents Relating to the Foundation and*

Antiquities of the Collegiate Church of Middleham. Camden Society, 1st Series, XXXVIII. London: Nichols, 1846.

Augustine of Hippo. *De Genesi ad litteram.* Vienna: Tempsky, 1894.

Bacon, Roger. *Communium naturalium.* In *Opera hactenus inedita,* fasc. 4–5. Ed. by Robert Steele. Oxford: Clarendon Press, 1909.

————. *De multiplicatione specierum.* In *Opus majus.* Ed. by Henry Bridges. London: Williams and Norgate, 1900.

————: *Opus majus.* Ed. and tr. by Robert Belle Burke. Philadelphia: University of Pennsylvania Press, 1928.

————. *Opus minus.* In *Opera quaedam hactenus inedita,* II. Ed. by J. S. Brewer. London: Longman, 1859.

————. *Opus tertium.* Ed. by A. J. Little. British Society of Franciscan Studies, IV. Aberdeen: The University Press, 1912.

Bartholomeus Anglicus. *De proprietatibus rerum.* Tr. by John of Trevisa, 1601. Reprinted, Frankfurt: M. Minerva, 1964.

Bernard of Clairvaux. *Epistolae.* In *Patrologia Latina,* 182. Ed. by J.-P. Migne. Paris: Garnier Frères, 1879. cols. 67–720.

————. *Vita S. Malachiae.* In *Patrologia Latina,* 182. Ed. by J.-P. Migne. Paris: Garnier Frères, 1879. cols. 1073–1118.

Blaauw, W. H. "Letters of Edward, Prince of Wales, Written in Sussex in the Year 1305," *Sussex Archaeological Collections,* II (1849), 80–98.

Catalani, Jordanes. *The Wonders of the East.* Tr. by Henry Yule. Hakluyt Society, 1st Series, XXXI. London: Richards, 1863.

Caterina of Genoa. *Treatise on Purgatory.* Tr. by Charlotte Balfour and Helen Irvine. London: Sheed and Ward, 1946.

Chaytor, H. J., ed. *Six Vaudois Poems.* Cambridge, England: Cambridge University Press, 1930.

The Chronicle of Muntaner. Tr. by Lady Goodeneough. Hakluyt Society, 2nd Series, XLVII. London: 1920.

Chronicle of Novgorod. Tr. by Neville Forbes and Robert Mitchell. Camden Society, 3rd Series, XXV. London: Offices of the Royal Historical Society, 1914.

Chronicles of the Crusades, Being Contemporary Narratives of Richard of Devizes and Geoffrey de Vinsauf. Tr. by J. A. Giles. London: Bohn, 1848.

Conrad of Eberbach. *Exordium magnum Cisterciense sive narratio de initio Cisterciensis Ordinis. Series scriptorum S. Ordinis Cisterciensis.* Rome: Editiones Cistercienses, 1961.

Contemporaries of Marco Polo. Consisting of the Travel Records of William of Rubruck, John of Pian de Carpini, Friar Odoric, and the Oriental Travels of Rabbi Benjamin of Tudela. Ed. by Manuel Komroff. New York: Boni & Liveright, 1928.

Curtis, Edmund. "Unpublished letters from Richard II in Ireland," *Proceedings of the Royal Irish Academy*, XXXVII (1924–27), Section C, 276–303.

Dá Cherda, Mac, tr. "Adamnán's Vision," *Fraser's Magazine*, n.s., III (1871), 184–194.

David, Charles W., ed. and tr. *The Conquest of Lisbon.* Records of Civilization, XXIV. New York: Columbia University Press, 1936.

Desclot, Bernardo. *Chronicle of the Reign of King Pedro III of Aragon (1276–1285).* Tr. by F. L. Critchlow. Princeton: Princeton University Press, 1928–34. 2 vols.

Documents inédits concernant la province de Picardie. Mémoires de la Société des Antiquaires de Picardie, VI. Amiens: Dumoulin, 1865.

Eadmer. *Vita Sancti Anselmi.* Ed. and tr. by Richard Southern. Nelson's Medieval Texts. London and New York: Thomas Nelson, 1962.

Eudes of Rouen. *The Registry of Eudes of Rouen.* Ed. by Jeremiah O'Sullivan. Tr. by Sidney M. Brown. Records of Civilization, LXXII. New York: Columbia University Press, 1964.

Eusebius of Caesarea. *Church History.* Tr. by A. C. McGiffert. In *A Select Library of Nicene and Post-Nicene Fathers*, 2nd Series, I. Ed. by Philip Schaff and Henry Wace. New York: Christian Literature Society, 1890.

Fitz-Thedmar, A. *Chronicles of the Mayors and Sheriffs of London, A.D. 1188 to A.D. 1274.* Tr. by H. T. Riley. London: Trübner, 1863.

Gervase of Canterbury. *On the Burning and Repair of the Church at Canterbury in the year 1174.* Ed. by Charles Cotton. Friends of the Canterbury Cathedral. Canterbury Papers, III. Cambridge, England: University Press, 1932.

Giraldus Cambrensis. *The Itinerary of Archbishop Baldwin through Wales.* Tr. by Sir Richard Hoare. London: Culmer, 1806.

Glanville-Richards, W. V. S. *Records of the Anglo-Norman House of Glanville.* London: Mitchell, 1883.

Grant, A. J. "Twelve Medieval Ghost Stories," *Yorkshire Archaeological Journal*, XXVII (1923–1924), 363–379.

Guibert de Nogent. *De laude S. Mariae.* In *Patrologia Latina*, 156. Ed. by J.-P. Migne. Paris: Garnier Frères, 1880. cols. 537–578.

————. *De pignoribus sanctorum.* In *Patrologia Latina*, 156. Ed. by J.-P. Migne. Paris: Garnier Frères, 1880. cols. 607–674.

Halphen, Louis, ed. *Recueil d'annales angevines et vendomoises.* Collection de textes pour servir à l'étude et à l'enseignement de l'histoire, fasc. 37. Paris: Picard, 1903.

Halliwell, J., ed. *The Chronicle of William de Rishanger. The Miracles of Simon de Montfort.* Camden Society, 1st Series, XV. London: Nichols, 1840.

Hennessy, William. "MacConglinny's vision; a humorous satire," *Fraser's Magazine*, n.s., XIII (Sept., 1873), 298–323.

Hildegard of Bingen. *Liber divinorum operibus simplicis hominis.* In *Patrologia Latina*, 197. Ed. by J.-P. Migne. Paris: Garnier Frères, 1882. cols. 739–1036.

Hitti, Phillip K., tr. *An Arab-Syrian Gentleman in the Period of the Crusades. Memoirs of Usamah Ibn-Munqidh.* New York: Columbia University Press, 1929.

Hugh of Saint Victor. *Adnotatiunculae elucidatoriae in Joelem prophetam.* In *Patrologia Latina*, 175. Ed. by J.-P. Migne. Paris: Garnier Frères, 1855. cols. 355–356.

Hugonis Metelli. *Epistolae.* In *Sacra antiquitatis monumenta historica, dogmatica, diplomatica*, II. Ed. by C. L. Hugo. Saint Dié: J. Charlot, 1731.

Innocent III. *Selected Letters of Pope Innocent III concerning England.* Ed. and tr. C. R. Cheney and W. H. Semple. Nelson's Medieval Texts. London and New York: Thomas Nelson, 1953.

[Isidore of Seville.] *An Encyclopedist of the Dark Ages.* Tr. by Ernest Bréhaut. Studies in History, Economics and Public Law, XLVIII, no. 1. New York: Columbia University Press, 1912.

Jacques de Vitry. *The Exempla, or Illustrative Stories from the Sermones Vulgares of Jacques de Vitry.* Ed. by Thomas Crane. Folklore Society Publications, XXVI. London: Nutt, 1890.

John of Fordun. *John of Fordun's Chronicle of the Scottish Nation.* Tr. by William Shene. The Historians of Scotland, IV. Edinburgh: Edmonton & Douglas, 1872.

Johnston, R. C. *The Crusade and Death of Richard I.* Anglo-Norman Texts, XVII. Oxford: Blackwell, 1961.

Jordan Fantosme. *Chronicle of the War between the English and Scots in 1173 and 1174.* Tr. by Francisque Michel. Surtees Society Publications, II. London: Nichols, 1840.

Khitrovo, Sofia, ed. and tr. *Itinéraries russes en Orient.* Société de l'Orient Latin, 1889. Reprint, Osnabrück: Zeller, 1966.

Knox, Ronald, ed. and tr. *The Miracles of King Henry VI.* Introduction by Shane Leslie. Cambridge, England: Cambridge University Press, 1923.

Krey, A. C., ed. and tr. *The First Crusade: The Accounts of Eye-Witnesses.* Princeton: Princeton University Press, 1921.

Latini, Brunetto. *Le Livre du Tresor.* Ed. by Francis J. Carmody. University of California Publications in Modern Philology, XXII. Berkeley: University of California Press, 1948.

The Letters of Abelard and Heloise. Tr. by C. K. Scott Moncrieff. New York: Alfred A. Knopf, 1926.

Macrobius. *Commentary on the Dream of Scipio.* Tr. by William H. Stahl. Records of Civilization, XLVIII. New York: Columbia University Press, 1952.

Major, Richard Henry. *Life of Prince Henry of Portugal, Surnamed the Navigator; and Its Results: Comprising the Discovery, Within a Century, of Half the World.* London: Asher, 1868.

Marbod of Rennes. In *Anglo-Norman Lapidaries.* Ed. by Paul Studer and Joan Evans. Paris: Champion, 1924.

Matthew Paris. *Matthew Paris' English History.* Tr. by J. A. Giles. 3 vols. London: Bohn, 1852–54.

Markham, Sir Clements, ed. and tr. *Book of the Knowledge of All the Kingdoms, Lands and Lordships that Are in the World. . . . Written by a Spanish Franciscan in the Mid-Fourteenth Century.* Hakluyt Society Publications, 2nd Series, XXIX. London: 1912.

Meyer, Kuno, ed. *The Vision of MacCongline.* London, 1892.

————, ed. and tr. *The Voyage of Bran, Son of Febal.* London: Grimm, 1895.

The Monks of Kublai Khan, Emperor of China, or The History of the Life and Travels of Rabban Sawma, Envoy and Plenipotentiary of the Mongol Khans . . . and Markos Who as Mar Yahbhallaha III Became Patriarch of the Nestorian Church in Asia. Tr. by Sir E. A. Wallis Budge. London: The Religious Tract Society, 1928.

Morris, Richard, ed. *Legends of the Holy Rood.* Early English Text Society, 1st Series, XLVI. London: Trübner, 1871.

229

Myrc, John. *Instruction for Parish Priests.* Ed. by Edward Peacock. Early English Text Society, XXXI. London: Trübner, 1868.

Napier, Arthur S., ed. *History of the Holy Rood-tree.* Early English Text Society, 1st Series, CIII. London: Trübner, 1894.

Nicholas of Cusa. *Vision of God.* Tr. by Emma Gurney Salter. London and Toronto: Dent, 1928.

Otto of Freising. *The Deeds of Frederick Barbarossa.* Tr. by Charles Mierow. Records of Civilization, XLIX. New York: Columbia University Press, 1953.

Paget, Valerian, ed. *The Revelations to the Monk of Evesham Abbey.* New York: McBride, 1909.

Peter the Venerable. *Contra Petrobrusianos haereticos.* In *Patrologia Latina,* 189. Ed. by J.-P. Migne. Paris: Garnier Frères, 1890.

———. *De miraculis.* In *Patrologia Latina,* 189. Ed. by J.-P. Migne. Paris: Garnier Frères, 1890. cols. 851–952.

Pierre d'Ailly. *Imago mundi.* Tr. by Edwin Keever. Wilmington, North Carolina: Imprint Co., 1948.

Raine, James, ed. *Historians of the Church of York and Its Archbishops.* Rolls Series, LXXI. London: Longmans, 1879–94.

Ralph of Diceto. *Ymagines historiarum.* Ed. by William Stubbs. London: Longmans, 1876. 2 vols.

Richard of Devizes. *The Chronicle of Richard of Devizes of the Time of King Richard I.* Ed. and tr. by J. T. Appleby. Nelson's Medieval Texts. London and New York: Nelson, 1963.

Rigord, Eudes. *Œuvres de Rigord et de Guillaume le Breton, historiens de Philippe Auguste.* Société de l'Histoire de France. Paris: Nogent, 1882–85. 2 vols.

Riley, H. T., ed. *Memorials of London and London Life in the Thirteenth, Fourteenth and Fifteenth Centuries.* London: Longmans, Green, 1868.

Robert of Clari. *The Conquest of Constantinople.* Tr. by E. H. McNeal. Records of Civilization, XXIII. New York: Columbia University Press, 1936.

Roger of Hoveden. *Annals of Roger of Hoveden.* Tr. by H. T. Riley. London: Bohn, 1853. 2 vols.

Sanuto, Marino, called "Torsello." *Secrets for True Crusaders to Help Them Recover the Holy Land.* Tr. by Aubrey Stewart. Palestine Pilgrims' Text Society Library, XII, no. 2. London: Palestine Pilgrims' Text Society, 1896.

Schade, Oskar, ed. *Visio Tnudali.* Halle: Libreria Orphanotrophei, 1869.

Stevenson, Joseph, ed. and tr. "Chronicle of the Isle of Man," *Church Historians of England,* V (1858), 383–405.

Stokes, Whitley. "Adamnán's Second Vision," *Revue celtique,* XII (1891), 420–443.

Thomas Aquinas. *De occultis operibus naturae.* Ed. and tr. by Joseph McAllister. Catholic University of America Philosophical Studies, XLII. Washington, D.C.: Catholic University Press, 1939.

Vielliard, J., ed. *Codex Calixtinus. Liber Quintus. Le Guide du pèlerin du S. Jacques de Compostelle.* Tr. into French by J. Vielliard. Bibliothèque de l'École des Hautes Études Hispaniques. Mâcon: Protat, 1963.

Walter of Guisborough. *The Chronicle of Walter of Guisborough.* Ed. by Harry Rothwell. Camden Society, 3rd Series, LXXXIX. London: Offices of the Royal Historical Society, 1957.

Walter Map. *De nugis curialium.* Tr. by M. R. James. Cymmrodorion Record Series, no. IX. London: Honorable Society of Cymmrodorion, 1923.

William Durand of Mende. *Rationale divinorum officiorum.* Tr. by John Neale and Benjamin Webb. 3rd ed. London: Gibbings, 1906.

———. *The Sacred Vestments.* Tr. by T. H. Passmore. London: Sampson Law, 1899.

William of Malmesbury. *The Marvels of Rome.* Tr. by Francis M. Nichols. London: no publisher indicated, 1889.

Worcester, John of. *The Chronicle of John of Worcester.* Ed. by J. R. H. Weaver. Anecdota Oxoniensa. Medieval and Modern Series, 4th Series, part 13. Oxford: Clarendon Press, 1908.

Zurara, G. E. de. *Conquests and Discoveries of Henry the Navigator.* Ed. by Virginia de Castro e Alameda. Tr. by Bernard Miall. London: Allen & Unwin, 1936.

SECONDARY WORKS

Adler, Elkan N., ed. *Jewish Travellers.* In *The Broadway Travellers,* XXIV. Ed. by Sir E. D. Ross and Eileen Power. London: Routledge, 1930.

Allworthy, T. B. *Women in the Apostolic Church: A Critical Study of the Evidence in the New Testament for the Prominence of Women in Early Christianity.* Cambridge, England: W. Heffer & Sons, 1917.

Arnheim, Rudolf. *Visual Thinking.* Berkeley: University of California Press, 1969.

Atiya, A. S. *Egypt and Aragon: Embassies and Diplomatic Correspondence between 1300 and 1330.* Abhandlungen für die Kunde des Morgenlandes, 23:7. Leipzig: Brockhaus, 1938.

Ault, W. O. "Village By-laws by Common Consent," *Speculum,* XXIX (1954), 378–394.

Baltrušaitis, Jurgis. *Le Moyen Age fantastique.* Paris: Armand Colin, 1955.

Barraclough, Geoffrey. *Papal Provisions.* Oxford: Basil Blackwell, 1935.

Becker, Ernest J. *Contributions to the Comparative Study of Medieval Visions of Heaven and Hell.* Baltimore: J. Murphy, 1899.

Bellamy, J. G. "The Coterel Gang: An Anatomy of a Band of Fourteenth-Century Criminals," *English Historical Review,* LXXIX (1964), 698–717.

———. *Crime and Public Order in England in the Late Middle Ages.* Toronto: University of Toronto Press, 1973.

Beresford, M. W. *The Lost Villages of Medieval England.* New York: Philosophical Library, 1954.

Berkeley, George. *A New Theory of Vision and Other Writings.* London: Dent; New York: Dutton, 1954.

Berry, Henry F. "Of the use of signs in the ancient monasteries," *Journal of the Royal Society of Antiquaries of Ireland,* 5th Series, II (1892), 107–125.

Beuzart, P. *Les Hérésies pendant le moyen âge et la réforme dans la région de Douai, d'Arras et du pays d'Alleu.* Paris: H. Champion, 1912.

Bloch, Marc L. *The Ile de France; the Country around Paris.* Tr. by J. E. Anderson. Ithaca, New York: Cornell University Press, 1971.

———. *Rois et serfs; un chapitre d'histoire capetienne.* Paris: Champion, 1920.

———. *Les Rois thaumaturges; étude sur le caractère surnaturel attribué à la puissance royale, particulièrement en France et en Angleterre.* Paris: A. Colin, 1961.

Boswell, C. S. *An Irish Precursor to Dante; a Study on the Vision of Heaven and Hell Ascribed to the Eighth Century Irish Saint Adamnán.* Grimm Library, XVIII. London: Nutt, 1908.

Brémond, H. *Histoire littéraire du sentiment religieux en France depuis la fin des guerres de religion jusqu'à nos jours.* Paris: Bloud & Gay, 1916–36. 11 vols.

Brentano, Robert. *The Two Churches: England and Italy in the Thirteenth Century.* Princeton: Princeton University Press, 1968.

Bretschneider, E. *Notes on Chinese Medieval Travellers to the West.* Shanghai: American Presbyterian Mission Press; London: Trübner, 1875.

————. *On the Knowledge Possessed by the Ancient Chinese of the Arab and Arabian Colonies, and Other Western Countries, Mentioned in Chinese Books.* London: Trübner, 1871.

Brooke, C. N. L. "Gregorian Reform in Action: Clerical Marriage in England, 1050–1200," *The Cambridge Historical Journal,* XII (1956), 1–21.

Browe, Peter, S. J. *Beiträge zur Sexualethik des Mittelalters.* Breslau: Müller & Seiffert, 1932.

————. *De ordaliis.* Pontifical Gregorian University. Textes et Documents, Series Theologica, IV and XI. Rome: Gregorian University Press, 1932, 1933.

Brown, William. "Trial by Combat," *Yorkshire Archaeological Journal,* 23 (1915), 300–312.

Brundage, J. "The Crusader's Wife: A Canonistic Quandary," *Studia Gratiana. Collectanea Stephen Kuttner,* XII (1967), 425–441.

————. "The Crusader's Wife Revisited," *Studia Gratiana. Collectanea Stephen Kuttner,* XIV (1967), 240–251.

Bryce, James. *The Holy Roman Empire.* 3rd ed., rev. London: Macmillan, 1871.

Byrne, E. H. "Easterners in Genoa," *Journal of the American Oriental Society,* 38 (1918), 176–187.

Castro, Philip de. "Travelling expenses in the thirteenth century," tr. by Joseph Hunter, in *Retrospective Review and Historical and Antiquarian Magazine,* 2nd Series, I (1827), 269–276, 465–469.

Cauwenbergh, Étienne van. *Les Pèlerinages expiatoires et judiciaires dans le droit communal de la Belgique au moyen âge.* Recueil de Travaux, Conférence d'histoire et de philologie, XLVIII. Louvain: Université de Louvain, 1922.

Clagett, Marshall, Gaines Post, and Robert Reynolds, eds. *Twelfth-Century Europe and the Foundations of Modern Society.* Madison: University of Wisconsin Press, 1966.

Constable, Giles. "The Second Crusade as Seen by Contemporaries," *Traditio*, 9 (1953).

Coulton, G. G. "A Visitation of the Archdeaconry of Totnes in 1342," *English Historical Review*, 26 (1911), 108–123.

Cox, J. C. *The Sanctuaries and Sanctuary Seekers of Medieval England*. London: Allen, 1911.

David, Charles W. *Robert Curthose, Duke of Normandy*. Harvard Historical Studies, XXV. Cambridge, Mass.: Harvard University Press, 1920.

Dawson, Christopher. *The Mongol Mission*. London and New York: Sheed and Ward, 1955.

Dejob, Charles. *La Foi religieuse en Italie au XIVème siècle*. Paris: Albert Fontemoing, 1906.

Delaruelle, Étienne, E.-R. Labande, and Paul Ourliac. *L'Église au temps du Grand Schisme et de la crise conciliaire*. Histoire de l'Église, XIV. Paris: Bloud & Gay, 1962–64.

Delhaye, Philippe. "Le Dossier anti-matrimonial de l'*Adversus Jovinianum* et son influence sur quelques écrits latins du XII siècle," *Mediaeval Studies*, XIII (1951), 65–86.

Delisle, Leopold. "Des Revenus publics en Normandie au XIIème siècle," *Bibliothèque de l'École des Chartes*, 3rd Series, I (1849), 400–451.

Denis, Ferdinand. *Le Monde enchanté; cosmographie et histoire naturelle fantastique du moyen âge*. Paris: A. Fournier, 1843.

Denomy, A. J. "An Inquiry into the Origin of Courtly Love," *Mediaeval Studies*, VI (1944), 175–260.

———. "Fin'Amors: the Pure Love of the Troubadours, Its Amorality, and Possible Source," *Mediaeval Studies*, VII (1945), 139–207.

Dept, G. G. *Les Influences angloises et françaises dans le comté de Flandre au début du XIIème siècle*. Université de Gand. Recueil de travaux, Faculté de philosophie et lettres, fasc. 59. Gand: Van Rysselberghe et Rombaut, 1928.

———. "Les Marchands flamands et le roi d'Angleterre," *Revue du Nord*, XII (1926).

Despois, L. *Histoire de l'autorité royale dans le comté de Nivernais*. Paris: Université de Paris, 1912.

Dickinson, John. "The Medieval Conception of Kingship and Some of its Limitations, as Developed in the Policraticus," *Speculum*, (1926), 308–337.

Dimier, A. "Violences, rixes et homicides chez les cisterciens," *Revue des Sciences Religieuses*, XLVI (1972), 38–57.

Dobiache-Rojdestvensky, Olga. *La Vie paroissiale en France au XIIIème siècle d'après les actes episcopaux.* Paris: Picard, 1911.

Doherty, J. J. "Bells, their origin, uses and inscriptions," *Archaeological Journal*, XLVIII (1891), 45–64.

Dondaine, Antoine, O.P. "Les Actes du concile albigeois de Saint Félix de Caraman," *Miscellanea Giovanni Mercati*, V. Studi e Testi, 125. Città del Vaticana: Biblioteca Apostolica Vaticana, 1946.

———. "La Hiérarchie cathare en Italie," *Archivum Fratrum Praedicatorum*, XX (1950).

———. *Un Traité néo-manicheen du douzième siècle: Le Liber de duo principiis, suivi d'un fragment de rituel cathare.* Rome: Istituto Storico Domenicano, 1939.

Dubois, Philippe, *Les Asseurements au XIIIème siècle dans nos villes du Nord; recherches sur le droit de vengeance.* Paris: A. Rousseau, 1900.

Duby, Georges. "Dans la France du nordouest au XIIème siècle: les 'jeunes,' dans la société aristocratique," *Annales: Economies, Sociétés, Civilisations*, XIX (1964), 835–846.

Dufour, Charles. "Situation financière des villes de Picardie sous Saint Louis," *Mémoires de la Société des Antiquaires de Picardie*, 2nd Series, V (1858), 583–692.

Eckenstein, Lina. *Woman under Monasticism.* Cambridge, England: Cambridge University Press, 1896.

Eisler, Robert. "Danse Macabre," *Traditio*, VI (1948), 187–225.

Engdahl, David E. "English Marriage Conflicts; Law Before the Time of Bracton," *The American Journal of Comparative Law*, XV (1966–67), 109–135.

Evans, Joan. *Magical Jewels in the Middle Ages and Renaissance.* Oxford: Clarendon Press, 1922.

Eyton, R. W. *Court, Household and Itinerary of King Henry II, Instancing also the Chief Agents and Adversaries of the King in His Governments, Diplomacy and Strategies.* London: Taylor, 1878.

Fliche, Augustin. *La Réforme grégorienne et la reconquête chrétienne.* Histoire de l'Église, VIII. Paris: Bloud & Gay, 1950.

———, R. Foreville and J. Rousset. *Du Premier Concile du Latran à l'avènement d'Innocent III*. Histoire de l'Église, IX. Paris: Bloud & Gay, 1946.

————, Christine Thouzellier and Yvonne Azais. *La Chrétienté romaine*. Histoire de l'Église, X. Paris: Bloud & Gay, 1950.

Forest, André and F. Van Steenberghen. *Le Mouvement doctrinal du XIème siècle*. Histoire de l'Église, XIII. Paris: Bloud & Gay, 1951.

Giraud, René. "Marriage in Avignon in the Second Half of the Fifteenth Century," *Speculum*, XXVIII (1953), 485–498.

Gillispie, Charles C. *The Edge of Objectivity*. Princeton: Princeton University Press, 1960.

Gougaud, L., O.S.B. "La Danse dans les églises," *Revue d'histoire ecclesiastique*, XV (1914), 5–22, 229–245.

Génicot, Leopold. *La Spiritualité mediévale*. Paris: Fayard, 1958.

Graf, Arturo. *La Leggenda del Paradiso Terrestre*. Torino: Löscher, 1878.

Gregorovius, F. A. *History of Rome in the Middle Ages*. Tr. by Annie Hamilton. London: Bell, 1894–1902. 8 vols.

Gwynn, Aubrey, S.J. "Archbishop Fitzralph and George of Hungary," *Studies, An Irish Quarterly Review*, XXIV (1935), 558–572.

Harding, Alan. *A Social History of English Law*. Baltimore: Penguin, 1966.

Heinrich, Mary Pia. *The Canonesses and Education in the Early Middle Ages*. Washington: Catholic University of America, 1924.

Herlihy, David. "Family Solidarity in Medieval Italian History," *Explorations in Economic History*, VII (1969–70), 173–184.

————. "Land, Family and Women in Continental Europe, 701–1200," *Traditio*, XVIII (1962), 89–120.

Hewitt, H. J. *The Black Prince's Expedition of 1355–1357*. Manchester, England: Manchester University Press, 1958.

Hopper, V. F. *Medieval Number Symbolism, Its Sources, Meaning and Influence on Thought and Expression*. New York: Columbia University Press, 1938.

Jamison, Ellen. *Admiral Eugenius of Sicily, His Life and Work*. The British Academy. London: Oxford University Press, 1957.

Jenkins, Claude. *The Monastic Chronicler and the Early School of St. Albans*. London: Society for Promoting Christian Knowledge, 1922.

Keen, M. H. *The Outlaws of Medieval Legend*. London: Routledge & Kegan Paul, 1961.

SUGGESTIONS FOR FURTHER READING

King, Charles W. *Antique Gems; Their Origin, Uses and Value as Interpreters of Ancient History.* London: Murray, 1860.

King, Georgiana G. *The Way of Saint James.* Hispanic Society of America. New York and London: Putnam, 1920. 3 vols.

Koch, Gottfried. *Frauenfrage und Ketzertum im Mittelalter.* Forschungen zur Mittelalterlichen Geschichte, IX. Berlin: Akademie Verlag, 1962.

Kunz, G. F. *The Curious Lore of Precious Stones.* Philadelphia and London: Lippincott, 1913.

——. *The Magic of Jewels and Charms.* Philadelphia and London: Lippincott, 1915.

Labitte, Charles. *Etude sur "La Divine Comédie" avant Dante.* Paris: no publisher indicated, 1853.

Labriolle, P. de. "Le 'Mariage spirituel' dans l'antiquité chrétienne," *Revue historique,* CXXXVI (1921), 204–225.

Lagarde, Georges de. *La Naissance de l'esprit laïque au déclin du moyen âge.* Vol. 1, 3rd ed. Louvain: Nauwelaerts, 1956.

Langlois, C. V. *La Société française au XIIIème siècle, d'après dix romans d'aventure.* 3rd ed. Paris: Hachette, 1911.

——. *La Vie en France au moyen âge d'après quelques moralistes du temps.* Paris: Hachette, 1908.

Law, Robert Adger. "In Principio," *Publications of the Modern Language Society of America,* XXXVII (1922), 208–215.

Leach, Henry G. *Angevin Britain and Scandinavia.* Harvard Studies in Comparative Literature, VI. Cambridge, Mass.: Harvard University Press, 1921.

LeBras, Gabriel. *Études de sociologie religieuse.* Vol. I: *Sociologie de la pratique religieuse dans les campagnes françaises.* Paris. Presses Universitaires de France, 1955.

——. *Institutions ecclésiastiques de la chrétienté médiévale.* Histoire de l'Église, XII. Paris: Bloud & Gay, 1959.

——. "Le Mariage dans la théologie et le droit de l'église du XIème au XIIIème siècle," *Cahiers de civilisation médiévale,* XI:2 (1968), 191–202.

Lehmann, Andrée. *Le Rôle de la femme dans l'histoire de France au moyen âge.* Paris: Berger-Lovrault, 1952.

Leclercq, Jean. "Documents sur les fugitifs," *Studia Anselmiana,* LIV (1965), 87–145.

————. "Violence and the Devotion to St. Benedict," *The Downside Review*, LXXXVIII (1970), 344–360.

Lecoy de la Marche, Albert. *La Chaire française au moyen âge.* 2nd ed. Paris: Renouard et Laurens, 1886.

Lee, F. G. "Episcopal Staves," *Archaeologia*, LI (1888), 351–382.

Leslie, Shane. *Saint Patrick's Purgatory.* London: Burns Oates, 1932.

Lewis, C. S. *The Discarded Image: An Introduction to Medieval and Renaissance Literature.* Cambridge, England: University Press, 1964.

Lindberg, David C. "Alhazen's Theory of Vision and its Reception in the West," *Isis*, LVIII (1967), 321–341.

————. "Lines of Influence in Thirteenth-Century Optics: Bacon, Witelo and Pecham," *Speculum*, XLVI:1 (Jan., 1971), 66–83.

Lot, Ferdinand. "La Frontière de la France et de l'empire sur le cours inférieur de l'Escaut," *Bibliothèque de l'École des Chartes*, LXXI (1910), 5–32.

Lottin, O. *Psychologie et morale aux XIIème et XIIIème siècles.* Louvain: Abbaye du Mont César, 1942. 6 vols.

Luchaire, A. *Social France at the Time of Philip Augustus.* Tr. by Edward Krehbiel. New York: Ungar, 1957.

Lunt, William. *Papal Revenues in the Middle Ages.* New York: Columbia University Press, 1934.

Macalister, R. A. "The Vision of Merlino," *Zeitschrift für celtische Philologie*, IV (1902–1903), 394–455.

McGinn, Bernard. "The Abbot and the Doctors: Scholastic Reaction to the Radical Eschatology of Joachim of Fiori," *Church History*, XL (1971), 30–47.

Magoun, F. P. "The Pilgrim Diary of Nikulas of Munkatherva: The Road to Rome," *Mediaeval Studies*, VI (1944), 314–354.

Mâle, Emile. "L'Art français de la fin du moyen âge: l'idée de la mort et la danse macabre," *Revue des deux mondes*, XXXII (1906), 647–679.

Mandonnet, R. P. "Les Idées cosmographiques d'Albert le Grand et de S. Thomas d'Aquin et la découverte de l'Amérique," *Revue Thomiste*, I (1893), 46–64.

Manning, Bernard Lord. *The People's Faith in the Time of Wyclif.* Cambridge, England: Cambridge University Press, 1919.

Matthews, T. *Welsh Records in Paris.* Carmarthen: no publisher indicated, 1910.

SUGGESTIONS FOR FURTHER READING

Martines, Lauro. *Violence and Civil Disorder in Italian Cities, 1200–1500.* Berkeley and Los Angeles: University of California Press, 1972.

Miller, William. *The Latins in the Levant; A History of Frankish Greece.* New York: Barnes & Noble, 1964.

Moorman, J. R. H. *Church Life in England in the Thirteenth Century.* Cambridge, England: Cambridge University Press, 1946.

Moule, A. C. "Brother Jordan of Sévérac," *Journal of the Royal Asiatic Society* (1928), 349–376.

Nansen, Fridtjof. *In Northern Mists: Arctic Exploration in Early Times.* Tr. by A. G. Chater. New York: Stokes, 1911. 2 vols.

Neilson, George. *Trial by Combat.* Glasgow: Hodge, 1890.

Newman, F. X. "St. Augustine's Three Visions and the Structure of the Commedia," *Modern Language Notes,* LXXXII (1967), 56–78.

Newman, W. M. *The Kings, the Court and the Royal Power in France in the Eleventh Century.* Toulouse: Cléder, 1929.

Nitze, W. A. "The Exhumation of King Arthur at Glastonbury," *Speculum,* IX (1934), 355–361.

Noonan, John T., Jr. *Contraception. A History of its Treatment by the Catholic Theologians and Canonists.* Cambridge, Mass.: Harvard University Press, 1966.

———. *The Morality of Abortion.* Cambridge, Mass.: Harvard University Press, 1970.

Olins, Peter Z. *The Teutonic Knights in Latvia.* Riga: no publisher indicated, 1925.

Oman, C. C. "The Jewels of Saint Alban's Abbey," *The Burlington Magazine,* LVII (1930), 81–82.

Owst, G. R. "*Sortilegium* in English Homiletic Literature of the Fourteenth Century," in James C. Davies, ed., *Studies Presented to Sir Hilary Jenkinson.* London: Oxford University Press, 1957.

Painter, Sidney. "The Family and the Feudal System in Twelfth-Century England," *Speculum,* XXXV (1960), 1–16.

Parks, George B. *The English Traveller in Italy.* Storia e Letteratura, XLVI. Rome: Edizioni di Storie e Letteratura, 1954.

Patch, H. *The Other World According to Descriptions in Medieval Literature.* Cambridge, Mass.: Harvard University Press, 1950.

Patetta, Frederico. *Le Ordalia, studio di storia del diritto e scienza del diritto comparato.* Turin: Università di Torino, 1890.

Petit-Dutaillis, Charles. *The Feudal Monarchy of France and England from the Tenth to the Thirteenth Century*. Tr. by E. D. Hunt. London: Trübner, 1936.

Phillips, E. D. *The Mongols*. London: Thames and Hudson, 1969.

Pike, Luke O. *A History of Crime in England*. London: Smith & Elder, 1873–76. 2 vols.

Poole, Austin. *From Domesday Book to Magna Carta, 1087–1216*. Oxford: Clarendon Press, 1951.

———. "Outlawry as a punishment of criminous clerks," in J. G. Edwards, V. H. Galbraith, and E. F. Jacob, eds., *Essays in Honor of James Tait*. Manchester: Butter and Tanner, 1933.

Power, Eileen. "The Position of Woman," in *The Legacy of the Middle Ages*. Ed. by C. G. Crump and E. F. Jacob. Oxford: Oxford University Press, 1927.

Raftis, J. A. *Tenure and Mobility: Studies in the Social History of the Medieval English Village*. Studies and Texts, VIII. Toronto: Pontifical Institute of Mediaeval Studies, 1964.

Reynolds, Roger E. "*Virgines Subintroductae* in Celtic Christianity," *Harvard Theological Review*, LXI (1968), 547–566.

Rhys, J. "Manx Folklore and Superstitions," *Folklore*, II (1891), 284–313.

Robertson, D. W. *A Preface to Chaucer: Studies in Medieval Perception*. Princeton: Princeton University Press, 1962.

Romefort, J. de. "Le Rhône de l'Ardèche à la mer, frontière des Capetiens au XIIème siècle," *Revue historique*, CLXI (1929), 74–89.

Roncière, Charles de la. *La Découverte de l'Afrique au moyen âge, cartographes et explorateurs*. Mémoires de la Société Royale de Géographie d'Egypte, V. Cairo: Institut Française d'Archéologie Orientale, 1924.

———. "De Paris à Tombouctou au temps de Louis XI," *Revue des deux mondes*, 7th Series, XIII (1923), 653–675.

Rordorf, Willy. "Marriage in the New Testament and in the Early Church," *Journal of Ecclesiastical History*, XX (1969), 193–210.

Ross, J. B. "A Study of Twelfth-Century Interest in the Antiquities of Rome," in James L. Cate and Eugene N. Anderson, eds., *Medieval Essays in Honor of James Westfall Thompson*. Chicago: University of Chicago Press, 1938.

Rousset, Paul. "La Femme et la famille dans l'Histoire Ecclésiastique d'Orderic Vital," *Zeitschrift für schweizerische Kirchengeschichte*, LXIII (1969), 58–66.

Sheehan, Michael M. "The Influence of Canon Law on the Property

Rights of Married Women in England," *Mediaeval Studies*, XXV (1963), 109–124.

Spargo, J. W. *Virgil the Necromancer*. Comparative Literature, X. Cambridge, Mass.: Harvard University Press, 1934.

Stenton, Doris. "Roger of Hoveden and 'Benedict'," *English Historical Review*, LXVIII (1953), 574–582.

Stones, E. L. G. "The Folvilles of Ashby-Folville, Leicestershire, and Their Associates in Crime, 1326–1341," *Transactions of the Royal Historical Society*, 5th Series, VII (1957), 117–136.

Stubbs, William. "The Medieval Kingdoms of Cyprus and Armenia," *Seventeen Lectures on the Study of Medieval and Modern History*. Oxford: Clarendon Press, 1878.

Thorndike, Lynn. *A History of Magic and Experimental Science*. New York: Columbia University Press, 1923–28. 8 vols.

Thornley, I. D. "Sanctuary in Medieval London," *Journal of the British Archaeological Association*, XC (1933), 213–315.

Thurston, Herbert. *The Roman Jubilee: History and Ceremonial*. Abrd. from "The Holy Jubilee." Edinburgh: Sands, 1925.

Toussaert, Jacques. *Le Sentiment religieux en Flandre à la fin du moyen âge*. Paris: Plon, 1960.

Trenholme, N. M. *Right of Sanctuary in England*. University of Missouri Studies, I, part 5. Columbus, Missouri: University of Missouri, 1903.

Tyler, James E. *Oaths; Their Origin, Nature and History*. London: Parker, 1834.

Vacandard, E. "Le Divorce de Louis le Jeune," *Revue des questions historiques*, XLVII (1890), 408–432.

Van Os, A. B. *Religious Visions. The Development of the Eschatological Elements in Religious Literature in Medieval England*. Amsterdam: H. J. Paris, 1932.

Viard, Jules. "L'Ostrevant, enquête au sujet de la frontière française sous Philippe VI," *Bibliothèque de l'École des Chartes*, LXXXII (1921), 316–329.

Vitry, Philippe de. "Le Chapel de fleurs de lis," *Roumania*, XXVII (1898), 55–92.

Ward, H. L. "Vision of Thurkill," *Catalogue of Romances in the British Museum*, II, 506–515. London: British Museum, 1893.

Wedel, T. O. *The Medieval Attitude Toward Astrology*. Yale Studies in English, LX. New Haven: Yale University Press, 1920.

Westropp, T. J. "Brasil and the Legendary Islands of the Atlantic," *Proceedings of the Royal Irish Academy*, 30:8, Section C (1944), 223–260.

Willard, James Field. "Inland Transportation in England during the Fourteenth Century," *Speculum*, I (1926), 361–374.

Wood, Charles T. *The Age of Chivalry: Manners and Morals, 1000–1450.* London: Weidenfeld and Nicolson, 1970.

Wright, J. K. *Geographical Lore of the Time of the Crusades.* American Geographical Society Research Series, XV. New York: American Geographical Society, 1925.

Wright, Thomas. *St. Patrick's Purgatory: An Essay on the Legends of Purgatory, Hell and Paradise Current during the Middle Ages.* London: John Russell Smith, 1844.

Index